PENGUIN PLAYS

PL 38

NEW ENGLISH DRAMATISTS 2

NEW
ENGLISH DRAMATISTS
2

THREE PLAYS, INTRODUCED BY
ALAN PRYCE-JONES AND EDITED BY
TOM MASCHLER

THE KITCHEN
Arnold Wesker

A RESOUNDING TINKLE
N. F. Simpson

EPITAPH FOR GEORGE DILLON
*John Osborne and
Anthony Creighton*

PENGUIN BOOKS

Penguin Books Ltd., Harmondsworth, Middlesex

AUSTRALIA: Penguin Books Pty Ltd., 762 Whitehorse Road,
Mitcham, Victoria

—

The Kitchen
First published by Penguin Books 1960
Copyright © Arnold Wesker, 1960

—

A Resounding Tinkle
First published by Faber and Faber 1958
Published by Penguin Books 1960
Copyright © Norman Frederick Simpson, 1958

—

Epitaph for George Dillon
First published by Faber and Faber 1958
Published by Penguin Books 1960
Copyright © John Osborne and Anthony Creighton, 1958

Made and printed in Great Britain
by Unwin Brothers Ltd.
Woking and London

CONTENTS

INTRODUCTION

THE three plays in this volume may be taken together, in terms of the contemporary British stage, as an example of sonata form. THE KITCHEN sketches in a high theme, A RESOUNDING TINKLE brings in a second subject *scherzoso*, and EPITAPH FOR GEORGE DILLON develops and rounds off the whole movement. The image is a fanciful one, I know; but I use it in order to stress the unity which binds together, below the surface, these three apparently very dissimilar plays.

Between them, they represent much of what is alive in our theatre today. To begin with, the necessity of a high theme. THE KITCHEN is summed up by Arnold Wesker himself in the words, 'The world might have been a stage for Shakespeare, but to me it is a kitchen: where people come and go and cannot stay long enough to understand each other, and friendships, loves, and enmities are forgotten as quickly as they are made.' Although this is a young man's play – and since writing it, Arnold Wesker has greatly enlarged both his range and his technique – the theme is brilliantly met. No heavy affirmative is struck – it is also part of the dramatist's intention to show that sooner or later 'all cooks are infused with a kind of madness' – but in the heat and tension of an overcrowded restaurant kitchen a cat's-cradle of activity is woven together so adroitly that the final explosion of violence, unexpected as it is, comes in retrospect to prove Arnold Wesker's point. The scurrying cooks and waitresses never have time to establish a human contact with one another; they can only hit out, get in each other's path, or give way to despair. The conclusion might have been a sentimental one, were it not that Arnold Wesker can bestow life on a character as soon as he opens his mouth. He can also be extremely funny. This is not his best play, but it is perhaps his most enjoyable one; and those who have seen it in performance will remember the exhilarating sense of virtuosity which carries its two short acts towards the clinching phrases of the final speech, made by the restaurant proprietor: 'I don't know what more to give a man. He works, he eats, I give him money. This is life, isn't it? I haven't made a mistake have I? . . . What is there more? What *is* there more?'

There is a lot more, N. F. Simpson would agree. But whereas Wesker is a realist, a Socialist, the constructive advocate of a new society, Simpson is very much slyer in his approach. A RESOUNDING TINKLE has no binding theme. It depends for its impact on a deadpan feeling for logic, and especially inverted Carroll-like logic, expressed in language of a deliberate flatness. The characters run on, as simple people run on in daily life; but extravagant things happen, never to their surprise.

7

The scope of a very ordinary day is extended to include a totally unassertive dimension of pure nonsense. In the later work of Simpson we are never nudged; and if this present play has a weakness it is that too direct an attempt is made to buttonhole an audience. The author harangues us in his own person, and in a sharply comic finale a group of critics joins him in an extended discussion which adds an unnecessary archness to the main action. But so long as Mr and Mrs Paradock hold the stage, supported by two comedians, a neighbour, some minor *personae*, and an unflagging spirit of fantasy, this play can qualify as one of the most amusing in the language. Furthermore, it reads as well as it acts. Others have pointed out that Simpson owes a debt to Ionesco. Perhaps he does, but only in the sense that the world of dreams is an impersonal world which anybody can enter. Mrs Paradock may come into the living room saying inattentively, 'There's somebody at the door wanting you to form a government', or there may be trouble with an elephant in the back garden, but what matters in this play is less the pretexts for talk than the talk itself.

Nonsense is an indigenous part of our literature – but this is a kind of nonsense nearer to Germany than to the France of Ionesco. Indeed, if Simpson's ideas have a parent at all outside his own imagination, they are like an extended version of Christian Morgenstern's GALGEN-LIEDER. He represents, however, an important element in our own theatre today: the element which likes a play to pose as a lightning improvisation rather than as a constructed work of art.

It is when we come to John Osborne's and Anthony Creighton's EPITAPH FOR GEORGE DILLON that we enter, for the first time in this collection, the world of the 'ordinary' professional three-act play. Except that this play is not ordinary unless in its classical lay-out, which wears with defiance the now unconventional garments of a beginning, a middle, and an end. Again, it is a trial trip of a play, an earnest of things to come, which only reached the professional stage after the success of LOOK BACK IN ANGER had launched the career of John Osborne. But it fully deserves to stand on its own as a study in failure. George Dillon sells out. Without the sustaining anger of Jimmy Porter, he abandons his dreams, and chooses the easier – though still not the easy – way. This is the play of a *milieu*, of a classical complex. There have been innumerable ironic plays, of late, about the dullness of dull people, and the effect upon them of an unexpected stranger, or an uncalculated event. George Dillon is the outsider in the suburban house of the Elliots. He may have a talent, he may be simply a scrounger. We never know, since he gives up too soon, throwing away his possible talent for a home and a little ready money. What makes the play memorable is less this fairly familiar situation than the skill with which the authors have caught the tone, the colour, the feeling of a middle-class household. It is a success which owes nothing to anger. Indeed, its characteristic is a certain sharp, no-nonsense kindness, exemplified best in the handling of Mrs Elliot – a suburban mother whom it would have been easy to guy, but who in fact is given a rather touching measure of sympathy and perception.

I should like to emphasize the fact that these three plays are all early works by dramatists who have gained in stature since writing them. Since all have been written in the last few years, and none by the middle-aged or elderly taking up the theatre as a second love, they must be considered foundation works in the British theatrical revival which is slowly taking shape. So auspicious a start would have seemed too much to hope for even five years ago.

1960   *Alan Pryce-Jones*

ARNOLD WESKER

The Kitchen

THE KITCHEN

First presented by The English Stage Society at The Royal Court Theatre, London, on 13 September 1959, with the following cast:

MAGI	Alan Howard
FIRST WAITRESS	Jennifer Wallace
MAX	Tenniel Evans
MANGOLIS	Peter Gill
PAUL	Alfred Lynch
RAYMOND	James Culliford
ANNE	Patsy Byrne
SECOND WAITRESS	Tarn Bassett
THIRD WAITRESS	Mary Miller
FOURTH WAITRESS	Jeanne Watts
DIMITRI	Charles Kay
HANS	Christopher Sandford
ALFREDO	Jack Rodney
GASTON	David Ryder
MICHAEL	James Bolam
BERTHA	Gwen Nelson
NICHOLAS	Anthony Carrick
KEVIN	John Briggs
PETER	Robert Stephens
FRANK, SECOND CHEF	Kenneth Adams
FIRST CHEF	Arnold Yarrow
FIFTH WAITRESS	Ida Goldapple
SIXTH WAITRESS	Brenda Peters
SEVENTH WAITRESS	Sandra Miller
EIGHTH WAITRESS	Ann King
MR MARANGO	Nigel Davenport
MONIQUE	Anne Bishop
HEAD WAITER	Cecil Brock
TRAMP	Patrick O'Connell

Directed by John Dexter

The action of the play takes place in the kitchen of the Tivoli Restaurant

INTRODUCTION AND NOTES FOR THE PRODUCER

THE lengthy explanations I am forced to make may be annoying; I am sorry, but they are necessary.

This is a play about a large kitchen in a restaurant called the Tivoli. All kitchens, especially during service, go insane. There is the rush, there are the petty quarrels, grumbles, false prides, and snobbery. Kitchen staff instinctively hate dining room staff, and all of them hate the customer. He is the personal enemy. The world might have been a stage for Shakespeare, but to me it is a kitchen: where people come and go and cannot stay long enough to understand each other, and friendships, loves, and enmities are forgotten as quickly as they are made.

The quality of the food here is not so important as the speed with which it is served. Each person has his own particular job. We glance in upon him, high-lighting as it were the individual. But though we may watch just one or a group of people, the rest of the kitchen staff does not. They work on.

So, because activity must continue while the main action is played out, we shall study, together with a diagram of the kitchen, who comes in and what they do.

The waitresses spend the morning working in the dining room before they eat their lunch. But throughout the morning there are about three or four who wander in and out carrying glasses from the glasserie to the dining room. Others wander into the steam room emptying their buckets of water; they carry mops and they have scarves on their heads. One or two others perform duties which are mentioned in the course of the play. During the service, the waitresses are continually coming out of the dining room and ordering dishes from the cooks. The dishes are served on silver, and the waitresses take about six plates out of the hot-plate immediately under the serving-counter. Stocks of plates are replenished all the time by the porters. These are highly efficient waitresses. They make a circuit round the kitchen calling at the stations they require. They move fast and carry large quantities of dishes in their arms.

The kitchen porters, who are mixed Cypriots and Maltese, are divided into various sections. Firstly, there are those who do the actual washing of cutlery, tins, and plates by machine; these we do not see. But we do see the two porters by the swill. During the service the waitresses bring their dirty plates to the swill and these two porters push the remains of food into two holes leading to bins under the counter and push the dirty plates (out of sight) to the men at the machine. Two other porters continually replace clean plates under the serving counter so that the waitresses can take them as required. Another sweeps up at regular intervals and throws sawdust around.

The woman who serves the cheeses and desserts we hardly and rarely see through the glass partition back of stage, but every now and then she comes to the pastry section to replenish her supplies of tarts and pastries. The coffee woman simply supplies cups of coffee from an urn to the waitresses as they call for it.

Now to the cooks. At this point it must be understood that at no time is food ever used. To cook and serve food is of course just not practical. Therefore the waitresses will carry empty dishes and the cooks will mime their cooking. Cooks being the main characters in this play, I shall sketch them and their activity here, so that while the main action of the play is continuing they shall always have something to do.

CHARACTERS OF THE PLAY
IN ORDER OF STATIONS

FRANK, *Second Chef, Poultry:* A prisoner of war for four years. Now at thirty-eight he has an easy-going nature. Nothing really upsets him, but then nothing excites him either. He drinks steadily throughout the day and by nightfall is blissfully drunk though instinctively capable. Flirts with the waitresses, squeezing their breasts and pinching their bottoms.

ALFREDO, *Roast:* An old chef, about sixty-five and flat-footed. Large-muscled and strong, though of medium height. He is a typical cook in that he will help nobody and will accept no help; nor will he impart his knowledge. He is the fastest worker there and sets-to straight away, not stopping till his station is all ready. He speaks little but has a dry sense of humour. He is the worker and the boss is the boss, and he probably despises the boss. He hums to himself as he works.

HANS, *Fry:* A German boy, nineteen, pimply, and adolescent. He is working in London through a system of exchange. He speaks very bad English and is impressed by anything flashy. Yet as a German he is sensitive.

PETER, *Boiled Fish:* Peter is the main character. Another young German aged twenty-three, who has worked at the Tivoli for the last three years. His parents were killed in the war. He is boisterous, aggressive, too merry, and yet good-natured. After three years at the Tivoli one might say he was living on his nerves. He speaks good English but with an accent, and when he is talking to people he tends to speak into their ear as though he were telling them a secret. It is a nervous movement. A strong characteristic of Peter is his laugh. It is a forced laugh, pronounced 'Hya Hya Hya' instead of 'Ha Ha Ha'. He turns this laugh into one of surprise or mockery, derision or simple merriment. There is also a song he sings (music on p. 18) which ends in exactly the same laughter. Somehow its maniacal tone is part of the whole atmosphere of the kitchen.

KEVIN, *Fried Fish:* The new young man, Irish, twenty-two. He spends most of his time being disturbed by the mad rush of the work and people around him. This is worse than anything he has ever seen.

GASTON, *Grill:* A Cypriot by birth, forty odd, slight, and dark-complexioned. Everyone-is-his-friend until he starts work, and then he is inclined to go to pieces and panic and cry at everyone. When this play starts he has a loud scratch down the side of his face.

15

MICHAEL, *Eggs:* There is nothing particular about this boy of eighteen. He is what his dialogue will make him; but he is a cook and before long all cooks are infused with a kind of madness.

MAX, *Butcher:* A stout man of fifty. Loud-mouthed, smutty, and anti-anything that it is easy to be anti about. He has a cigarette continually drooping from his mouth and like Frank drinks steadily all day till he is drunk.

NICHOLAS, *Cold Buffet:* Nicholas is a young Cypriot who has lived in England three years and can therefore speak reasonable English but with an accent. Speaking the language and working in a capacity socially superior to his compatriots, who are dishwashers, he behaves with a wild heartiness, as one who is accepted. And as one who is accepted he imitates, and he chooses to imitate Frank and Max by becoming drunk by the end of the day.

RAYMOND AND PAUL, *Pastrycooks:* Paul is a young Jew; Raymond is an Italian who speaks almost perfect English but with an accent. These two pastrycooks, as opposed to the madmen in the kitchen, are calm and less prone to panic. The rush of the kitchen does not affect them, they work hard and straight through without the afternoon break but have no direct contact with the waitresses. Raymond is emotional. Paul is suave though not unpleasant.

CHEF: A large man of about fifty-nine with a tiny moustache. If he could he would work elsewhere – preferably not in the catering trade at all. The less that is brought to his attention, the happier he feels. In such a large kitchen the organization carries itself almost automatically. He rarely speaks to anyone except Frank, the Second Chef, Max who works near him, and Nicholas who is immediately under him. He will not say good morning or communicate any of the politeness expected of a chef. Familiarity, for him, breeds the contempt it deserves.

MR MARANGO, *Proprietor:* An old man of seventy-five, stout – but not fat – with flabby jowls and a sad expression on his face. A magnificent curtain of grey hair skirts the back of his bald head and curls under itself. His sad look is really one of self-pity. The machine he has set in motion is his whole life and he suspects that everyone is conspiring to stop it.

THE ACTIONS OF THE COOKS

For the purposes of the action of this play the following dishes have been allotted to the cooks. Of course they cannot go through all the actions necessary for the cooking of these dishes. The two important things are:

1. That they have some actions to mime throughout the play in between speaking their parts and gossiping among themselves; and

2. That by the time the service is ready to begin they have an assortment of neatly arranged trays and pots of 'dishes and sauces' ready to serve to the waitresses as requested.

FRANK: Roast pheasant – chips. Roast chicken – pommes sauté. Mushrooms. Pour salt in twenty chicken carcasses; place in oven. Slice carrots and onions and boil for gravy. Salt and place pheasants in oven. (Both carcasses are cleaned elsewhere.) Chop mushrooms and fry together with sauté.

ALFREDO: Roast veal – spaghetti. Boiled ham – boiled potatoes. Roast beef for staff. Season and cook veal and beef in oven. Boil spaghetti in salt water. Chop onions and carrots and make sauce. Place ham in pot to boil.

HANS: Sausages – baked rice. Pork chops – white beans. Vegetables for the staff. Cut up ham, tomatoes, onions, and mushrooms, and sauté for rice. Boil white beans. Pork chops are fried during service. Collect from cold cupboard and heat yesterday's vegetables for staff.

PETER: Mixed fish – sauce. Cod meunière – boiled potatoes. Boiled turbot – sauce hollandaise. Beat egg yellows on slow heat; add melted margarine for sauce hollandaise. This takes a long time. Slice cod and turbot into portions. Slice lemons for garniture.

KEVIN: Grilled sardines – boiled potatoes. Grilled salmon – boiled potatoes. Fried plaice – chips or potatoes. Slice lemons for plaice. Cut salmon into portions. Arrange four trays on bench: one for oil, one for milk, one for flour, and one with required fish. Clean grill with wire brush.

GASTON: Grilled chops – chips. Grilled steak – chips. Most of his work is done during service. Clean grill with wire brush. Collect from veg. room and then blanch chips. Aid Kevin.

MICHAEL: Hamburger – egg on top – chips. Ham omelette. Onion soup. Cut ham for omelette. Cube stale bread for onion soup. Crack eggs in tin ready for omelette. We assume enough soup left over from yesterday.

MAX: Mainly carting of huge meat carcasses from coldroom to bench where he then proceeds to cut and dissect them.

NICHOLAS: Cold roast beef – potato salad. Cold ham – Russian salad. Slice meats and arrange various trays of salad. Also roll and slice in portions chopped meat for Michael's hamburgers.

CHEF: Mainly clerical and organizational work of course. He will mind his own business as much as possible.

PAUL AND RAYMOND: Bands of apple and pear tart. Pastry called 'religieuse'. First bake trays of tarts prepared day before. Spread custard sauce and then slice fruit to lay on top. Make more pastry. Mix flour and fat, add water, roll out. Cut into more bands ready for tomorrow. Fill pastry with cream from cloth bag. Peel fruit.

BERTHA: Hitherto unmentioned because part is small. She is the *veg. cook*. Assume all her vegs., sprouts, cabbage, spinach, and sauté, were cooked day before. She merely has to heat them over. Otherwise gossips with coffee woman.

NOTE: Cooks are continually moving between stations and plate room in order to get pots and pans for cooking in.

Any producer is at liberty to abstract this set if he can also get over the atmosphere.

PETER'S SONG

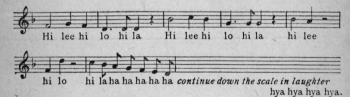

Hi lee hi lo hi la Hi lee hi lo hi la hi lee

hi lo hi la ha ha ha ha ha *continue down the scale in laughter*
hya hya hya hya.

ACT ONE

There is no curtain to this act. The kitchen is always there. It is in semi-darkness. A figure is seen sleeping by the oven. Nothing happens until the audience is quite seated (at the usual time for commencement that is).

The figure rises. It is the night porter, MAGI. *He stretches, looks at his watch, and then stands still, realizing where he is. It is seven in the morning. He switches on a light which just barely lights the kitchen. Then with a burning (?) sheet of paper in his hand he lights the ovens. Into the first shoots a flame. There is smoke and flame, and soon the oven settles into a steady burn and with it comes its hum. It is the hum of the kitchen, a small roar. It is a noise that will stay with us to the end. As he lights each oven the noise grows from a small to a loud ferocious roar. There will be this continuous battle between the dialogue and the noise of the ovens. The producer must work out his own balance.*

The porter exits. Some seconds later he returns with a hefty woman. They are pushing a chariot on which are two cauldrons of potatoes. They lift these on to the oven. 'The spuds', mutters the woman. They exit and as they do MAX *passes them on his way in. 'Good morning', he says. He makes his way to his corner, switches on his light, pulls out the drawer beneath his table, and places his belongings in it. At the same time he takes out a bottle of beer, opens it, and drinks. Then he goes to his coldroom offstage and drags out another vat filled with beef. This he hauls to Alfredo's station. Meanwhile the night porter and the hefty woman return with another cauldron of spuds. They hoist it on to the oven.*

HEFTY WOMAN: There.

MAX [*to Magi*]: Magi, give us a hand, please.

    [*They raise the beef on to Alfredo's oven. As they do this* PAUL *and* RAYMOND *enter with their tools under their arms. They go to their own corner and switch on their lights and electric oven.*]

PAUL [*to anybody*]: Good morning, good morning, good morning.
    [*to Max*] And to you too, Max.

MAX [*his soul not yet returned*]: Good morning.

RAYMOND: Max, it's escallop of veal on . . . today.

MAX: How many?

RAYMOND: Three. I'll take them now and put them in my box, before the others get here.

[MAX *goes to the coldroom and returns with three escallops which he slaps down on his table and* RAY *collects.*]

MAX: And don't forget my puff pastry tomorrow.

RAYMOND: Usual?

MAX: Usual.

PAUL [*to Ray as he returns*]: It's religieuse today?

RAYMOND: Yes. But you do the fruit bands. Leave the pastries, I'll do them.

[*A woman enters from the dining room with a glass stand in her hand. This is* ANNE, *the dessert woman.*]

PAUL: Good morning, Anne.

RAYMOND: Good morning, sweetheart.

ANNE [*Irish, pretty, thirty-five, speaks with slow, cloying lilt*]: Hello, boys, hello, Max.

MAX [*his soul returned*]: Top o' the mornin' to you, Anne.

ANNE [*putting coffee in metal jug to warm on oven*]: An' the rest o' the day to yersel', dear. [*Stretching herself*] Ah, me bed was lovely.

RAYMOND [*lasciviously*]: I bet it was.

ANNE: Hey, Raymond, tell me, what happened to Peter in the end, you know, last night?

RAYMOND: Now he's a silly boy, eh? Don't you think so? I don't even know what it was all about anyway. You know, Paul?

PAUL: All I know is he had a fight with Gaston. Why? I don't know. Over a ladle I think, or maybe a . . .

MAX: He's a bloody German, a fool, that's what he is. He is always quarrelling, always. There's no one he hasn't quarrelled with, am I right? No one! That's some scheme that is, exchanging cooks! What do we want to exchange cooks for? Three years he's been here – three years!

ANNE: Ah, the boy's in love.

RAYMOND: What love! You ever see him? When Monique does a turn as hostess by the stairs he watches her through that mirror there. [*Points to glass partition.*] And he walks round the kitchen and looks to see if she's talking or flirting with any of the customers. You don't believe me?

PAUL: And they quarrel in front of everybody as well. They shout at each other. Shout! You know, sometimes she doesn't even look at him and waits for her orders with her back turned.

ANNE: The poor boy. He's no parents you know. But what happened last night? I want to know.

MAX: Ask Magi.

[MAGI *is the night porter. He is a Cypriot. He has dressed himself now and is ready to go.*]

MAGI: Any coffee, Anne?

ANNE: Sure dear. [*Pours.*]

RAYMOND: Hey, Magi, what happened with Peter last night, uh?

MAGI [*unconcerned*]: They nearly killed him.

ANNE: Oh no!

MAGI: He talk a lot and get away. 'Everyone for me', he say, 'is the same. It makes no difference', he say. A very lucky boy, I tell you.

RAY [*gesticulating*]: But what was it all about, tell me? I don't know nothing, me.

MAGI: Well, *you* should know that – I wasn't here.

PAUL: All we know is that they suddenly started shouting at each other. And you know Peter, always shouts more than the other, and you can always hear Peter – well, so then it stopped, and then a few seconds later they were fighting and I saw Gaston raise a pallet knife and Peter knock it out of his hand, and then . . .

RAYMOND: And then he lifted Gaston up and nearly sat him on the stove and . . .

PAUL: And then the chef came along and . . .

ANNE: Well, *I* saw the chef separate them and I heard Gaston say, 'I haven't finished yet, it's not over yet', but I still don't know what it was all about.

PAUL: Who cares? I say good morning to Peter but never good night.

MAGI: Well, I came in at nine last night. The boys were changing and suddenly Peter comes and Gaston follows him. Gaston says Peter called him a lousy Cypro and the boys make circle round him and want to murder him! All of them, they all wanted to hit him! And he was scared! I never seen him so white.

ANNE: But what was it about to begin with?

MAX: A ladle, I tell you.

PAUL: Who knows? There's always fights. Who knows how they begin?

MAGI [*laying down cup*]: He was a lucky boy, I tell you. Well, I'm going.

ANNE: And I must get started too. [*Looks round empty kitchen.*] You wouldn't think this place will become a mad house in two hours would you now? [*Moves off with* MAGI.]

[RAY, PAUL, *and* MAX *continue to work in silence.*]

MAX: Any luck on the pools, Ray?

RAY: Huh!

MAX: Norwich and Leyton let me down. Twenty points. Twenty points!

[*Pause.*]

PAUL: Read about the man in the mental home who won £35,000?

RAY: And his wife turned up after eighteen years?

PAUL: Eighteen years!

[*Pause.* DIMITRIOS *enters – a Cypriot kitchen porter, young, good-looking, and intelligent. He is carrying in his hand a home-made portable record player. He is happy as he takes it to Paul. He speaks with an accent.*]

DIMITRI: I make it, Paul, I make it. There! [*Lays it on table nearby.*] She does not look handsome. I'm sorry for that.

PAUL: Ah, you good boy, Dimitri. Can we play it?

[*He looks round to see if authority is in sight. Only two young waitresses approach. One has a bucket in her hand and her hair is tied up with a scarf. The other one is similarly attired and carries a feather duster.*]

Any one around?

FIRST WAITRESS [*pointing to portable*]: What is it, Paul?

PAUL: Is Marango around yet?

SECOND WAITRESS: Not yet. Whose is it?

PAUL: It's mine. Dimitri here made it.

RAYMOND: You made it on your own? All those little wires and plugs? Tell me, what are you doing here? Why you waste your time with dishes in this place? You can't get a job in a factory?

DIMITRI: A factory? You think I find happiness in a factory? What I make there? Uh? This little wire, you see it? This I would make, or that what you call it . . .

PAUL: Knob.

DIMITRI: Knob. That perhaps I could put in. All day I would screw in knobs. I tell you, in a factory a man makes a little piece till he becomes a little piece, you know what I mean?

FIRST WAITRESS [*stupidly*]: Yeah, he's right, you know.

DIMITRI: Sure I know, my brother, he works there. I know all right.

RAYMOND: Hey, Dimitri, *you* know what happened to Peter last night?

DIMITRI: They nearly kill him. Why?

SECOND WAITRESS: Oh, my Gawd.

DIMITRI: But you think it was all Peter's fault? They all wanted to fight. Listen, you put a man in the plate room all day, he's got dishes to make clean and stinking bins to take away and floors to sweep, what else there is for him to do – he wants to fight. He got to show he is a man someway. So – blame him!

PAUL: I got a record with me – can we play it?

DIMITRI: Sure.

[*They plug in the pick-up and play a rock 'n' roll tune.* PAUL *takes a waitress and begins to dance. The other waitress tries to persuade* DIMITRI *to dance but he is shy and will not, so she hops on her own till some others come from the dining room and they either dance or clap their hands. After some seconds a waitress rushes in and cries out* 'Marango is in the dining room'. *There is a scramble to restore*

23

everything to normal: work is resumed, PAUL *puts away the pick-up, and* DIMITRI *vanishes into the plate room.*

Enter ALFREDO.]

ALFREDO: Good morning, gentlemen.

MAX [*pointing to Alfredo's station*]: The veal is there.

ALFREDO [*studying the menu on the board*]: Thank you, thank you.

PAUL [*shouting*]: Is the new cook here?

ALFREDO [*shrugging his shoulders*]: He didn't ask for me.

[*At this point* GASTON *enters first and goes to his station. A few seconds later* MICHAEL *comes in and sets out his business, to be followed by* HANS *who escorts* KEVIN. *Sooner or later they all arrive to glance at the menu on the board.*]

HANS [*to Kevin*]: I not know where you work. On fish perhaps. [*To Paul*] Paul, new cook.

PAUL: Hello.

[*They continue to work while* KEVIN *watches them and the rest of the kitchen.*]

KEVIN: Is there much doing here?

PAUL: You'll see. Two thousand customers a day.

[*While* KEVIN *has been introduced and is talking to the pastrycooks,* BERTHA *has entered. She goes to the cold cupboard and after looking around inside takes out a tray of sliced cold potatoes. Following behind about to start his work is* NICHOLAS. *He has a bottle of beer in his hand which he is drinking.*]

NICK [*to Bertha*]: Where you go with that?

BERTHA: I need it for sauté.

NICK [*taking tray*]: Oh no, no, no, no. That's for me. Me, I prepared that yesterday. That's for me, for my salad.

BERTHA [*trying to hold on to tray*]: You get your salad from the veg. room.

NICK: Ah no, bloody hell! You get *yours* from the veg. room. That is for me, that is what I get ready.

BERTHA [*nastily*]: You don't bloody hell me, my son. You bloody hell in your own country. [*To others*] What d'you think of him, eh? the little . . .

NICK: This is my country.

BERTHA: The lavatory is your country.

NICK [*taking tray eventually*]: The lavatory is *your* country, and the sewers, you know that? The sewers!

BERTHA [*taking out another tray*]: I'll pay you, sonny. You cross me once, that's all, just once. Lousy little foreigner, you!

NICK [*cheekily*]: For her I'm gonna starve. Listen to her . . .

ALFREDO [*approaching cupboard for his own goods*]: Excuse me, friends, you can carry on in a minute. [*But the quarrel has died down.*]

NICK [*approaching pastry-section*]: D'you hear her? Uh? The cow! Paul, you got some tart or cake or something? I'm starving. [PAUL *hands him tart. To Kevin*] You the new cook?

KEVIN: Yes.

NICK: Good luck to you! [*Laughs to the others.*] You know where your station is?

KEVIN: I don't even know what stations there are.

NICK: Here, I'll show you. [*Takes him over to right of stage.*] Well, at that end there, you see that fat bitch? [*Points.*] She's a veg. cook. And next to her we got the second chef, Frank, on poultry; and then Alfredo on the roast; and Hans he does staff and rice and cutlets and you know; and – oh yes, that's the menu. The chef, he writes it out each night. And there is where Peter works, boiled fish and all that. He's not here yet. And over there . . .

[*By this time he has to take Kevin back to left of stage and points out the other stations. As he talks on,* PETER *enters in a great hurry. He is late. He laughs his laugh.*]

PETER: Hya, hya, hya . . . *auf geht's, auf geht's.*

HANS: *Auf geht's, mein Lieber! Was hat dich zurückgehalten heute früh?*

PETER: *Ach, die Frau, die Frau.*

NICK: Peter, the new cook. I give him to you.

PETER: So what shall I do with him? [*To Kevin*] You know where it is you work?

KEVIN: Not yet I don't.

PETER: What restaurant you work in before?

KEVIN: Parisito, Shaftesbury Avenue.

PETER [*rubbing his thumb and finger together*]: Good pay?

KEVIN [*shaking his head*]: That's why I came here.

PETER: Oh, you get good money here – but you work! [*Raising his hands in despair*] Oh, yes! Now, you help me. Can you make a sauce hollandaise? You know – eggs and – [*Makes motion of whisking.*]

KEVIN: Yes, yes.

PETER [*briskly*]: The eggs are already in a tin in the cold cupboard. There is a pot, the whisk is in the drawer and I melt margarine for you.

[*By now almost everybody is working. Waitresses are making an appearance; they are carrying glasses back and forth. One waitress is handing out the printed menu for the day, another is taking round bread for lunch for the kitchen staff. As she reaches the pastry cooks,* HANS *approaches her shyly and tries to flirt with her. She rebukes his advances and moves off up right stage.* FRANK, *the second chef, enters and kisses her as she passes. He approaches cold cupboard out of which he takes a bottle of beer.*]

MAX [*to Frank*]: We got no lamb cutlets.

FRANK: Three carcasses came in yesterday.

MAX: So?

FRANK: So!

MAX: So you come and help me cut them up. I'm on my own today.

FRANK: What you got?

MAX: Veal cutlets.

FRANK: O.K., so veal cutlets then. [*Moving to* KEVIN.] New cook?

KEVIN [*sweating and still beating his sauce*]: Yes, Chef.

FRANK: Right, you work on the fried fish this morning.

PETER [*approaching from cutting table*]: Thank you, thank you; but I got six dishes to prepare.

FRANK: Co-Co is off today. Someone must do the fry.

PETER: Bloody house this is. The middle of summer and we got no staff. I got six dishes.

[FRANK *takes* KEVIN *to the friture and leaves* GASTON *to explain what has to be done. The* CHEF *enters now. He walks straight to his*

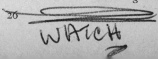

table, ignoring HANS *who says* 'Good morning, Chef.' FRANK *approaches him, talks a while, and then returns to his own station. Meanwhile –*]

HANS [*to Peter*]: *Er hat dich beinahe erwischt gestern Abend.*

PETER: *Nur zusammen sind sie mutig.*

HANS: *Haben sie nicht für dich draussen gewartet?*

PETER: *Ja, da waren einige, aber ich war zusammen mit Monika. Ha! jetzt spricht sie nicht mehr mit mir. Ach, nun – auf geht's!* [*Sings his song, in which* HANS *joins him, ending in laughter.*]

GASTON [*passing at that moment*]: Madmen, madmen!

PETER: Hey, Gaston. I'm sorry – your black eye, I'm sorry about it.

GASTON: DON'T TALK TO ME.

PETER: I say I'm sorry, that's all.

GASTON: You sorry because half a dozen Cypriot boys make you feel sorry – but we not finished yet!

PAUL: Gaston! What's the matter with you? A man is saying sorry – so accept!

GASTON: Accept? He give me this [*pointing to black eye*] and I must accept? [*To Peter*] We not finished yet I'm telling you.

PETER: What you not finished with? Tell me! What you want to do now? You want to give me a black eye? That make you feel happier? All right! Here, give me one and then we'll be finished, eh? [*Adopts quixotic stance.*]

GASTON: Don't laugh, Peter. I'm telling you, it gets worse, don't laugh. [PETER *adopts another quixotic stance.*]

PAUL [*to Peter*]: So what are you tantalizing him for? Lunatic! [*To Raymond*] Nobody knows when to stop. A quarrel starts and it goes on for months. When one of them *is* prepared to apologize so the other doesn't know how to accept – and when someone knows *how* to accept so the other . . . ach! Lunatics. [*Throws a hand of disgust.*]

FRANK [*shouting from his station to Nick*]: Nicholas! Twelve chickens, please.

NICHOLAS [*looking in cupboard*]: There is only six here.

FRANK: Well, order some more, then.

HANS [*joining in the shouting*]: *Auf geht's*, Nicholas, come on, Nicholas. [*At this point* RAYMOND *passes on way to plate room.*] *Buon giorno, Raymondo. Come state?*

RAYMOND: *Bene, bene, grazie. Su con il lavoro!*

HANS: *Una lunga vita ai lavoratori!*

MAX [*suddenly and violently to Hans*]: You're in England now, speak bloody English. [HANS *is nonplussed for the day.*] Everybody speaking in a different language, French, Italian, German. [*To Hans*] You came here to learn English, didn't you? Well, speak it then!

PETER: What's the matter, Max? You frightened of something? Have another beer.

MAX: I'm not frightened of you, I tell you that straight. So *you* can keep quiet.

PETER [*approaching close to Max and talking in his ear*]: You know your trouble, Max? You been here too long.

MAX [*moving away from him*]: Yes, yes, yes, Peter, all right.

PETER [*following him*]: How long have you been here? Twenty-one years? You need a change.

MAX [*moving away again*]: Yes, yes.

PETER [*following him*]: Why don't you go work a season in Germany?

MAX: Sure to.

PETER: Visit other kitchens? Learn more!

MAX: Yes, yes. Get on with your work.

PETER: Don't you worry about my work.

HANS: *Ach, verlass ihn.*

PETER: You can't bear a change, can you? A new face upsets you.

MAX: Let's drop it, uh? Enough, yes?

HANS: *Es lohnt sich nicht, mein Lieber.*

CHEF: All right, Peter, let's have some work, yes?

[PETER *returns to his work and winks at Raymond in passing. Now* MR MARANGO *enters. He is walking slowly round the kitchen, inspecting everything, placing his hand on the hot plate to see if it is still working. It is a mechanical movement – sometimes he puts a hand on the cold pastry slab to see if it is still hot – it is a mechanical tour. Meanwhile –*]

28

KEVIN [*to Peter*]: Is it like this every day? [*Wiping sweat from fore-head.*] Look at me, I never sweated so much since me glorious honeymoon.

PETER: It is nothing this. This is only how it begins. Wait till we start serving, then! [*Raises his hands.*] You in place?

KEVIN: More or less. I got me salmon to cut.

PETER: Good, we eat soon.

MARANGO [*gently to Kevin*]: You're the new cook?

KEVIN [*wiping his brow again*]: Yes, sir.

MARANGO: It's hot, eh, son?

KEVIN: Sure, an' a bit more.

MARANGO: Never mind, I pay you well. Just work, that's all, just work well. [*Continues tour.*]

KEVIN [*to Peter*]: He seems a kind old man.

PETER: You think he is kind? He is a bastard! He talks like that because it is summer now. Not enough staff to serve all his customers, that is why he is kind. You going to stay till winter? Wait till then, you'll see. The fish is burnt! Too much mis-en-place! The soup is sour! He is not a man, he is a restaurant, I tell you. He goes to market at five-thirty in the morning; returns here, reads the mail, goes up to the office, and then comes down here to watch the service. Here he stands, sometimes he walks round touching the hot plate, closing the hot plate doors, looking inside this thing and that thing. Till the last customer he stays. Then he has a sleep upstairs in his office. Half an hour after we come back he is here again, till nine-thirty, maybe ten at night. Every day, morning to night. What kind of a life is that, in a kitchen! Is that a life, I ask you? Me, I don't care, soon I'm going to get married and then whisht – [*Makes movement with his arm to signify 'I'm off'.*]

HANS [*approaches with large tray in his hand which he later puts in cold cupboard*]: Auf geht's, Irishman. I must not speak German to you. This is England, Irishman. [*Loudly as he moves off.*] Auf geht's, hya, hya, hya.

[*At this point* MONIQUE *passes by where* PETER *is working. She is*

Peter's girl, a pretty, petite blonde. Really she is a waitress, but today is the Hostess's day off and she takes over. She is carrying glasses. All she says to Peter is 'Bully'. They have been quarrelling.]

PETER [*to Monique*]: Go to hell! [*To Kevin proudly*] That's my wife or she will be soon. Look – [*takes out card from wallet*] – this card she sent me when she was on holiday. [*Reading aloud.*] 'I am not happy till you come. I love you very much.' And look, her lipstick marks. She is very lovely, yes?

KEVIN: She looks like a girl I knew, all bosom and bouncing, you know?

PETER [*not really understanding what Kevin said*]: We eat soon, eh? [*KEVIN goes off to peruse his printed menu. To Hans*] Hans, hilf' mir. [*They take a large, heavy pot off the oven and pass the contents through a strainer into a small pot which PETER has prepared on the ground.*]

KEVIN [*showing menu to Peter*]: Look here, it says on the printed menu fried plaice and on the board it says fried sole.

PETER: See the chef.

KEVIN [*approaching chef*]: Good morning, Chef. Look, it says here fried plaice and on the board it's got fried sole.

CHEF: I don't know anything about it, it was my day off yesterday. See the second chef.

KEVIN: Have we got any plaice?

CHEF [*sarcastically looking inside his apron*]: It's not here.

KEVIN [*moves away to Raymond*]: Now that's a helpful person for you. Doesn't he care about anything?

RAYMOND: He don't want to know nothing, only when it's gone wrong.

[*MONIQUE again passes in front of PETER to glasserie. PETER is angry. Tries to make his quarrel secret, but of course this is impossible.*]

PETER: Why do you still call me bully, all day you call me bully.

MONIQUE [*moves away across front of stage*]: Bully!

PETER [*following her and talking, as is his habit, in her ear*]: You think to make me angry? What is it you wanted me to do? Let him fight me?

MONIQUE [*turning to him at last*]: He's got a black eye now, you see?

PETER: I see, I see. But he raised a knife to me.

MONIQUE: Bully. [*She turns away.*]

PETER [*following her like the pathetic, jealous lover*]: And remember, you're hostess today, I can see you in the glass. No flirting, do you hear? [*Grips her arm.*] No flirting.

MONIQUE: I shall talk to who I like. [*Moves off.*]

PETER [*hoping no one can hear him*]: Cow! Disgusting cow! All the restaurant can see you.

[*At this point* HANS *draws out the table from the pastry section more to the centre of the stage and begins to lay it with cutlery and glasses and bread ready for lunch.* ALFREDO *also lays himself a place on the counter between where* PETER *and* HANS *work.* MAX, NICHOLAS, *and* FRANK *prepare to eat at Max's table.* KEVIN, MICHAEL, PETER, *and* HANS *will eat at the table* HANS *is now laying.* GASTON *will not eat because he will not sit with* PETER. *These two continue to ignore each other throughout the day.*]

MICHAEL [*shouting*]: Who has the strainer? Gaston? Peter?

PETER: I got it here, you'll have to clean it. [*To a kitchen porter who is nearby.*] Hey, Mangolis, you clean this for Michael, please?

[MANGOLIS *makes a rude sign with his hand and moves off.* PETER *shrugs his shoulders and* MICHAEL *heaves up strainer himself and carts it off. A waitress stops in her work to speak to Peter.*]

WAITRESS [*as though she wants him to confide in her only*]: Hey, Peter, what happened last night? They didn't . . .

PETER [*briskly, she only wants to gossip*]: No, no. Cowards all of them. It was nothing.

PAUL [*to same waitress as she passes his section*]: Hettie, did you go last night?

HETTIE [*ecstatically*]: Mmm.

PAUL: He's a good actor?

HETTIE [*even more ecstatically and hugging herself*]: What a man! I simply melt – oh, one night, just one night with him and then I wash dishes all my life. [*Moves off.*]

RAYMOND [*to Paul*]: So what chance do we stand? You wonder my wife doesn't make love like she used to?

PAUL: And that's why I'm not going to get married. I buy picture books and I'm happy.

WAITRESS: All right, boys, staff meal coming up.

[*While* PAUL *and* RAYMOND *are talking, a long procession of straggling, gossiping, and giggling waitresses have come down stage on the left and are moving around in front of Peter's station and up the other side to* HANS *and* ALFREDO *who have laid trays of food on the serving counter. Beside food are piles of plates. The waitresses help themselves.*]

FIRST WAITRESS: What've you got for us this morning?

ALFREDO: Curried cats and dogs.

SECOND WAITRESS: Is this cabbage from yesterday?

HANS: It's all right, it's all right, eat it, eat.

THIRD WAITRESS: What are these?

HANS: Very good, very good. Cauliflower and white sauce.

FOURTH WAITRESS: White sauce? It smells.

FIFTH WAITRESS: Got anything good, Hans?

HANS: If you don't like, go to chef.

SIXTH WAITRESS: Got any boiled potatoes?

HANS: Not cooked yet, not ready, ach. . . .

[HANS *moves away in disgust leaving them to serve themselves. He watches Peter working a second and then goes into steamroom. As the waitresses are serving themselves and grumbling and eventually moving off to the dining room, we discover that* NICHOLAS *has been arguing with a very tall and heavily made-up waitress near to the glasserie. He is making his quarrel much too public for her liking. He is probably a little drunk already.*]

NICK [*urging her*]: Come with me and ask him. Come on.

WAITRESS: No Nicky, no – now stop.

NICK: Well, why don't you believe me then? If I tell you I got to stay the afternoon why don't you believe me? [*Shouting*] Frank! Frank! Where is he now? [*Wanders off in search of Frank while waitress waits wondering what he is going to do.*]

RAYMOND [*shouting to waitress*]: Hit him! Go on, you're big enough. [*Nudges* PAUL, *they laugh.*]

FRANK [*As he is dragged into the scene by* NICHOLAS]: What do you want me for? What is it now, eh?

WAITRESS: Oh, Nicky, don't be a fool. [*To Ray and Paul despairingly.*] Oh, for Christ's sake, what do you think of him now?

NICK: No, ask him, go on. You don't believe me.

FRANK: Ask him what for hell's sake?

NICK: Have I got to work in the afternoon or haven't I?

FRANK [*moving away incredulous that he has been called away for this*]: You called me for *that*? You mad or something? Do me a favour and leave me out of this will you. [*Grinning to the others*] Asks me to solve his marriage problems. [*To Nick*] I'll tell you how to do it as well, ha, ha, ha!

[*Crashing in on laughter is a loud scream from the steamroom.* HANS *comes running out with his hands covering his face. He curses in German:* 'Zum Kuckuck noch mal! Verdamnt! Zum Teufel!' *A number of people run and crowd him.*]

FRANK: What is it, Hans?

HANS: Who bloody fool put a pot of hot water on steamer?

PETER: It fell on you?

HANS [*moving away from crowd*]: Bastard house! I never worked before so bad. Never, never . . . [PETER *takes him away for some first aid.*]

A WAITRESS [*calling after them*]: Put some of that yellow stuff on him.

FRANK: He'll live. [*To the crowd*] All right, it's all over, come on. [*Crowd disperses,* FRANK *moves to Chef.*] No matter how many times you tell them they still rush around.

CHEF [*he is not interested, shrugs shoulders*]: Is the new chap all right?

FRANK: He seems to be. Look out. [MARANGO *approaches.*]

MARANGO: What happened to the boy?

CHEF [*as though concerned*]: I don't know. I wasn't there. Frank, what happened?

FRANK [*wearily*]: Someone left a pot of boiling water on one of the steamers and he tipped it over his face.

MARANGO: He's burnt his face. It's not serious [*to Chef*] but it might have been. [*He shakes his head sadly and moves away.*]

CHEF: What can I do, Mr Marango? They rush about like mad, I tell them but they don't listen.

[MARANGO *moves off, shaking his head still.*]

CHEF [*to Frank*]: Much he cares! It interrupts the kitchen so he worries. Three more years, Frank, three, that's all and then whisht! retire, finish! Then you can take over.

FRANK: Oh no! Not this boy. I'm in charge one day a week – enough! They can find another madman.

CHEF: Do you think I'm mad?

FRANK: Do you enjoy your work?

CHEF: Who does?

FRANK: So on top of not enjoying your work you take on responsibility – that isn't mad?

CHEF: I've got a standard of living to keep up – idiot!

FRANK [*moving off*]: So go mad!

[PETER *and* HANS *return.* HANS' *face is now a curious red and yellow.* KEVIN *and* PAUL *go up to them.*]

KEVIN: You all right?

[HANS *makes a movement of his hands to say* 'Ach, I'm fed-up, forget it'.]

PAUL: You look beautiful.

KEVIN: A Red Indian.

PETER: Come on, let's eat.

[*They all move to their places to eat.* PAUL *returns to his work. There is less activity in the kitchen now, the calm before the storm. A few waitresses wander around, a porter sweeps the floor.*]

KEVIN [*to Peter*]: How long have you been here?

PETER: Three years.

KEVIN: How did you stick it?

MICHAEL: Sick already?

KEVIN: I don't think I'll last the day.

PETER: People are always coming and going.

HANS [*he is not eating much*]: I think me I'll go soon.

MICHAEL [*to Kevin*]: The worse is to come. [*To others*] Am I right? You wait till the service, ah . . . But you'll get used to it after a while.

PETER: We all said we wouldn't last the day, but tell me what is there a man can't get used to? Nothing! You just forget where you are and you say it's a job.

MICHAEL: He should work on the eggs. Five dishes I've got, five! Hey Paul, any cakes?

PAUL: They're all gone – I got some tart from yesterday. [*Raising his shoulders*] Sorry!

PETER [*not too loudly*]: Liar!

KEVIN: I thought you could eat what you liked here.

MICHAEL: You can, but you have to swipe it. Even the door for cooking. If I want to make an onion soup that's any good I go to the coldroom and I take some chicken's wings to make my stock. No questions, just in and out – whisht!

HANS: I think I go to America.

KEVIN: America?

HANS [*grins sheepishly, he is about to surprise Kevin*]: I been to New York already.

KEVIN: You have?

HANS: I already been twice. [*Nods head to say 'what do you think of that!'*] Worked on a ship. [*Pause.*] On a ship you waste more than you eat. [*Lets this sink in.*] You throw everything into the sea before you come on land. [*Sinks in further.*] Whole chickens! The gulls, you know, they eat it.

KEVIN: What about New York?

HANS [*kissing his fingers*]: The Empire State Buildings . . . ! And Broadway, Broadway – you heard of Broadway? [KEVIN *nods with his mouth full.*] Ah . . . Beautiful city.

KEVIN: I heard it, yes.

HANS [*in his stride now. Grimace, meaning – no question of it!*]: Three in the morning, you know? Women! Night clubs! Rush here, rush there. [*More grimace. Secretly*] This house not very good here.

KEVIN: It's not, eh?

PETER: You got to turn out food hot and quickly. Quality – pooh!
No time!

KEVIN: Even in the small restaurants they're not after carin[g]
much.

MICHAEL [*lighting cigarette*]: Why should they! It's this [*rubs thumb
and finger together*] that counts, you know that.

KEVIN: Oh, I don't know. You'd've thought it was possible to run [a]
small restaurant that could take pride in its food and make mone[y]
too.

PETER: Of course it's possible, my friend – but you pay to eat in it!
It's money. It's all money. The world chase money so you chas[e]
money too. [*Snapping his fingers in a lunatic way*] Money! Money!
Money! [*An idea*] Aha! Watch, watch how Frank hates me.

  [PETER *picks up a glass with water in it and moves gently to where*
  FRANK *eats. His back is to Peter.* PETER *places glass in the cup o[f]*
  Frank's tall white hat and creeps back laughing his laugh to himsel[f]
  FRANK *of course moves and the water spills over him. More laughte[r]*
  from Peter.]

FRANK [*shouting across to him*]: One day you'll lay an egg too many
and it'll crack under you. Yes – you laugh.

PETER: Frank is also unhappy. [*Waitress approaches table.*] Yes?

WAITRESS [*lays hand on Michael's shoulders; he lays his on her buttocks*]
Who's on fish today?

MICHAEL: Do you love me?

WAITRESS: I think you're irresistible. Who's on fish?

KEVIN: Me.

WAITRESS: Right, I order four plaice. [*Moves off.*]

PETER [*easing Kevin back to seat because he has just risen to serve that
order*]: You got time. You not finished your lunch yet. The
customer can wait. [*To Kevin*] Be like Mr Alfredo. Nothing
disturbs Mr Alfredo. Mr Alfredo is a worker and he hates his boss.
He knows his job but he does no more no less and at the right time.
Mr Alfredo is an Englishman – look!

  [*At this point* MR ALFREDO *comes to the front of the stage and looks
  around to see no one is watching. No one is. He tucks something first*

into the right of his apron, then, still looking to see no one has seen, he tucks something into the left of his apron. Then straightening himself out he returns to pick his teeth. A waitress approaches FRANK.]

WAITRESS: Mr Marango wants a leg of chicken and some sauté.

FRANK: Mr Marango can go to hell, I'm eating.

WAITRESS [*moves off*]: I'll call for it in five minutes.

FRANK: They don't give you a chance to eat here.

MAX: Hey, you heard they nearly killed Peter last night?

FRANK: Don't talk to me about that boy. He's mad. I've had too much of him already. . . . Three years.

NICK: They should kill 'em off! Kill 'em off! The lot! Bosch! I hate them you know. I don't hate no one like I hate them. And they want to abolish hanging now. You read about it?

MAX [*to Frank*]: Do you think that Bill 'll go through?

FRANK: How should I know! I suppose it's worth a try.

MAX: They'll be sorry, I'm telling you.

NICHOLAS [*self-righteously*]: What I say is, if a man he kills another then he should be killed too.

MAX [*approvingly*]: An eye for an eye.

NICHOLAS: And we should use the electric chair. It's no good the hanging.

MAX [*enjoying what he is about to say*]: Remember those two they put on the chair in America not long ago, for spying? The bloody thing misfired – ha – they had to do it again. I bet the electrician on that job copped out. . . .

[MONIQUE *walks past* PETER *to front of stage and waits for him by his station. She has a cup of tea in her hand.* PETER *jumps up and goes to her. They do this every meal break.*]

PETER: Where are you going tomorrow?

MONIQUE: Dancing at the Astra.

PETER: Why do you have to go there? All the prostitutes go there.

MONIQUE: I'm going with Monty.

PETER: Listen, Monique. Tell Monty tonight. Ask for a divorce, eh? We can't go on like thieves, we do damage to ourselves, you know that?

MONIQUE: Peter, not here, please. I can't tell him yet.

PETER: Here – inside here [*knocks at his head with his hand*] we do
damage. We insult ourselves. I'm not going to wait much longer
you'll see. You think I like this Tivoli? You don't believe me I
won't wait do you?

MONIQUE: Please yourself.

PETER [*despairingly*]: What do you want me to do? Do you want to
make me something to laugh at? Three years I'm here now, three ..

[MONIQUE *leaves him, saying 'Not now'.* PETER *is about to
become furious but controls himself and as though in high spirits kicks a
cardboard margarine box that has been lying around.*]

PETER [*shouting*]: *Auf geht's,* Irishman. Finish now. *Auf geht's.*

[PETER *sings his song and* HANS *and* KEVIN *join in with him as
they – and indeed all the cooks – clear away their plates and prepare
to face the service.* CHEF *approaches* KEVIN.]

CHEF: You all right?

KEVIN: Yes, Chef.

CHEF: In place and everything?

KEVIN: Yes, Chef.

[CHEF *moves in to show* KEVIN *how it's done. First dip fish into
milk, then flour and the friture.*]

PETER [*to Hans*]: Watch him now, the Irishman. Hya, hya, hya!
Soon he won't know what is happening. Watch. Hya, hya, hya!

[*The waitresses begin to enter, shouting their orders at the required
station. They take plates from hot plate, cradle them in their arms,
and order. They appear in greater numbers as the service swings into
motion. Queues form in front of first one cook, then another.*]

HANS [*shouting to Max*]: Veal cutlets and sausages, please!

MAX: Ye-es. [*Takes them in tray to Hans.*]

GASTON [*shouting to Max*]: Send up the steaks and mutton chops!

MAX [*angrily*]: Wait a bloody minute, will you!

GASTON [*in panic*]: I got six steaks ordered already.

MAX: So what am I supposed to do?

GASTON [*to nobody in particular*]: Everybody the same. I've always
got a big queue before I start. [*Returns mumbling.*]

FIRST WAITRESS [*to Kevin*]: Three plaice, please.

KEVIN: Three plaice? Right.

SECOND WAITRESS: Two grilled salmon, do we order it?

KEVIN: Yes, five minutes.

THIRD WAITRESS: Three grilled sardines, please.

KEVIN [*rushing around*]: Right away!

FOURTH WAITRESS: Four plaice, please.

KEVIN: All right, all right.

PETER [*shouting while he serves*]: Ha! ha! Hee! hee! Ho ho! They're here! They come!

FIRST WAITRESS [*to Peter*]: Two turbot.

PETER: Two turbot!

SECOND WAITRESS: Three dishes of fish.

PETER [*rushing around*]: Three dishes of fish!

THIRD WAITRESS: Are my six cod ready yet?

PETER: When did you order them?

THIRD WAITRESS: Five minutes ago. I came past and you were talking to Hans – remember?

PETER: I remember nothing. Come back in five minutes. Next?

THIRD WAITRESS: You weren't listening, that's what it was.

PETER [*rudely*]: You ordered nothing I say, now come back five minutes' time. Next? [*Next one orders.*]

HANS [*shouting to his waitresses who aren't in a queue*]: You wait yes? You can't see the cutlets cook?

[*The* CHEF *is wandering around in all this as though he were searching for something further ahead. It is his way of making the cooks believe he is not really watching them. As he stands by the pastry section a* HEAD WAITER *comes up to him.*]

HEAD WAITER: Ten minutes ago Daphne ordered six cod and they are not ready yet.

CHEF [*walks up to Peter*]: The cod – not ready yet?

PETER [*in the midst of his rush*]: She's a liar, you know the one, Chef? She ordered nothing. Here. [*Hands six cod.*]

[CHEF *passes on cod to* HEAD WAITER *and moves on.* PETER *makes a face after him and when it is safe he begins to sing his song while working. Half-way through he breaks off and rushes to oven. There is something vast and Shakespearian in the way* PETER *moves; he is always wanting to play the fool.*]

PETER: Oh God! She burns! The cod! Hya, hya, hya. She burns, Irishman. No good, no good. [*Rushes the frying-pan with the burnt fish to the dustbin nearby and covers it with paper.*] Ssh, sssssh. Hya, hya, hya.

HANS [*to Peter, loudly, in the midst of his own work*]: That is not too good work, Peter, not good work *mein Lieber*. Pig's work. [*Laughs and points to Kevin who has large queue at his station.*] We have busy time, Irishman, yes?

KEVIN: For God's sake help me. [PETER *rushes to his aid laughing.*]

PETER: Let's go, Irishman, let's go. [*To a waitress.*] The next?

FIRST WAITRESS: Two salmon.

PETER: Right. [*He serves while* KEVIN *replenishes the supply.*] And the next?

SECOND WAITRESS: Three sardines.

PETER: And the next?

[*He rushes like mad crying, 'And the next, the next!' They each give him their order. Meanwhile* HANS *dashes between his own station and Peter's. The whole tempo of work is speeded up suddenly. Waitresses rush around with dishes in their arms. Porters clear away dirty pots. Orders are being shouted; every station has its share of waitresses. At this moment a queue has formed at Peter's station and he now rushes there laughing like a merry fool going into battle.*]

PETER: Look at this – hya, hya – good morning ladies – and the next. . . .

FIRST WAITRESS [*to Peter*]: Three mixed fish. [PETER *serves her and cries out, 'Next, next', and so on.*]

SECOND WAITRESS: Two cod.

THIRD WAITRESS: One turbot.

FOURTH WAITRESS: One cod.

KEVIN [*to Peter*]: I've run out of lemons!

PETER [*with rude indifference*]: Well, cut some more then. The next?

KEVIN: Let me borrow your cutting board then, please. [*He moves to take it from Peter's bench.*]

PETER [*he stops his work and jumping on* KEVIN *grabs board. In the kitchen it is each man for himself now*]: Oh no, no, no, no, my friend. The plate room, the plate room, in the plate room you'll find them. This is mine, I have need of it.

KEVIN: But I'll give it back in a few seconds.

PETER [*pointing*]: The plate room. [*Slams his hand down on the board for emphasis. To a waitress –*] What do you want?

KEVIN [*surprised at this change in Peter*]: Well, speak a little human like, will yer, please?

PETER: No time, no time.

WAITRESS [*to Peter*]: Will you please serve me with three turbot?

PETER: I've only got two left, in five minutes, five minutes, come back in five minutes. [*Dashes off to steamroom to get a new plate of turbot in water ready to boil.*]

    [*Meanwhile* KEVIN *is being harassed at his station. While he is busy cutting up some more lemons a queue of demanding waitresses begin to pester him. As the first waitress calls for her order the* CURTAIN *begins to fall very, very, very slowly so that when it is completely fallen we can still hear Peter cry, 'Auf geht's.'*]

FIRST WAITRESS [*to Kevin*]: Me sole, luvvy, got me sole?

KEVIN: Wait a minute, can yer?

SECOND WAITRESS: You should have it all ready, Paddy, me boy. No time for breathing here. [*She turns for confirmation to her friends who agree.*]

KEVIN [*still rushing around*]: Jesus, is this a bloody madhouse or something? You all gone mad?

    [*The waitresses laugh among themselves, a rather fiendish laughter.*]

THIRD WAITRESS: Come on, Paddy.

PETER [*in the midst of his own rushing*]: *Auf geht's, auf geht's.* [*He laughs his laugh, and the lights fade on the Kitchen's rush.*]

INTERLUDE

Lights fade up on the sound of a guitar.
It is afternoon break.
The sounds of the oven are at half.
PAUL *and* RAYMOND *are working in their corner. These are the only two who stay through the afternoon.*
KEVIN *is flat out on his back on a wooden bench – exhausted.*
DIMITRI *is slowly sweeping up.*
PETER *is sitting by a table waiting for Monique.*
HANS *is in a corner singing 'Ah sinner-man' in German to a guitar.*

KEVIN: Finished! I'm done! I'm boiled! You can serve me up for supper!

PAUL [*as if ordering a meal*]: Two portions of boiled Irishman, please! With garnish!

RAYMOND [*also calling*]: Two fried tomatoes on his ears, potatoes round his head, and stuff his mouth with an extra helping of peas.

PAUL: Sprinkle with shamrock and serve with chips – if you please.

KEVIN: I'll produce me own gravy! But did you see it? Did-you-see-that? Fifteen hundred customers and an' half of them eating fish. *I* had to start work on a Friday!

RAYMOND: It's every day the same, my friend.

KEVIN [*raising himself up*]: Look at me. I'm soaking. Look at this jacket. I can wring it out. That's not sweat, no man carries that much water. [*Flopping back again.*] Kevin, you'll drop dead if you stay. I'm warning you, Kevin, take a tip from a friend, hop it! Get out! You've got your youth, Kevin – keep it! This is no place for a human being – you'll drop dead, I'm telling yous.

DIMITRI: Hey, Irishman, what you grumbling about this place for? Is different anywhere else? This stinking kitchen is like the world – you know what I mean? It's too fast to know what happens. People come and people go, big excitement, big noise. [*Makes noise, gesticulates and runs wildly about, and then stops.*] What for? In the end who do you know? You make a friend, you going to be all your life his friend, but when you go from here – pshtt! you forget! Why you grumble about this one kitchen?

PETER: You're a very intelligent boy, Dimitri.

DIMITRI: And you're a bloody fool. I'm not sure I want to talk with you.

KEVIN: Oh, not the Gaston row again. All the morning I hear how Peter give Gaston a black eye. It's the break, no rows, please, it's peace. Can you hear it? It's lovely. It's silence. It's nothing – ahhh! [*Moves.*] Oooh – I'm drowning, in me own sweat. Christ! What a way to die.

DIMITRI [*to Peter*]: A bloody fool you!

[PETER *picks up a cardboard box and puts it over Dimitri's head.* DIMITRI *flings it off angrily and is about to throw it back, but he sees* PETER *with his head in his hands. Instead he takes out a cigarette box and begins rolling Peter a cigarette. He gives the paper to* PETER *to lick, then continues folding it and hands it to him.*]

PETER: Hey, Irishman, I thought you didn't like this place. Why don't you go home and sleep.

KEVIN: Me home is a room and a bed and a painting of the Holy Virgin. It'll always be there.

PETER: Like this place, this house – this too, it'll always be here. That's a thought for you, Irishman. This – this mad house, it's always here. When you go, when I go, when Dimitri go – this kitchen stays. It'll go on when we die, think about that. We work here – eight hours a day, sweat our guts, and yet – it's nothing. We take nothing. Here – the kitchen, here – you. You and the kitchen. And the kitchen don't mean nothing to you and you don't mean to the kitchen nothing. Dimitri is right, you know – why do you grumble about this kitchen? The world is filled with kitchens – only some they call offices and some they call factories. There, Irishman – what do you say to that?

KEVIN: You want to come in one morning and find it gone?

PETER: Just one morning. Imagine it, eh? Gone. All this gone.

KEVIN: So you'd be out of work!

PETER: So I'd die?

KEVIN: It doesn't worry you, I suppose.

HANS: *Du träumst schon wieder, mein Lieber.*

KEVIN: What's he say?

PETER: He say – I'm dreaming. [*Starts to sing his rowdy 'Hi lee hi lo' song, but stops and lets* HANS *continue his guitaring.*] Hey, Irishman, how do you dream?

KEVIN: How's that?

PETER: Listen, Irishman – I give you a chance to dream – hey Paul, Raymondo, Dimitri – stop work a minute, you got time. Here, come here. [*All but* RAYMOND *gather round.*] We are all given a chance to dream. The ovens are low, the customers gone, Marango is gone, it's all quiet. God has given us a chance now! So dream. Go ahead and dream. Dimitri, you! You dream first.

DIMITRI [*after a pause*]: In this place? With iron around me? And dustbins? And black walls?

PETER: Pretend! The walls are sky, yes? The iron, it's rocks on a coast. The dustbins [*thinks*] they're bushes, and the ovens are the noise of winds. Look at the lights – stars Dimitri.

[*The others gasp and make rude noises at this poetry.*]

HANS: Dreaming, *mein Lieber*, dreaming, dreaming.

PETER [*angrily*]: I want to dream. I feel like it. Dimitri – dream – a little dream, what you see?

DIMITRI [*after a longer pause*]: A little, a little er – what you call it – a small house, sort of –

PAUL: A hut?

DIMITRI: No –

KEVIN: A shed?

DIMITRI: That's right, a shed. With instruments, and tools, and I make lots of radios and television sets maybe, and . . .

PETER: Ach! Silly boy. A hobby he dreams of! Hey, Irishman – you – you dream.

KEVIN: Sleep, me. Most people sleep and dream, me – I dream of sleep!

PETER: Hans – you, what are your dreams?

[HANS *sings on, as though not answering the question. Then –*]

HANS: *Geld! Mein Lieber!* Money. With money I'm a good man,

I'm generous, I love all the world. Money, *mein Lieber, Geld!* [*Continues to sing.*]

PETER: How can you talk of money, Hans, when you're singing?

HANS: Dreaming, *mein Lieber*, dreaming, dreaming.

PETER: Raymondo?

RAYMOND: Women!

PETER: Paul?

PAUL: Listen, Peter – I'll tell you something. I'm going to be honest with you. You don't mind if I'm honest? Right! I'm going to be honest with you. I don't like you. Now wait a minute, let me finish. I don't like you! I think you're a pig! You bully, you're jealous, you go mad with your work, you always quarrel. All right! But now it's quiet, the ovens are low, the work has stopped for a little, and now I'm getting to know you. I still think you're a pig only now – not so much of a pig. So that's what I dream. I dream of a friend. You give me a rest, you give me silence, you take away this mad kitchen so I make friends, so I think – maybe all the people I thought were pigs are not so much pigs.

PETER: You think people are pigs, eh?

PAUL: Listen, I'll tell you a story. I agree with Dimitri also. The world is filled with kitchens – and when it's filled with kitchens you get pigs. I'll tell you. Next door me, next door where I live is a bus driver. Comes from Hoxton; he's my age, married and got two kids. He says good morning to me; I ask him how he is, I give his children sweets. That's our relationship. Somehow he seems frightened to say too much, you know? God forbid I might ask him for something. So we make no demands on each other. Then one day the busmen go on strike. He's out for five weeks. Every morning I say to him, 'Keep going mate, you'll win.' Every morning I give him words of encouragement, I say I understand his cause. I've got to get up earlier to get to work but I don't mind. We're neighbours, we're workers together, he's pleased. I give him money for the strike fund. I can see he's pleased. Then, one Sunday, there's a peace march. I don't believe they do much good but I go, because in this world a man's got to show he can still say his piece. The next morning he comes up to me and he says, now listen to this, he says, 'Did you go on that peace march yesterday?' So I says yes, I did go on that peace march yesterday. So then he turns round to me and he says: 'You know what? A bomb should've been dropped on the lot of them! It's a pity', he says, 'that they had children with them 'cos a bomb should've been dropped on the lot!' And you know what was upsetting him? The march was holding up the traffic, the buses couldn't move so fast! Now I don't want him to say I'm right, I don't want him to agree with what I did, but what makes me so sick with terror is that he didn't stop to think that this man helped me in my cause so maybe, only *maybe*, there's something in his cause, I'll talk about it. No! The buses were held up so drop a bomb, he says, on the lot! And you should've seen the hate in his eyes, as if I'd murdered his child. Like an animal he looked. And the horror is this – that there's a wall, a big wall between me and millions of people like him. And I think – where will it end? What do you do about it? And I look around me, at the kitchen, at the factories, at the enormous bloody buildings going up with all those offices and all those people in them and I think Christ! I think. Christ, Christ, Christ! [*He moves round and round with his hand on his head.*] I agree with you, Peter – maybe one morning we should wake up and find them all gone. But then I think: I should stop making pastries? The factory workers should stop making trains and cars? The miner should leave the coal where it is? [*Pause.*] *You* give *me* an answer. You give me your dream.

KEVIN: Hush, patissier! Hush! It's quiet now. Gently now.

[*There is a long silence.* HANS *who had stopped playing now continues. The ovens hum.*]

PETER: I ask for dreams – you give me nightmares.

PAUL: So I've dreamt! Is it my fault if it's a nightmare?

KEVIN: We're waiting for your dream now, Peter boy.

DIMITRI [*jumping up suddenly*]: This is the United Nations, eh? A big conference. Is Russia here, and America and France and England – and Germany too. Is all here. And they got on a competition. Is finished the wars, is finished the rows. Everybody gone home. We got time on our hands. A prize of one million dollars for the best dream. Raymondo, he want a new woman every night. Me, I want a workshop. Paul, he wants a friend. Irishman, he wants a bed, and Hans, he just want the million dollars. Big opportunity! Come on, Peter, a big dream.

PETER [*looking around*]: All this gone?

DIMITRI: You said so. One morning you come here, to this street here, and the kitchen is gone. And you look around for more kitchens and is none anywhere. What you want to do? The United Nations wants to know.

[PETER, *suddenly confronted with his own idea, becomes embarrassed and shy. He laughs his silly laugh.* 'Hya, hya, hya, hya.' *Kicks the cardboard box.* 'Hya, hya, hya.' *And then* MONIQUE *arrives, bringing in the last dishes, and* PETER *forgets everything and becomes the all-consumed lover, the excited child.*]

MONIQUE: Ready?

PETER: Finished? I come, I come. Hey, Irishman, you'll soon be coming back. Go home. Change. You catch pneumonia. [*Excitedly.*] *Auf geht's, auf geht's!*

[*The mad* PETER *rushes out with his* MONIQUE.
The rest are left.
The guitar and the hum of the ovens.]

DIMITRI [*shouting at the absent Peter*]: Fool! Bloody fool! We wait for a dream.

PAUL: I don't know what you see in him.

DIMITRI: I don't know what I see in him either. Bloody fool!

KEVIN: Bloody volcano, if you ask me. I'm away. [*Rises.*]

PAUL [*returning to his work*]: He hasn't got a dream.

KEVIN: It's all mad talk if you ask me. I don't see no point in it. I don't see no point in that Peter bloke either. He talks about peace and dreams and when I ask him if I could use his cutting board to cut me lemons on this morning he told me – get your own. Dreams! See yous!

[KEVIN *exits.*

HANS *is still playing.*

DIMITRI *returns to his sweeping.*]

PAUL [*to Dimitri*]: So *you* tell me that point of all that. I don't even know what I was saying myself.

DIMITRI: Why should I know? Sometimes things happen and no one sees the point – and then suddenly, something else happen and you see the point. Peter not a fool! You not a fool! People's brain moves all the time. *All* the time. I'm telling you.

[DIMITRI *sweeps on.*

HANS *continues singing.*

The LIGHTS *slowly fade.*]

ACT TWO

Everyone has returned for the evening work. The waitresses have been served with their food, the cooks have settled down some five minutes ago to their own meal. As the curtain rises PAUL *and* RAYMOND *are in the last stages of their day's work.* MICHAEL, KEVIN, GASTON, *and* HANS *are at the table near the pastry cooks.* ALFREDO *and* PETER *are eating at Alfredo's usual spot.* FRANK, MAX, *and* NICHOLAS *were seated as in the morning. The* CHEF *is by his table writing. Some of the porters are leaning by the walls talking, one or two waitresses wander in or out. The coffee woman is eating with* BERTHA. PETER *is lying with his head in his arms.*

ALFREDO [*to Peter*]: You are not ill, are you?

PETER [*his head all the time in his arms*]: No.

ALFREDO: Good! You have all your teeth?

PETER: Yes.

ALFREDO: Good! You have good lodgings?

PETER: Yes.

ALFREDO: You eat enough, don't you?

PETER: Yes.

ALFREDO: So tell me what you're unhappy for.

PETER [*raising his head*]: Alfredo, you are a good cook, uh? You come in the morning, you go straight to work, you ask nobody anything, you tell nobody anything. You are ready to start work before we are, you never panic. Tell me, is this a good house?

ALFREDO [*drily*]: Depends. It's not bad for Mr Marango, you know.

MICHAEL [*approaching Peter*]: Peter, give me a cigarette, please! [PETER *does so.* MICHAEL *stays on to listen.*]

ALFREDO: I'm an old man. It's finished for me. Mind you, I've worked in places where I could do good cooking. But it doesn't matter now. Now I work only for the money.

MICHAEL: Quite right! A match, Peter, please.

PETER [*to Michael, as he looks for matches*]: You like it here, don't you? No, I got no matches.

49

MICHAEL: The ovens, I love the sound of the ovens.

PETER: Idiot! He loves the sound of the ovens! You stand before them all day! They're red hot! You fry first a bit of ham and an egg in a tin; then someone orders an onion soup and you put soup and bread and cheese in another tin and you grill that. Then someone orders an omelette and you rush to do that. Then someone throws you a hamburger and you fry that. You go up, you go down, you jump here, you jump there; you sweat till steam comes off your back.

MICHAEL [*moving across to* NICK *for a light*]: I love it.

PETER [*returning head to arms*]: Good luck to you.

MAX [*to Nick*]: What did you marry her for then?

MICHAEL [*holding out his hand to Nick*]: Got a light, Nick?

NICK [*loudly (they are both drunk) as he feels for matches*]: Because I love her, that's why. Ha – [*digs Frank*] – did you hear that? Why did I marry her? Because I love her. And you? [*Hands* MICHAEL *matches.*] Here.

MAX [*enjoying his joke uproariously and also digging Frank*]: Because she told me I was big for my age. [*When his laughter has died down*] Hey, did you read about the man who took a young girl into his house, his wife was there, and they all sat undressed watching television. His wife was there! With him! All undressed! Watching television!

FRANK [*drily, he too is drunk*]: So what happened? They caught cold? [MICHAEL *wanders back to the third table.*]

KEVIN: I'll be taking *my* leave tonight, by Christ.

GASTON: But you'll get used to it. It's good money.

[*At this point a waitress strolls up to listen.*]

KEVIN: To hell with the money an' all. I like me pay but not for this. It's too big here, man; it's high pressure all the time. An' the food! Look at the food! I never cooked so bad since I was in the army. An' no one is after caring much either!

WAITRESS: And what about the waitresses? We're the animals! Here, you know at the banquet the other day, when we had Minestrone soup . . .

HANS: Huh! Minestrone soup! A drop of meat stock and salt!

WAITRESS: . . . there were about ten of us, some extras as well. Well, the head waiter gave us the signal to get out plates, and oh my God, the mad rush. Everybody pushing everybody else out of the way. Look – [*shows arm*]. One of the extras did it. It makes you an animal it does; I was telling my . . .

HANS [*to Kevin*]: Marango will try to make you stay.

KEVIN: Now there's a man. Have you watched him? One of the girls dropped some cups by there this morning and he cried 'Me wages', he cried. 'All me wages down there!' And do you take notice of the way he strolls among us all? I thought he'd a kind face but when he's done talking with you his kindliness evaporates. In thin air it goes, sudden, and his face gets worried as though today were the last day and he had to be a closing for good and he were taking a last sad glance at everything going on. This mornin' he watched me a while and then walked away shaking his head as though I were dying and there was not a drop of hope for me left an' all.

HANS [*to Gaston*]: What he has said?

[GASTON *laughs and digs* KEVIN. *The waitress wanders away, but not before she flirtatiously kisses* PAUL *who has just strolled up.*]

PAUL [*to those at the table*]: Bon appétit.

GASTON: Paul, you got some cake?

PAUL [*to Ray*]: Ray, we got any cake? [RAY *brings some over*] [*To Hans.*] You got over this morning yet?

HANS [*taking one of the cakes* RAY *is offering round*]: This morning, ach! He's a big fool that Max. He's like a dustbin.

RAY: So why you take notice? Look at them.

[FRANK *is still eating*, MAX *and* NICHOLAS *are standing up and pointing at each other in some sort of argument, waving fingers, pulling faces, and swaying.*]

RAY: The first thing in the morning they come in and drink a bottle of beer. Then they're happy. All day they drink. [*Returns to work.*]

PAUL [*to Hans*]: What did Max say then, exactly?

HANS: He doesn't like I talk in German. [*Tragically.*] You know,

Paul, you – you are a Jew and me – I'm a German; we suffer together. [*Nods his head to emphasize the sad situation.*] We suffer together.

[PAUL *laughs ironically, slaps Hans on the back, and returns to his work.*]

KEVIN: Is that a Jew then?

HANS [*sentimentally*]: A very good boy.

KEVIN: Well, who'd have thought that now!

[*At this point a* TRAMP *wanders into the kitchen. He is looking for the* CHEF. *Everyone stares at him and grins.*]

MAX [*shouting across to Bertha*]: Bertha, ha, ha, is this your old man come after you? [*General laughter.*]

[*The* TRAMP *comes over to the group of young men and talks to Kevin.*]

TRAMP: 'Scuse me. The Chef please, which'n is he?

[*The* CHEF *wanders slowly up to the man, trying to assume an intimidating expression. He says nothing but merely raises his head questioningly.*]

TRAMP: 'Scuse me, Chef. [*Touching his knee.*] War disabled. I don't usually ask for food, but I lost me pensions book, see? I don't like to ask but . . .

[*The* CHEF *turns to* MICHAEL *and points to the soup. At the same time he says to a porter, 'Clean a tin,' and then he returns to his place.*]

TRAMP [*to Kevin*]: Don't usually do this. Can't do anything till they trace me book. [*To Hans*] Got it in the desert, 'gainst Rommel.

[HANS *looks away. After an embarrassing few seconds silence* MICHAEL *returns with a fruit tin full of soup and hands it to the tramp.*]

TRAMP [*realizing he hasn't received much, tries again*]: Got a cigarette?

MAX: Go on, 'op it, be quick, we got work.

PETER [*goes up to tramp and looks in the tin. He takes tin from tramp and offers it to Max*]: You drink it?

MAX: Ah, get out of it, you and your high and bloody mighty gestures. *I* work for my living. Fool!

[PETER *ignores him and tosses the tin into the dustbin. Then he moves to Hans' station and brings back two meat cutlets which he gives to the tramp.*]

PETER: Take these cutlets. [*Gently pushing him.*] Now go, quick, whist!

[*But he is not quick enough. The* CHEF *approaches and stands looking on.*]

CHEF [*quietly*]: What's that?

PETER: I gave him some cutlets.

CHEF [*still quietly*]: Mr Marango told you to give him?

PETER: No, but . . .

CHEF: You heard me say perhaps?

PETER: No, I . . .

CHEF: You have authority suddenly?

PETER [*impatiently*]: So what's a couple of cutlets, we going bankrupt or something?

CHEF: It's four and six, that's what, and it's me who's Chef that's what and – [PETER *moves away muttering* 'Ach'. *The* CHEF *follows him, annoyed now.*] Don't think we're too busy I can't sack you. Three years is nothing you know; you don't buy the place in three years, you hear me? You got that? Don't go thinking I won't sack you.

[*By this time* MR MARANGO *appears on his round, hands in pocket.* TRAMP *finds this an opportunity to go. With a gesture of the head* MARANGO *asks what is the matter.* CHEF *does not wish to make any more fuss.*]

CHEF: The tramp, Peter gave him a cutlet, it was his own supper.

[CHEF *returns to his work, dispersing the crowd on the way.* MR MARANGO *simply nods his head at Peter. It is a sad nodding, as though Peter had just insulted him. He walks from right of stage to the left in a half circle round Peter nodding his head all the time.*]

MARANGO [*softly*]: Sabotage. [*Pause.*] It's sabotage you do to me. [*Sadly taking his right hand out of his pocket and waving it round the kitchen.*] It's my fortune here and you give it away. [*He moves off muttering* 'Sabotage'.]

PETER: But it . . .

MARANGO [*not even bothering to look round*]: Yes, yes, I'm always wrong – of course – yes, yes. [*Moves off into dining room.*]

[*Everyone settles back into place.* PETER *goes to get a cup of coffee and makes faces at Marango's back; then he returns beside Alfredo.* HANS *joins them.*]

HANS: *Er ist wirklich hinter dir, her?*

PETER: *Ach, er erwartet, dass die ganze Welt auf seine Küche aufpasst.*]

KEVIN: I seem to remember being told not to grumble by someone.

PETER: A bastard man. A bastard house.

KEVIN: And he also said you could get used to anything.

PETER: But this house is like – is like –

PAUL: Yeah? What is it like?

PETER: God in heaven, I don't know what it's like. If only it – if only it –

KEVIN: Yes, yes, we know all that – if only it would all go.

PETER: Just one morning – to find it gone.

PAUL: Fat lot of good you'd be if it went – you couldn't even cough up a dream when it was necessary.

PETER: A dream?

HANS: Yes, *mein Lieber* – the dream, remember? You walked out on us.

PETER: A dream! [*Thinks about it sadly.*] I can't dream in a kitchen. [*As if to prove the point the work in the kitchen is heard extra loud.* MONIQUE *comes front of stage and leans on centre of counter with a cup of coffee.* PETER *goes up to her.* MICHAEL *and* HANS *wander back to their table.*]

MONIQUE [*with great sentimentality*]: Did you see that tramp? Isn't that a shame?

PETER: You didn't hear?

MONIQUE: Hear what?

PETER [*boasting and laughing*]: I had a row about him. Mr Marango and the Chef there. They wanted to give him a dirty tin full of soup so I threw it away and gave him some cutlets.

MONIQUE: Oh you didn't, Peter. . . . And Marango caught you?

PETER [*imitating*]: 'Sabotage', the old man said. 'Sabotage, all my fortune you take away.'

MONIQUE [*pushing him playfully with her hand*]: Oh, Peter!

PETER [*tenderly*]: I brought your birthday present.

MONIQUE [*placing her arm round his neck joyfully*]: Tell me, tell me, what is it, ah? What is it?

PETER [*taking her in his arms*]: You wait, yes?

[MONIQUE *embraces him and her hand slips to his buttocks which she nips. They playfully struggle for a few seconds in which time another waitress passes them and takes Monique's hand off Peter's behind and places it on his shoulders, crying, 'Now then, Monique, watch it!'*]

MONIQUE [*coyly replacing her hand*]: But it's nice.

PETER: Can you eat me?

MONIQUE: Oh, don't be silly, Peter.

PETER: How do you want me? Grilled? Fried? Underdone? Well done?

[*While* PETER *and* MONIQUE *continue to talk affectionately a sudden cry comes up from the back of the kitchen. That waitress who has just passed Peter and Monique has doubled up in pain and passed out. A crowd rushes to her – it all happens very quickly, hardly noticed. The boys at the table simply glance round and watch but do not move.* PETER *and* MONIQUE *do not even hear it. We can only hear a few confused voices.*]

FIRST VOICE: What's happened?

SECOND VOICE: Winnie has passed out.

THIRD VOICE: All right, now, don't crowd round, take her into the dining room. Don't crowd round. [*Crowd disperses as* WINNIE *is taken into dining room.*]

KEVIN: Well, what was all that now?

GASTON: The heat. Always affecting someone. Terrible.

[*Meanwhile. . . .*]

PETER [*to Monique*]: Did you – er – you still going to do it? I mean I . . .

MONIQUE: Don't worry, Peter, I shall see to it now. It's not the first time, is it?

PETER: You don't think we should go through with it? I don't mind being responsible, you know that.

MONIQUE: Enough, I'm not going to talk about it any more.

PETER: You told Monty about us, then?

MONIQUE [*finishing her coffee*]: You really must stop rowing with Marango, darling.

PETER: Did you speak to Monty as we said?

MONIQUE: They won't stand it all the time, you know. I'm always telling you about this, Peter.

PETER: Listen, Monique, I love you. Please listen to me that I love you. You said you love me but you don't say to your husband this thing.

MONIQUE: Now not this again.

PETER: You are not going to leave him, are you? You don't really intend it?

MONIQUE: Oh, Peter, please.

PETER: What do you want I should do then?

MONIQUE: Did the Chef say much?

PETER: We could leave any day. We could go for a long holiday first. Ski-ing in Switzerland perhaps.

MONIQUE: I am going to the hairdresser tomorrow as well.

PETER: Monique, we row this morning, we row in the afternoon too, this evening we are almost in love again. Answer me.

MONIQUE: Monty has promised we shall soon have our own house.

PETER [*screaming*]: MONIQUE!

[MONIQUE *looks round in embarrassment and, muttering* 'You fool', *stalks off. A waitress approaches Peter.*]

WAITRESS: You serving yet, Peter? I want three turbot. Special for Marango.

PETER: It's half-past six yet?

WAITRESS: It's nearly . . .

PETER: Half-past six is service.

WAITRESS: But it's special . . .

PETER: HALF-PAST SIX!

[PETER *goes off to find some beer. Service is just beginning. Evening service is not so hectic and takes a longer time to start up. Waitresses*

56

appear, most people are at their stations, the people at the table near the pastry section are just rising.]

KEVIN: Me, I'd have a Jaguar. It's got a luxury I could live with.

GASTON: Have you seen the new French Citroen? Just like a mechanical frog it looks.

HANS: And the Volkswagen? It's not a good car?

KEVIN: Now there's a good little car for little money.

HANS: No country makes like the Volkswagen.

KEVIN: You've gotta hand it to the German.

[PETER *has returned with a bottle of beer. He cries out his laughter and sings his song. More waitresses are coming in but the service is easy and orders ring out in comfort. One waitress, however, breaks her journey round the kitchen and, wiping some plates which she has just taken from the hot plate, goes up to the* CHEF *to gossip.* MAX *and* NICHOLAS *stand by listening.*]

WAITRESS: Heard what happened to Winnie? She's been rushed to hospital.

MAX: What did she do wrong then?

WAITRESS: She was pregnant.

MAX: She didn't look it.

WAITRESS: I know. She didn't give herself a chance.

CHEF: Misfired?

WAITRESS: I'll say, and it weren't no accident neither.

MAX [*shaking his head*]: Silly woman, silly woman.

CHEF: She's got seven children already, though.

WAITRESS: That's right. Marango's hopping mad. It started happening on the spot, in there, in the dining room. May and Sophie had to take her away.

MAX: What did she do then?

WAITRESS: She took pills, that's what. And I'll tell you something else, there are four other girls here took the same pills. There! Four of them! And you know who one of the four is? [*She inclines her head in Peter's direction.*]

MAX: Monique?

WAITRESS [*nodding her head triumphantly*]: Now don't you tell anyone

I told you, mind. But you ask Hettie, ask her, she bought the stuff.
[*Continues on the round.*]

MAX: Knew this would happen. Knew it! Can't be done though.
What makes them think that by taking a tablet through the mouth
it'll affect the womb? There is only one way, the way it went in!
What happens with a tablet? Nothing! Nothing can. The stomach
is irritated that's all, squeezed, see? Forces the womb, presses it.

NICHOLAS: Now what do you know about this? A doctor now!

MAX: Oh, I know about this all right. Only one drug is effective
through the mouth. [*Secretively.*] And you know what that is?
Ergot? Heard of it? Only thing to do it. And that's rare. Oh yes,
I studied this in the forces when I had nothing else to do. Very
interesting, this psychology. Complicated. I knew Winnie was
pregnant soon as she came here.

[*All this time the pastry cooks have been clearing away their station
and are now ready to go. They are saying good-bye to everyone.* MAX
shouts to them as they go.]

MAX: Some people have it easy!

[*The pastrycooks leave and as they do so an argument flares up
suddenly at Peter's station.* PETER *takes a silver plate with fish in it
out of a waitress's hand and smashes it to the floor. She had just
helped herself to her order while* PETER *had been busy and his back
turned.*]

PETER: You wait for me, yes? *I* serve you. You ask *me*.

WAITRESS: But you were busy.

PETER: I don't care. This is my place and there [*points to the side of
bar*], there is for you.

WAITRESS: Now you wait a bloody minute, will you? Who the hell
do you think you are, you?

PETER: You don't worry who I am. I'm a cook, yes? And you're
the waitress, and in the kitchen you do what I like, yes? And in
the dining room you do what you like.

WAITRESS [*taking another plate from the oven*]: I won't take orders
from you you know, I . . .

PETER [*shouting and smashing the plate from her hand for a second time*]:

Leave it! Leave it there! I'll serve you. Me! Me! Is *my* kingdom here. This is the side where *I* live. *This.*

WAITRESS: You Bosch you. You bloody German bastard!

[*She downs plates on the bar and walks off.* PETER *follows her. There is a general uproar and protest from the other waitresses who are impatient to be served.*]

PETER: What you call me? What was it? Say it again. [*But she has gone right off into the dining room. He screams at her.*] SAY IT AGAIN!

[*This scream calls the attention of most people to him. They all stare at him as at a frightened animal.* PETER *stands aroused, left back of stage, with his back to the audience. Suddenly he wheels round and in a frenzy searches for something violent to do. First he darts forward, then stops; then he rushes to his right and stops again. Then with a cry of 'Auf geht's' he dashes to a part under the serving counter near Michael and picking up a chopper from the bar smashes something underneath. There is a slow hiss and all the fires of the oven die down. There is a second of complete silence before anybody realizes what has happened, and then* FRANK *and two others are upon him, trying to hold him down. The* CHEF, *at last moved to do something, rushes to the scene, but* PETER *breaks away and flees to the dining room.* FRANK *and others follow. All this has happened too quickly for anyone to do a great deal about it, but in the scuffle the following cries are heard:*]

MICHAEL: He's broken the gas lead! Someone turn off the main!

FRANK: Hold him, grab hold of him!

KEVIN: Jesus Christ, he'll murder her.

HANS: *Sei nicht dumm! Beherrsch dich! Lass' ihn laufen!*

[*When* PETER *has rushed into the dining room there is another silence as everybody waits to hear what will happen next. Some are not even sure what has already happened. A crowd has gathered by the glass partition through which can be seen the dining room. Suddenly there is a tremendous crash of crockery to the ground. Some waitresses and, presumably, customers scream.*]

KEVIN: Holy Mother o' Mary, he's gone berserk.

GASTON: The lunatic! He's swept all the plates off the table in there.

MICHAEL [*who is one of the crowd by the glass partition, moves away down to the front of stage*]: He's ripped his hands.

KEVIN: I knew something like this would happen, now I just knew it. When you take away a man's dignity he is fighting mad. Can you see that now? Can you understand it now?

[*The crowd by the entrance to the dining room make way as* FRANK, ALFREDO, *and* HANS *bring* PETER *back. Peter's hands are covered in blood. Some smears have reached his face. He looks terribly exhausted. They bring him down stage.* MICHAEL *hurriedly finds a stool.*]

CHEF [*to Michael*]: Phone an ambulance.

WAITRESS: Monique is doing that now.

[MONIQUE *pushes through the crowd. She is sobbing, but she carries the medical box and a table cloth.* ALFREDO *snatches the cloth from her and rips it up. She tries to dab some liquid on Peter's hands; he jumps. This is too much for her: she leaves it all and rushes away.* ALFREDO, *however, simply takes Peter's hands and ties them up.*]

PETER: It hurts, Christ, it hurts.

ALFREDO: Shut up!

CHEF [*bending close to Peter*]: Fool! [*He straightens up and finding nothing else to say for the moment bends down to repeat again:*] Fool! [*Pause.*] So? What? The whole kitchen is stopped. Fool!

PETER [*to Alfredo*]: Now he cares.

CHEF [*incredulous and furious*]: What do you mean, 'Now he cares'?

ALFREDO [*gently moving* CHEF *out of the way that he might tie up Peter's hands*]: Leave him, Chef, leave him now.

CHEF [*reaching Peter another way*]: What do you mean, 'Now he cares'? *You* have to make me care? Forty years and suddenly you have to make me care? You? You? Who are you, tell me? In all this big world who are you, for Christ's sake?

[*At this point the crowd breaks away to let* MARANGO *in. He looks like a man who has just lost all his money at the stock exchange, as though he might have a fit. At first he is unable to speak. All he does is gesticulate with his arms in the air showing Peter what he has done –*]

60

MARANGO: You have stopped my whole world. [*Pause.*] Did you get permission from God? Did you? [*He looks to the others – perhaps they heard God give Peter permission. Then to* PETER.] There-is-no-one-else! You know that? NO ONE!

FRANK [*taking Marango's shoulder*]: All right, take it easy, Marango. The boy is going, he's going. He's ill, don't upset yourself.

MARANGO [*turning to Frank and making a gentle appeal*]: Why does everybody sabotage me, Frank? I give work, I pay well, yes? They eat what they want, don't they? I don't know what more to give a man. He works, he eats, I give him money. This is life, isn't it? I haven't made a mistake, have I? I live in the right world, don't I? [*To Peter.*] And you've stopped this world. A shnip! A boy! You've stopped it. Well why? Maybe you can tell me something I don't know – just tell me. [*No answer.*] I want to learn something. [*To Frank.*] Is there something I don't know? [PETER *rises and in pain moves off. When he reaches a point back centre stage* MARANGO *cries at him.*] BLOODY FOOL! [*Rushes round to him.*] What more do you want? What is there more, tell me? [*He shakes Peter but gets no reply.* PETER *again tries to leave. Again* MARANGO *cries out.*] What is there more? [PETER *stops, turns in pain and sadness, shakes his head as if to say – if you don't know I cannot explain. And so he moves right off stage.* MARANGO *is left facing his staff who stand around, almost accusingly, looking at him. And he asks again –*] What is there more? What *is* there more?

[*We have seen that there must be something more and so the* LIGHTS *must slowly fade.*]

CURTAIN

N. F. SIMPSON

A Resounding Tinkle

A RESOUNDING TINKLE

First presented in a shortened and rearranged version by The English
Stage Society, at The Royal Court Theatre, London, on 1 December
1957, with the following cast:

FIRST COMEDIAN	Graham Crowden
SECOND COMEDIAN	Toke Townley
TECHNICIAN	Leslie Glazer
PRODUCER	Patrick Barton
FIRST CLEANER	Rita Webb
SECOND CLEANER	Fanny Carby
BRO PARADOCK	Nigel Davenport
MIDDIE PARADOCK	Wendy Craig
UNCLE TED	Marigold Sharman
AUTHOR	John Wood

Directed by William Gaskill

SCENE: A suburban living room
TIME: The present

CHARACTERS OF THE PLAY

BRO PARADOCK
MIDDIE PARADOCK, *his wife*
FIRST COMEDIAN, *Hamster*
SECOND COMEDIAN, *Bug*
TECHNICIAN
AUTHOR
MRS NORA MORTICE, *a neighbour*
FIRST CLEANER
SECOND CLEANER
DON PARADOCK, *daughter of Bro and Middie Paradock*

MUSTARD SHORT ⎤
DENZIL PEPPER ⎟
MISS SALT ⎬ *critics*
MRS VINEGAR ⎟
CHAIRMAN ⎦

MAN IN BOWLER HAT
PRODUCER

ACT ONE

SCENE I

A suburban living room. Evening. The silence between BRO PARADOCK, *who stands with a glass in his hand looking out of the window, and his wife,* MIDDIE PARADOCK, *whose glass stands beside her on the small table by which she is sitting, has clearly just fallen. It is not broken for nearly half a minute.*

MRS PARADOCK: So don't flatter yourself.

[BRO PARADOCK *turns from the window, empties his glass, and, picking up Middie Paradock's glass, goes to a side table to fill both from one of two bottles containing a brightly purple liquid.*]

MR PARADOCK: I'm not flattering myself. And in any case we had all this out before.

MRS PARADOCK: And now we're having it out again.

[BRO PARADOCK *hands one of the two glasses to his wife. Both raise their glasses perfunctorily, grunt, and sip. They are far from certain what to make of the bliss they come upon for the second time, and* BRO PARADOCK, *after another two sips, takes up the bottle and looks steadily at the label.*]

MR PARADOCK: I've never known this to happen before.

MRS PARADOCK: It doesn't have to have happened before.

MR PARADOCK: I can feel it hurrying through my veins like smoke.

MRS PARADOCK: It's happened now. That's all you need concern yourself with.

MR PARADOCK: My lines seem to be coming to me in bits. Or what seem to be bits. This is like some unspecified milk of paradise.

MRS PARADOCK: What you can't remember you can make up.

MR PARADOCK: And what I can't make up can go unsaid.

MRS PARADOCK: No one minds with this kind of play. No one notices. You can be eight sheets in the wind or whatever it is practically from the word Go and the more the merrier from the author down. Or up. So don't for God's sake start having any qualms over remembering your lines or anybody else's lines. Just put it down to the ambrosia. Let ambrosia look after it.

MR PARADOCK: Ambrosia is what they eat. Not what they drink.

MRS PARADOCK: What who eat?

MR PARADOCK: You mean nectar. Let the nectar look after it. Not ambrosia.

MRS PARADOCK: Who said anything about nectar?

MR PARADOCK: You can't *drink* ambrosia for God's sake! Ambrosia is the food of the immortals. It's what the gods eat.

MRS PARADOCK: I don't know what it is you're trying to prove with your slick emendations of every damn remark I make, but whatever it is you can go right ahead and prove something different.

[*A knock.*]

MRS PARADOCK [*going out to answer the knock*]: What the hell do you think you make me look like by comparison?

[BRO PARADOCK *takes up a newspaper.* MIDDIE PARADOCK *returns and begins tidying the room, speaking as she does so.*]

MRS PARADOCK: There's somebody at the door wanting you to form a government.

[BRO PARADOCK *looks at her in astonishment. Several seconds elapse.*]

MR PARADOCK: What does he look like?

MRS PARADOCK: He says he's working through the street directory.

[*Pause.*]

MRS PARADOCK: I shall want this cork opened in case we have to offer him a drink. [*Pause.*] He was wearing an old raincoat. He looked as if he was trying it on for size.

MR PARADOCK: Give me the bottle. You can't open a cork. You should know that. You open the bottle. [*He begins to remove the cork.*] If it's an old raincoat what would he be trying it on for?

MRS PARADOCK: It might not be as old as the one he had before.

MR PARADOCK: I don't know why you wanted this bottle opened when the other one's more than half full.

MRS PARADOCK: The coat he had before may have been in tatters. It may have been black with grease. Or mud.

[*With a preoccupied air* BRO PARADOCK *takes a pipe from the mantelpiece and begins filling it.*]

MR PARADOCK: How can I start forming a government at six o'clock in the evening?

MRS PARADOCK: You'd be saying the same thing if it were six o'clock in the morning. [*She takes a torn and dirty raincoat from a cupboard.*] Look at this thing. How do you know his mightn't have been in a worse state than this one? Look at the sleeves. And the collar – look at it. His was probably as bad or worse.

MR PARADOCK: It's the Prime Minister's job.

MRS PARADOCK: Oh yes. If you want to shelve your responsibilities I dare say it is the Prime Minister's job.

MR PARADOCK: It's no concern of mine at all.

MRS PARADOCK: There's a man at the door waiting for your answer. [*Pause.*]

MR PARADOCK: How do you know he isn't wanted by the police?

MRS PARADOCK: Why should he be?

MR PARADOCK: If he is we ought to turn him over.

MRS PARADOCK: If he's a criminal, he's in plain clothes – that's all I can say.

MR PARADOCK: I'm going to turn him over. [*He moves to the door.*]

MRS PARADOCK: You may never get another chance to form a government.

MR PARADOCK: That goes for anything I ever choose not to do.

MRS PARADOCK: So what's it to be?

MR PARADOCK: I'll see what he looks like.

[*He goes out.* MIDDIE PARADOCK *clears the table, sets out paper, ashtrays, water, and glasses as for a board meeting.* BRO PARADOCK *returns, takes up a newspaper, and sits down in silence. Pause.*]

MR PARADOCK: It was Uncle Ted having a joke.

MRS PARADOCK: I would have recognized him.

MR PARADOCK: He was disguising his voice. He said I looked like Gladstone.

MRS PARADOCK: And did you?

MR PARADOCK: He wanted me to be taken in – I could see that.

MRS PARADOCK: So I suppose you obliged?

MR PARADOCK: That sort of thing cuts no ice with me.

MRS PARADOCK: You should have led him on by pretending to think it was 1868.

MR PARADOCK: It was all of a piece with his asking me to form a government.

MRS PARADOCK: I hope you didn't start saying: My mission is to pacify Ireland?

MR PARADOCK: It cut no more ice with me than Gladstone would have done if I'd been Queen Victoria. And God knows there's little enough of the Empress of India about me.

MRS PARADOCK: It would have been playing into his hands to say: My mission is to pacify Ireland.

MR PARADOCK: I know it would have been playing into his hands.

MRS PARADOCK: I can't think why I didn't recognize him.

MR PARADOCK: He said he was round canvassing for the Whigs.

MRS PARADOCK: Surely Uncle Ted knows you've never been a Whig?

MR PARADOCK: I suppose he thought he could talk me round like last time, when he had me voting for some candidate who refused to stand.

MRS PARADOCK: You should have let him come in for a few minutes to try your overcoat on.

MR PARADOCK: My overcoat would never fit Uncle Ted. Uncle Ted is broader across the shoulders than I am.

MRS PARADOCK: Exactly.

MR PARADOCK: He's a bigger man altogether than I am. He'd never get into my overcoat. I doubt whether he could even wear it like a cloak.

MRS PARADOCK: You don't see what I'm leading up to, do you? I know your overcoat is too small for him. It's too small for you except when you're in one of your pint-size moods. But if he'd tried it on I could have seen at a glance he wasn't a man of your build. I might after a time have been able to narrow it down to Uncle Ted. As it is I don't know what to think.

MR PARADOCK: I've already told you it was Uncle Ted having a joke with us. It's just the kind of joke Uncle Ted would think up.

MRS PARADOCK: And what happened about the government? Did you agree to form one or not?

MR PARADOCK: I wasn't approached.

MRS PARADOCK: That's a likely story.

MR PARADOCK: He probably forgot.

MRS PARADOCK: If he forgot how do you know it was Uncle Ted? It looks to me as if you've let yourself in for something with your bland assumptions about it being Uncle Ted having a joke with us. You'll be getting somebody round before you know where you are with papers to prove it's 1868.

MR PARADOCK: But not that I'm Gladstone.

MRS PARADOCK: If it's 1868 it makes precious little difference whether you're Gladstone or Disraeli.

[*A knock.*]

MR PARADOCK: Tell them I'm in conference.

MRS PARADOCK: It'll be the concert party I expect.

[MIDDIE PARADOCK *goes out.* BRO PARADOCK *sits down at the head of the table as though presiding at a directors' meeting of four, whose names around the table anti-clockwise from himself are Black, Green, White, and Brown.* BRO PARADOCK *appears to be following a discussion which is passing back and forth across the table. Occasionally he intervenes to clarify a point, to invite a comment or to call someone to order.* MIDDIE PARADOCK *returns.*]

MRS PARADOCK: I've sent them upstairs to get their make-up on. It's the concert party.

MR PARADOCK: Where are they going to do their act? There's no room in here for them.

MRS PARADOCK: It doesn't last more than ten minutes or so.

MR PARADOCK: They've still got to have somewhere to do it.

MRS PARADOCK: They can do it in the room next door. We can watch through the serving hatch there. We've done it before.

MR PARADOCK [*shrugs*]: As long as they're satisfied. Give me a hand to get this board meeting out of the way before they come down, Middie.

MRS PARADOCK: If I can find my shorthand.

[MIDDIE PARADOCK *fetches a notebook and pencil, quickly tidies her hair as she passes a mirror, puts on stylishly elegant spectacles, and sits down beside Bro Paradock. The mime continues for a few moments, and* BRO PARADOCK *then rises to close the meeting.*]

MR PARADOCK: Gentlemen. We have several proposals before us. I think we have three, to be exact – unless Mr Black's last point is to be taken as expanding the total to three and a half! [*He acknowledges laughter.*] The question is whether by continuing the meeting for another three or four hours we can reduce those three – and a half – proposals to one, or whether it would be better to congratulate ourselves on the progress we have already made and postpone a final decision for later consideration. As you know, gentlemen, and it is a melancholy thought – whatever we may decide, whatever plans we may make for the future of the company, it is beyond any of us to predict the conditions under which those plans will have to work, since no one can forecast – and perhaps least of all the government itself, what the government's future policy towards typewriter ribbons is to be. [*He acknowledges laughter.*] We have cleared a great deal of useful ground here this afternoon, and I think you will agree with me when I say . . .

[FIRST COMEDIAN, *wearing a white coat and carrying a stethoscope, enters.*]

MRS PARADOCK: Here they are.

FIRST COMEDIAN: The other one's coming in a moment. Where would you like us?

MRS PARADOCK [*opening the door, right, into an adjoining room*]: We thought perhaps in here would be rather nice.

[MIDDIE PARADOCK *leads* FIRST COMEDIAN *out, switching on the light to reveal a small adjoining room containing a wash-basin, a light, long wooden table, and a desk.* BRO PARADOCK *puts his head through the hatch.*]

MRS PARADOCK: We haven't got a stage for you I'm afraid, but there's any amount of hot water upstairs if you want to wash the make-up off afterwards.

MR PARADOCK: We thought for the moment you were Uncle Ted back.

MRS PARADOCK: We thought nothing of the kind. He thinks it's 1868 and you've come to ask him to form a government. It's all he ever thinks about.

FIRST COMEDIAN: I'd like an old blanket on this table, Mrs Paradock, and two or three cushions if you could manage it.

MRS PARADOCK: I can manage the blanket; I'll see what I can find for you to use as cushions.

FIRST COMEDIAN: A pillow would do. I only want to prop his head up.

MRS PARADOCK: I'll find something. And say nothing to him whatever you do about Edward Cardwell. He's only waiting for a chance to have you reforming the Army. He thinks he's Gladstone.

MR PARADOCK: I'm not deaf and I don't need humouring, thank you.

MRS PARADOCK: Cushions and a blanket.

[MIDDIE PARADOCK *goes out.*]

MR PARADOCK: There's plenty of hot water in the bathroom upstairs.

[FIRST COMEDIAN *continues in silence to set his scene, placing the table near the front of the stage and arranging papers on the desk.* MIDDIE PARADOCK *comes in with blanket and cushions.*]

MR PARADOCK: I was telling our friend here there's plenty of hot water upstairs if they want it afterwards.

MRS PARADOCK: A spotlight would be more to the point. They can't do their act in total darkness.

MR PARADOCK: It isn't what they can do that matters. Or what they can't do. It's what we can see them doing. That's the thing that matters.

FIRST COMEDIAN [*placing cushions under the blanket with which he covers the table to form an improvised couch as for a doctor's patient*]: I

71

think we're about ready now if you wouldn't mind giving my friend a shout. He can come through the same door there when you've put out the light in your room.

MRS PARADOCK: Do you hear that, Bro? We're to have our light out. You'd better have your torch ready.

[MIDDIE PARADOCK *goes out and returns almost immediately.*]

MRS PARADOCK: He's just coming down. Where's your torch, Bro, before I switch out the light?

MR PARADOCK: It's here ready. I've had it ready all the time while you've been talking.

MRS PARADOCK: Isn't this exciting?

[*She switches off the light. By the light of the torch she finds her way to the hatch.* FIRST COMEDIAN *is sitting at his improvised desk writing. He leans forward, presses a button, and says* 'Ping'. *The door from the living room opens to admit a man of no particular age between forty and sixty, whose nondescript appearance and defeated air contrast with the brisk ebullient manner the First Comedian has assumed. This is the* SECOND COMEDIAN. *He approaches the desk and sits diffidently down. When after a few minutes the* FIRST COMEDIAN *disengages his attention from what he is writing, the* SECOND COMEDIAN *leans forward.*]

SECOND COMEDIAN: It's my feet, Doctor.

FIRST COMEDIAN: What's the matter with your feet?

SECOND COMEDIAN: I was rather hoping you might be able to tell me that, Doctor.

FIRST COMEDIAN: Let me see them.

[SECOND COMEDIAN *takes off shoes and socks.*]

SECOND COMEDIAN: They're all right now. It's when they suddenly swivel round they catch me.

[SECOND COMEDIAN *holds out both legs quite straight in front of him.* FIRST COMEDIAN *stands over them.*]

FIRST COMEDIAN: What are these?

SECOND COMEDIAN: They're my kneecaps, Doctor.

FIRST COMEDIAN: They ought to be much higher up your legs than this.

SECOND COMEDIAN: I can't seem to keep them up, Doctor.

FIRST COMEDIAN: Take everything off except your trousers and lie down over there.

[FIRST COMEDIAN *goes to wash-basin where he begins washing his hands, while* SECOND COMEDIAN *goes into the corner, where the desk conceals him, to undress.*]

FIRST COMEDIAN: Eardrums still getting overheated?

SECOND COMEDIAN: Only when I listen to anything, Doctor.

[SECOND COMEDIAN *comes out and lies down on the couch.* FIRST COMEDIAN *examines his chest.*]

FIRST COMEDIAN: Breathe in deeply. Again. Yes – you're having trouble with your breathing. Breathe out. Do you notice any difference?

SECOND COMEDIAN: None at all, Doctor.

FIRST COMEDIAN: And do you know why? The reason you notice no difference is that there isn't any. All the time while you're breathing out, there's air forcing its way in. It's trying to push past. Breathe in again. [*He reflects for a moment.*] Do you ever feel as though the air you're getting is the wrong kind of air?

SECOND COMEDIAN: I just don't get the air, Doctor.

FIRST COMEDIAN: Somebody must have it if you don't.

SECOND COMEDIAN: It's my lungs, Doctor.

FIRST COMEDIAN: Nonsense. There's nothing wrong with your lungs. They're both perfectly fit.

SECOND COMEDIAN: I don't think they hit it off, Doctor. They're at daggers drawn practically the whole time. Over the air.

FIRST COMEDIAN: And your breathing's twisted to blazes as a result. Let me see your tongue. Open your mouth. [*He looks inside.*] You've had this jaw to pieces, haven't you?

SECOND COMEDIAN: It was some years ago, Doctor.

FIRST COMEDIAN: It doesn't matter how long ago it was. It's not a question of time. You laymen start dismantling these parts, but you've no idea how to put them together again. Here's a tooth which has been put back upside down. You're biting on the root.

[FIRST COMEDIAN *begins to use the stethoscope.*]

SECOND COMEDIAN: I've been told I can expect all my teeth to turn turtle eventually.

FIRST COMEDIAN: What are you doing about it?

SECOND COMEDIAN: Consulting you, Doctor.

FIRST COMEDIAN: I thought you'd come to me about your feet.

[FIRST COMEDIAN *grimaces as he continues to sound* SECOND COMEDIAN'S *chest.*]

FIRST COMEDIAN: What on earth are you carrying round in this blood stream of yours?

SECOND COMEDIAN: Only my blood, Doctor.

FIRST COMEDIAN: You've got a hell of a noisy circulation.

SECOND COMEDIAN: I have, Doctor. It keeps me awake.

FIRST COMEDIAN: I should think so. It sounds like a mobile iron foundry. You need a silencer for it. I'll give you a letter to take to the King's Cross Blood, Brain, and Bowel Hospital. You can have it under the National Health.

SECOND COMEDIAN: I'd like them to look at my arteries while I'm there as well, Doctor. They seem to have venous blood in them.

FIRST COMEDIAN: It's when you get arterial blood in the veins that you need to begin worrying. Turn over and let me look at your back.

[SECOND COMEDIAN *turns painfully over and* FIRST COMEDIAN *stands looking for some moments in silence.*]

SECOND COMEDIAN: I've had it some time, Doctor.

FIRST COMEDIAN: I can see that. And we can write off these kidneys.

SECOND COMEDIAN: I hardly ever use them, Doctor.

FIRST COMEDIAN: How long have your ribs been like this?

SECOND COMEDIAN: As long as I can remember, Doctor.

FIRST COMEDIAN: And how long is that? Months? Years?

SECOND COMEDIAN: I can't altogether recall, Doctor.

[FIRST COMEDIAN *goes back to his desk where he takes up a pen and begins writing briskly.*]

FIRST COMEDIAN: You can get your clothes on.

[*While* SECOND COMEDIAN *gets dressed*, FIRST COMEDIAN *goes on writing. When* SECOND COMEDIAN *reappears, he puts down his pen.*]

FIRST COMEDIAN: Sit down, Mr Avalanche.

[SECOND COMEDIAN *sits down hesitantly and waits for* FIRST COMEDIAN *to begin.*]

FIRST COMEDIAN: I don't suppose there's much I can tell you that you don't know already. It's an obsolete body, of course, as you realize. And I'm afraid you'll have to do the best you can with it. You must learn to cooperate with your organs.

SECOND COMEDIAN: The small of my back is too big, Doctor.

FIRST COMEDIAN: There's nothing to be gained by pretending it isn't. In fact I'll be quite frank with you, Mr Avalanche – it's a great deal larger than it should be. Not only in your case, but with a surprisingly large number of people. But there's absolutely no need for you to have any misgivings about it. People go on – some of them with far less wrong with them than you have by a long way – they go on living active lives sometimes for years. There's no reason at all, Mr Avalanche, why given time you shouldn't have a good twenty or thirty years in front of you.

SECOND COMEDIAN: With a transparent pelvis, Doctor?

FIRST COMEDIAN: The main thing is to keep that blood circulating. Take precautions, but don't overdo it. Sleep whenever you can with your eyes closed. Keep off strong poisons of all kinds – and breathe. Breathe all the time. If it doesn't seem to be showing results, make sure it isn't because you're under water. Keep at it: the more you breathe the better you'll feel.

SECOND COMEDIAN: I've been having a lot of trouble with my slanting bowel since I became allergic to smells, Doctor.

FIRST COMEDIAN: You will for a time, but it's nothing to worry about. Take this letter to the Blood, Brain, and Bowel Hospital and they'll give you a thorough overhaul.

SECOND COMEDIAN: I shall feel a lot easier, Doctor.

FIRST COMEDIAN: And get those feet seen to. They'll be no good to you while they swivel. You should be seeing somebody about them. The feet should never swivel. Hand that letter in to the almoner and you can come back here when the specialist has seen you.

SECOND COMEDIAN: Thank you, Doctor. And I'll come in again as you say when I've been examined.

FIRST COMEDIAN: Next Thursday. I can't see you before then. And I'll give you something for those elbows to see if we can't get them bending the right way.

SECOND COMEDIAN: Very good, Doctor.

[SECOND COMEDIAN *goes listlessly out, switching off the light as he does so. As he enters the living room he switches that light on.* BRO *and* MIDDIE PARADOCK *withdraw from the hatch and close it.* MIDDIE PARADOCK *half opens the door into the passage through which the* SECOND COMEDIAN *has gone.*]

MRS PARADOCK: You can find your own way upstairs I expect. You'll find plenty of hot water up there.

[*She closes the door.*]

MR PARADOCK: It's Aunt Chloe's birthday next week.

MRS PARADOCK: So you keep saying.

MR PARADOCK: We shall have to think of something.

MRS PARADOCK: Unless we send Doris round when she comes home from school?

MR PARADOCK: There's never anything she wants. If you think of anything, she's always got it. Everything you think of she's got already.

MRS PARADOCK: Listen. Hear them? Hear them washing their make-up off upstairs?

MR PARADOCK: What's the good of sending Doris round?

MRS PARADOCK: Not if she were to burst a paper bag in Aunt Chloe's ear? We could get her a deaf-aid.

MR PARADOCK: I don't see why we should go to all that trouble. It isn't as if it's her twenty-first.

MRS PARADOCK: I thought that was rather novel when he said: You've had this jaw to pieces.

MR PARADOCK: I was expecting him to make some remark about dry rot in the roof of his mouth.

MRS PARADOCK: It was very unpredictable.

MR PARADOCK: Except at the end. That bit about the elbows bending the wrong way. I could see that coming.

MRS PARADOCK: That wasn't till right at the end.

MR PARADOCK: I could see it coming.

MRS PARADOCK: You mean you think you could see it coming. You're being wise after the event again. If you could see it coming why didn't you say so before it came? That would have been the time to say it instead of waiting till it was all over.

MR PARADOCK: Because if I'd said so before it came it would have spoiled it for you.

MRS PARADOCK: How did you know I hadn't seen it coming myself?

MR PARADOCK: Because you'd have said so.

MRS PARADOCK: And spoiled it for you?

MR PARADOCK: You wouldn't have spoiled it for me because I saw it coming all along as you well knew.

MRS PARADOCK: One of these days you'll be wise after the event once too often. Did we give them supper last time?

MR PARADOCK: We've never had them before.

MRS PARADOCK: We would never have had them this time if it had been left to you. You'd better ask them what they want to drink when they come down.

[BRO PARADOCK *goes to the table behind the door where he is unseen at first by the two* COMEDIANS, *who enter, wearing dark lounge suits, as* MIDDIE PARADOCK *goes out.*]

MRS PARADOCK: Here they are. There'll be something ready for you in a few minutes if you'll excuse me while I get it served up.

[*She closes the door behind her.*]

FIRST COMEDIAN: I thought they were going to send us off without anything.

[*They catch sight of* BRO PARADOCK. *A difficult pause.*]

MR PARADOCK: You'd like a drink, I expect. I'll get you some clean glasses.

[SECOND COMEDIAN *opens the door and closes it behind* BRO

PARADOCK *who goes out with the tray.* FIRST COMEDIAN *shrugs, picks up a magazine, and sits with his back to the audience.*]

SECOND COMEDIAN: You're being a bit casual, aren't you? What about all these people?

FIRST COMEDIAN: Well?

SECOND COMEDIAN: We can't sit down and read magazines.

FIRST COMEDIAN: It's not my job to spoon-feed them.

SECOND COMEDIAN: They'll get restive.

FIRST COMEDIAN: Let them talk among themselves for a time.

[SECOND COMEDIAN *sits doubtfully down with a magazine, but is increasingly ill at ease. He gives up the effort to read, and standing up, looks across to the* FIRST COMEDIAN. *Convulsively he turns and makes an agonized attempt to address the audience direct.*]

SECOND COMEDIAN [*inarticulate for a few moments*]: Good people ... [*He can get no further and turns angrily on* FIRST COMEDIAN, *who is now watching him with interest.*]

SECOND COMEDIAN: Don't just sit there!

FIRST COMEDIAN [*putting down his magazine*]: Now listen to me, Bug. Just take it easy, will you? Sit down and take that look off your face. Give it to a rabbit to wear when it meets a stoat. You look like death.

[SECOND COMEDIAN *sits miserably down.*]

SECOND COMEDIAN: Maybe it isn't your job to spoon-feed them. But it's not mine either.

FIRST COMEDIAN: Then we can both stop worrying. If they don't want to amuse themselves they can make do with silence.

SECOND COMEDIAN: They'll never stand for it.

FIRST COMEDIAN: We can break it up with dialogue from time to time if it would make you any easier. And silence isn't so easy to come by as all that, either, if it comes to that.

SECOND COMEDIAN: It's not what you go to a theatre for. You go to other places for silence. Not a theatre. They'll feel cheated.

FIRST COMEDIAN: It's possible. I've known people feel cheated about some odd things. I've known people buy a bath sponge and do calculations to show that two-thirds of the sponge is made up of holes. And it galls them to think that two-thirds of what they've paid good money for isn't really there. Of course they feel cheated. They have every right to feel cheated. They've been overcharged. They've been overcharged two hundred per cent.

SECOND COMEDIAN: Not with a sponge. They've no right to feel cheated over a sponge. A sponge is where you expect to find holes. But a theatre is not where you expect to find silence. That's the difference. The holes are there for a purpose in a sponge. They're there to soak up the water.

FIRST COMEDIAN: Now you're bringing a new element into it. Start talking about purpose and you'll have the whole argument bedevilled. Before we know where we are we shall be splitting hairs. No. Leave purpose out of it. They're not there *to* soak up the water. The holes in a sponge soak up the water. It's not the same.

SECOND COMEDIAN: Which is what I said in the first place. The holes are there for a purpose.

FIRST COMEDIAN: Purpose purpose purpose! It isn't purpose – it's coincidence! They happen to be there and they happen to soak up the water. The holes were there long before you or anybody else ever used a sponge in a bath. And that goes for everything else. It goes for sponges and it goes for ... for everything else. What, for instance, is the purpose of the sea? Is it so that sponges can have somewhere to grow? To give fish somewhere to use their gills? Perhaps you want to tell me that oceans exist to cater for submarines? Rather than waste all those submarines on dry land, God in His all-seeing wisdom made the sea. That's how you're arguing. You're arguing from effect back to cause and it's disastrous.

SECOND COMEDIAN: You're going too fast for me. Your mind doesn't work the way mine does. Let me come to it in my own way.

FIRST COMEDIAN: Good God, we're going to be at it all night. Surely you can see the analogy with a sponge. We don't have to run a bath for you and let you get into it, do we? With your ducks and your boats, before you can see a simple analogy?

SECOND COMEDIAN: Offensive swine!

FIRST COMEDIAN: All I'm trying to say is that anyone who starts with the idea of sponge, and starts squeezing water over himself out of it before he lets his mind wander slowly back through the millennia to the beginnings of things, is going the wrong way about it. He'll end up in a paroxysm of wonder. He'll want to start worshipping something, on the spot, while he's still dripping with water and his glasses are steamed up. And for no better reason, for no more compelling reason, than that the entire evolutionary processes of the cosmos seem to him to have been geared for several million years to the task of providing him with something to wash himself with. How marvellous are Thy ways, O Lord! The seasons always working out just right for the crops; the flowers never forgetting what colour they have to be to attract the right kind of insect and repel the wrong kind, blessed be God! Isn't it wonderful the way it all works out? And if it had worked out quite differently that would have been pretty wonderful too.

SECOND COMEDIAN: What none of this alters, or even begins to make any impression on as far as I can see, is the irrefutable fact that five minutes of dead silence, or even two or three minutes of it, is going to open the flood-gates of their indignation like the bottom coming out of a bag of cement. They won't stomach it.

FIRST COMEDIAN: At the end of three or four minutes of silence, if it would put your mind at rest, we could have a hunting horn.

SECOND COMEDIAN: Where would that get any of us?

FIRST COMEDIAN: Or a horse whinnying. To break the tension. Kettle-drums. Anything like that.

SECOND COMEDIAN: Bringing a neighing horse on to the stage is going to present us with more problems than its solves.

FIRST COMEDIAN: A whinnying horse. I said nothing about a neighing horse.

SECOND COMEDIAN: People won't stand for it.

FIRST COMEDIAN: As for problems, of course a horse on the stage presents problems. Of course it does. And suppose we solve all the problems it presents? What happens? We end up with more problems than we started with. Because that's the way problems propagate their species. A problem left to itself dries up or goes rotten. But fertilize a problem with a solution – you'll hatch out dozens. It's better than breeding budgerigars. There isn't anything very challenging about a budgerigar. There's a limit to what you can do by way of experiment. Horse-breeding and dog-breeding and all the other hobbies people have to occupy them when they're not breeding problems are not for you and me. The people who count are the ones who devote their lives to a search for the sterile solutions from which no further problems can be bred. I hope they never find it. The moment they do the world ends.

SECOND COMEDIAN: Don't let my presence on the stage cramp your style. Go on as if I weren't here. Make a full-blooded soliloquy of it while you're in voice. Open the hatches and disgorge. Give us all plenty to flounder in and damned be him that first cries, 'Hold, enough!' Only count me out.

[As SECOND COMEDIAN makes to fling open the door, MIDDIE PARADOCK enters, carrying a tray of food.]

MRS PARADOCK: Oh. [She pauses uncertainly, and then goes to the table to put down the tray.] I hope I haven't interrupted you both in the middle of a quarrel.

[BRO PARADOCK enters with a tray of drinks which he puts down on the small table behind the door.]

MR PARADOCK: You'd like an aperient I expect.

MRS PARADOCK: Put it down and leave it. They can pour their own in a moment.

MR PARADOCK: Oh.

[MIDDIE PARADOCK takes BRO PARADOCK aside.]

MRS PARADOCK: We've come in at the wrong moment. They were about to have a set to.

[They go towards the door.]

MR PARADOCK: Is there anything you need? Or can you manage?

MRS PARADOCK: Of course they don't need anything. There are knives in the drawer if they want to go at each other in that way.

[BRO *and* MIDDIE PARADOCK *go out and close the door.* SECOND
COMEDIAN *goes to the small table where he pours out two glasses of
the purple drink and brings them to the larger table on which* FIRST
COMEDIAN *has set out the food.*

*They sit and begin their meal, eating and drinking for some time in
silence.*]

SECOND COMEDIAN [*holding up his glass*]: This is like the milk of
paradise.

[*They continue to eat in silence.*]

SECOND COMEDIAN: It'll save time if we test for humour now.

FIRST COMEDIAN: Afterwards.

SECOND COMEDIAN: Where I get baffled is over isolating the
quintessential comic element.

[*Pause.*]

SECOND COMEDIAN: You could get rid of the linguistic overtones
by using Esperanto, but that means evening classes for comedian
and audience alike while they're all learning Esperanto.

FIRST COMEDIAN: They might not like the joke any more in
Esperanto than they did in English.

SECOND COMEDIAN: And after months of part-time study they'd
be in a pretty ugly mood.

FIRST COMEDIAN: It's the wrong approach altogether. If you want
to isolate the quintessential comic element, the only way you can
do it is through your laughter response index.

SECOND COMEDIAN: You mean through my own, personal laughter
response index? Because if so there's nothing doing there. Every
joke I've ever thought of has been tried out on myself first.

FIRST COMEDIAN: And what's your laughter response index?

SECOND COMEDIAN: I get a nil reading. I've got no sense of
humour.

FIRST COMEDIAN: I doubt that. You may have a low laughter
quotient. Many people have. But it's ridiculous for a comedian
to be without a sense of humour altogether.

SECOND COMEDIAN: I keep it under control. I like to keep my
satiric vision unimpaired.

IRST COMEDIAN: Satiric vision my sun-glasses! You've got about as much satiric vision as a hawk with bi-focals has got eyes like a lynx. Or vice versa as far as that goes. You remind me of a lark walking the plank with its eyes closed. Slowly. Cautiously. Feeling its way step by step, making a false move and clutching convulsively at the air before hitting the water.

[*They continue the meal in silence.*]

IRST COMEDIAN: You remind me of a pigeon coming down by parachute.

[*Silence.*]

IRST COMEDIAN: Coming down by parachute because it likes to keep its neuroses airborne as long as possible.

ECOND COMEDIAN: You're as smug as a parrot.

FIRST COMEDIAN: You remind me of a cormorant.

SECOND COMEDIAN: As smug as a parrot from the Azores. I only hope when you hit the water you don't find it frozen over. Or that if you do you're wearing your skates. If you're wearing your skates when you hit the water and find it frozen over, you can be as smug as you like till kingdom come and I wish you joy of it. Till then leave it to the parrots, please.

FIRST COMEDIAN: You remind me of a cormorant with a beak a yard long tapping out a manifesto to the cosmos on a second-hand typewriter. I affirm letter by tipsy letter that I exist! I am in revolt (with reservations) against revolt! I do not choose not to be! Beak first it plunges like a kingfisher into the glutinous mud, sticks fast and quivers like a tuning-fork.

[*They eat the rest of their meal in silence, and then pushing back their chairs get up from the table.*]

FIRST COMEDIAN: I wonder what kind of an allegory they'll make of that.

SECOND COMEDIAN: We shall know soon enough.

[*They move in an unsettled way about the room, picking up and putting down books and ornaments, looking out of the window, yawning.*]

FIRST COMEDIAN: I suggest we have one more drink and then see what we can do on the strength of it by way of getting the curtain down.

[*He pours two drinks, one of which he hands to* SECOND COMEDIAN.]

FIRST COMEDIAN: Go for spontaneity. Just give the dialogue its head – it's bound to be almost played out by now.

SECOND COMEDIAN: This seems a damned hit or miss way to me of doing things.

FIRST COMEDIAN: It won't when you've had some more nectar. Drink up. A sort of rallentando close should do it very nicely but don't try to force it. Let it take its course.

[FIRST COMEDIAN *takes up a position at the window.*]

FIRST COMEDIAN: The stars are a long way off tonight.

[SECOND COMEDIAN *joins him for a moment at the window, looks up as though to verify* FIRST COMEDIAN'S *observation, and then turns away.*]

SECOND COMEDIAN: The planets are not much nearer.

[SECOND COMEDIAN *stands looking intently at a goldfish in a bowl.* FIRST COMEDIAN *comes away from the window.*]

FIRST COMEDIAN: In 1751 Dr Joseph Priestley was distressed that he could not feel a proper repentance for the sin of Adam.

[SECOND COMEDIAN *continues to stare into the goldfish bowl.* FIRST COMEDIAN *has something on his mind which he is uncertain how best to put into words. He takes up a position behind a high-backed chair as though in front of a rostrum.*]

SECOND COMEDIAN: The open sea is a closed book to this goldfish.

[*Pause.* SECOND COMEDIAN *turns away from the goldfish.*]

FIRST COMEDIAN: I concede that the earth could be flat. But I doubt it. I doubt it for a number of reasons which I don't intend to go into now. I'd like to put it to the test. I'd very much like to put the whole theory to the test simply by sailing west as far as I could go. If my reckoning is reliable, and if the earth is, as I believe, spherical, I ought eventually, unless there happens to be other land in the way, to arrive on the coast of China.

SECOND COMEDIAN: It's a persuasive theory.

FIRST COMEDIAN: It opens up so many possibilities. Take the sun. We talk about sunrise and sunset. How do we know that what we imagine to be the sun rising and the sun setting, and what we imagine to be the sun moving from east to west across the sky, aren't all in fact a simple optical illusion? How do we know that it isn't we who are moving, while the sun remains motionless in the heavens?

SECOND COMEDIAN: I suppose anything could be an optical illusion.

FIRST COMEDIAN: Look at it this way. This is very tentative, but you've been in a train often enough, haven't you, when another train is drawn up alongside it. Now. One train begins to move. You can feel nothing, but you look through the window and decide that it's the other train which is moving backwards. As you gather speed, however, the movement of your own train as it begins to sway tells you that in fact it is you who are moving forwards.

SECOND COMEDIAN: I think some of this has been gone into before.

FIRST COMEDIAN: You'd get exactly the same effect as you got with the trains if the earth were to be spinning in the opposite direction to the apparent movement of the sun across the sky.

SECOND COMEDIAN: In fact there are a good many people who seem to organize their lives on some such assumption.

FIRST COMEDIAN: I don't intend to let this rest here. If Columbus was right on this score, he was very likely right on other things too. But no one will ever know what those things were until someone takes the trouble to find out. And people aren't going to go to the trouble of finding out until he's been proved right on this point first. That's why it's up to me to vindicate him if I can. I'm certain he was right.

SECOND COMEDIAN: He bides his time who's stuck knee-deep in lime.

FIRST COMEDIAN: I can't see what that's got to do with it.

SECOND COMEDIAN: It's a proverb.

FIRST COMEDIAN: You seem to set precious little store by relevance, I must say.

SECOND COMEDIAN: I prefer to go off at a tangent.

FIRST COMEDIAN: And damned smug you sound about it, too!

SECOND COMEDIAN: I stand for the line of least resistance.

FIRST COMEDIAN: Then let's both doze off.

[*They sit opposite each other and close their eyes. Both begin muttering under their breath. At last* FIRST COMEDIAN *opens his eyes suspiciously. Suspicion turns to anger, and leaping up he gestures violently to where* SECOND COMEDIAN *is sitting bolt upright and with eyes now open.*]

FIRST COMEDIAN: You cavalier bastard! You've been talking in my sleep!

SECOND COMEDIAN: How was I to know whose sleep it was?

FIRST COMEDIAN: You could have asked, couldn't you?

SECOND COMEDIAN: What the hell!

FIRST COMEDIAN: It was a pretty cavalier thing to do, that's all I'm saying. You might ask next time.

[*Both subside. There is a pause.* SECOND COMEDIAN *gets up from his chair.*]

SECOND COMEDIAN: Not a year passes but I am older.

[*Pause.*]

FIRST COMEDIAN: By how much I grow older, by so much am I nearer my end.

[*Pause.*]

SECOND COMEDIAN: When the end comes there is no more.

[*Both look up at the curtain, which begins to fall very slowly. They follow it down a short way with their eyes, turn to look at each other in mutual search for confirmation, find it, and rush to pour themselves another drink. They drink to success as the* CURTAIN *comes quickly down.*]

SCENE 2

Later the same evening. In front of the curtain appears a man of perhaps thirty-five, well-dressed and easy-mannered; he would pass for a third generation estate agent with an office in Knightsbridge. He represents the author. He has a glass in his hand, which is half full of a bright, purple liquid.

AUTHOR: I agree. A pretty epileptic start. We're going to see what we can do in the next scene about pulling the thing together. Because this isn't at all, of course, how I wrote the play. You must have realized that. We're all – what shall I say? – we're all just a thought oiled over on this side of the footlights. I expect you've gathered that. And, of course, the thing was by no means as straightforward as I could have wished even before this crate arrived backstage. It really is remarkable stuff, I might say. Milk of paradise is . . . well, it's not what I would have called it but I can see the connexion; anyone casting around for some phrase to just hit it off with might well seize on one like that. And of course one is quite possibly not as clear-headed after two or three glasses of this as to be able to explain altogether clearly what it is one is trying to do. Conversely, as it were, such an explanation would hardly have been needed had one not failed – rather lamentably, I must admit – to achieve what one was trying to achieve. How close we're getting to the original tonight is anybody's guess – it would have been anybody's guess whether this nectar had arrived so unexpectedly or not. Because I know hardly a word of Portuguese, and of course Portuguese is precisely the language, unfortunately, in which the play – or most of it – came to me. I was pretty much in the dark, I can tell you, until I got to work with a dictionary. I had someone help me, naturally, and between us we've hammered out something, but I'm far from happy about the whole thing. I think what you'd all better do is to visualize if you can a regimental sergeant-major on a kitchen chair in the middle of a bare stage with his back to you. He has a megaphone through which quite suddenly he'll begin reciting 'Jabberwocky' over and over again for three hours at top speed. I want that image to be clear in your minds, and I want you to hold it there throughout this performance of ours tonight. It is our sheet anchor. Without that image in our minds we shall lose all sense of proportion about what we're going through here and now. For let us make no mistake about it, we are in this together and we must do what we can to see that no one of us suffers more than another. There is no desire, no intention on my part, or on the part of any of us on this side of the footlights, to impose upon you any ready-made idea of our own as to what this play ought to turn out to be. So often the author – we have all known him – moves invisibly among his audience nudging one and distracting another, muttering and mouthing among his betters. Or he leans forward from time to time to make simultaneous overtures of sumptuous impropriety to every Aunt Edna in the house. Such has never been my conception of the relationship that should exist between us. No. It is together that we must shape the experience which is the play we shall all of us have shared. The actors are as much the audience as the audience themselves, in precisely the same way that the audience are as much the actors as the actors themselves. We are all spectators of one another, mutual witnesses of each other's discomfiture. Each of us as he receives his private trouncings at the hands of fate is kept in good heart by the moth in his brother's parachute, and the scorpion in his neighbour's underwear. So let us in the name of that *Schadenfreude* that binds us each to each work from now on together, you on your side of the footlights, and we on ours. We shall need all you can give us. Dramatic situations, plot, glamour, spectacle, lyricism. And some tragic relief. And if we could possibly step up the intellectual content at all? Some of you these days are travelling in from places as far out as Harrow and Morden, and you just have to have your minds stimulated more than in the days when the illusion of thought had to last no farther than Hammersmith or Putney. So there it is. I'll go off now into the wings. We'll leave the stage quite empty for a moment or two, and I think that if like Quakers we all compose our minds in a kind of mystic amalgam, something may come of it.

[*He goes off as the curtain rises on the living room as it was at the end of the first scene. The two* COMEDIANS *are sprawled, fast asleep, in armchairs.* BRO *and* MIDDIE PARADOCK *have just come in.*]

MRS PARADOCK: I'm not saying it's your fault.

MR PARADOCK: Not a drain.

MRS PARADOCK: I'm not saying it's your fault. All I'm saying is that to give them two bottles, both practically full, is hardly the best way to go about things if you want to conserve your nectar.

MR PARADOCK: They might have shown a bit more restraint than to swallow the lot. They call themselves comedians. I'd like to know what's supposed to be comic about drinking to excess.

MRS PARADOCK: They haven't got to be comic the whole time.

MR PARADOCK: I wouldn't employ them to sell typewriter ribbons.

MRS PARADOCK: Neither would anybody else while they were in that state.

MR PARADOCK: It doesn't take you long to leap to their defence, I notice. I wonder if you'd find it so comic if I started drinking to excess.

MRS PARADOCK: You've never done anything to excess in your life. That's just your trouble.

MR PARADOCK: I happen to prefer moderation.

MRS PARADOCK: You make a vice of it. You never know when not to stop.

MR PARADOCK: I wouldn't employ them to sell typewriter ribbons for me.

MRS PARADOCK: So you keep saying.

MR PARADOCK: No more would I.

MRS PARADOCK: And while you're not employing them selling typewriter ribbons other people are stealing a march on you in some other trade.

MR PARADOCK: Comedians! I'd like to know what's comic about them now. Look at them. It isn't as if they're lying where anyone could trip over them and fall flat on his face. That might raise a laugh if it were someone else; but who's going to fall over them there?

MRS PARADOCK: They'll come round presently.

MR PARADOCK: All I can say is that I hope you're right.

MRS PARADOCK: I wish that were all you could say. Except that you'd go on saying it all day long like a mentally deficient parakeet.

MR PARADOCK: A parakeet wouldn't necessarily have to be mentally deficient to keep saying the same thing over and over again. If that's all it's been taught, how can it say anything else? There's nothing mentally deficient about a parakeet acting according to its nature. It may be educationally subnormal, but that's another matter.

MRS PARADOCK: And when these two come round, which is more to the point, they're going to want some help in making us laugh. You'd better get down Bergson.

MR PARADOCK: They may hit us over the head with it when they come round. [*He goes to the bookshelf.*]

MRS PARADOCK: It isn't very heavy. It's only a small book. I can see it from here – on the shelf. Not that one – that's right – now to the left next to the blue one.

MR PARADOCK [*taking down the book*]: *Laughter*. Henri Bergson.

MRS PARADOCK: It's not big enough to do any damage even if they do hit you over the head with it. Now turn to page thirty-two and read out what it says.

MR PARADOCK [*reads*]: The fundamental law of life . . . [*Gestures to the audience.*] Will they want to take notes?

MRS PARADOCK: They can read it for themselves when they get home.

MR PARADOCK: Oh. [*Reads.*] The fundamental law of life . . . is a complete negation of repetition! But I find that a certain movement of head or arm, a movement always the same, seems to return at regular intervals. If I notice it and it succeeds in diverting my attention, if I wait for it to occur and it occurs when I expect it, then involuntarily I laugh. Why? Because I now have before me a machine that works automatically. This is no longer life, it is automatism established in life and imitating it. It belongs to the comic.

MRS PARADOCK: Good. And what does he say on page fifty-eight?

MR PARADOCK: He says: We laugh every time a person gives us the impression of being a thing. You've marked it, but where does all this get us?

MRS PARADOCK: You'll see. These two are Bergson trained.

MR PARADOCK: They'll be like that for hours yet.

[*The two* COMEDIANS *begin to stir.*]

MRS PARADOCK: Will they?

[*The two* COMEDIANS *look around them as though coming out of a trance.* SECOND COMEDIAN *leaves his chair and advances to the front of the stage.* FIRST COMEDIAN *follows.*]

SECOND COMEDIAN: You could call this intellectual slapstick.

FIRST COMEDIAN: We are, metaphysically, the Marx Brothers.

SECOND COMEDIAN: Presenting the custard pie comedy of the abstract.

FIRST COMEDIAN: Quintessentially.

SECOND COMEDIAN: And working to a blueprint.

FIRST COMEDIAN: The fundamental law of life is a complete negation of repetition! But I find that a certain movement of head or arm, a movement always the same, seems to return at regular intervals. [BRO PARADOCK *looks, as he begins to recognize these words, with some astonishment towards his wife, who with a complacent half-smile sits down in one of the vacated armchairs and takes up some knitting.*] If I notice it and it succeeds in diverting my attention, if I wait for it to occur and it occurs when I expect it, then involuntarily I laugh. Why? Because I now have before me a machine that works automatically. This is no longer life, it is automatism established in life and imitating it. It belongs to the comic.

SECOND COMEDIAN: We laugh every time a person gives the impression of being a thing.

[BRO PARADOCK *comes forward to join them. The two* COMEDIAN
adopt stage American accents.]

MR PARADOCK: Tell me something about this Bergson method.

FIRST COMEDIAN: You've never seen Bergson?

MR PARADOCK: Not that I can remember.

FIRST COMEDIAN: He's never seen Bergson.

SECOND COMEDIAN: I thought everybody had seen Bergson some
time or another.

FIRST COMEDIAN: You can't put it into words. You've just got to
see it.

MR PARADOCK: I understand he does it all by machinery.

SECOND COMEDIAN: He just comes on. That's all. He comes on
like he's a machine.

MRS PARADOCK [*without looking up from her knitting*]: It sound
richly comic.

SECOND COMEDIAN: Remember that time he came on the way he
was an electronic computer, and then had them put straw in his
hair?

MR PARADOCK: Can he do anything else? Can he do typewriters?

FIRST COMEDIAN: He never has. What about it, Bug? Can Bergson
do a typewriter?

MRS PARADOCK: He only wants to start selling you typewriter
ribbons. It's a new sideline. Take no notice.

SECOND COMEDIAN: Typewriters don't make out too good comedy-
wise, I guess.

MR PARADOCK: I want to be made up to look like an electronic
computer. I want to raise a laugh.

FIRST COMEDIAN: It's no good looking like an electronic computer.
You've got to *be* an electronic computer.

MR PARADOCK: If Bergson can be an electronic computer for the
laughs, so can I. What does an electronic computer do?

FIRST COMEDIAN: Electronic computer? It's . . . well, it's electronic. What would you say was the difference, Bug?

SECOND COMEDIAN: What difference?

FIRST COMEDIAN: It's like the human brain except it's electronic.

SECOND COMEDIAN: It's just the way they do things. They do it different. Why can't you stop asking questions?

FIRST COMEDIAN: It thinks. Does calculations. Almost any calculation you like to think of as long as you feed the data into it first.

MR PARADOCK: Why don't we do calculations?

SECOND COMEDIAN: Hell.

MR PARADOCK: For the laughs. Multiply. Subtract. Like an adding machine.

FIRST COMEDIAN: But there are three of us.

MR PARADOCK: A comptometer then. What does it matter? Tell me to do something. Go on. Feed me some data.

FIRST COMEDIAN: What sort of data?

MR PARADOCK: Any sort. Just feed me. Tell me to add a hundred and ninety-three to six hundred and thirty-eight. Any damn thing.

SECOND COMEDIAN: For crying out loud a comptometer's got rows of black keys all over the top of it for crissake with numbers on!

MR PARADOCK: Eight hundred and thirty-one!

SECOND COMEDIAN: They gotta be pressed down.

MR PARADOCK: That's the operator's job. Feed me some data.

FIRST COMEDIAN: And where's your lever mechanism?

MR PARADOCK: Did Bergson say anything about lever mechanism? The cube root of fifty thousand six hundred and fifty-three. . . .

FIRST COMEDIAN [to Second Comedian]: Unless he's electrically operated?

SECOND COMEDIAN: It'd be more kinda realistic to have him bending forward like he was the right shape for a comptometer.

MR PARADOCK: Thirty-seven!

FIRST COMEDIAN: I want him plugged in somewhere.

MR PARADOCK: Three hundred and ninety-six thousand gallons of petrol at three and ninepence three farthings a gallon allowing two per cent wastage . . .

[FIRST COMEDIAN *passes his hands over* BRO PARADOCK *in*

search of something, finds what he wants in his left pocket, and putting
his hand into the pocket brings out a three-pin plug attached to a
length of flex. This pays itself out from Bro Paradock's pocket.]

SECOND COMEDIAN: Bend him forward.

FIRST COMEDIAN: Like this?

SECOND COMEDIAN: He ought to look more like he's got keys.

MR PARADOCK: Seventy-five thousand five hundred and ninety-four
pounds fifteen shillings!

SECOND COMEDIAN: Get him plugged in. For God's sake get him
plugged in.

MR PARADOCK: Feed me some data.

FIRST COMEDIAN: Pay that flex out, Bug, will you? I'll plug him in
to the power point.

MR PARADOCK: Five times the cube root of pi r squared! Give me
a value for r. In centimetres. Furlongs. Cubits. Any damn thing.
[FIRST COMEDIAN *fits plug into socket.*]

SECOND COMEDIAN: Switch it on.

FIRST COMEDIAN: Oh. [*He does so.*] There. Now he's live.
[BRO PARADOCK *twitches and becomes tense. His face begins to*
work. Suddenly words burst out in a rapid torrent.]

MR PARADOCK: Paraparaparallelogrammatical. Eighteen men on a
dead man's chest at compound interest is not what it's for for four
in the morning when the square on the hypotenuse is worth two
in the circle two in the circle two in the circle two in the circle . . .

FIRST COMEDIAN [*looks across, alarmed, at* SECOND COMEDIAN]:
He's shorting!

SECOND COMEDIAN: The voltage wants fixing.
[BRO PARADOCK *continues his monologue while* FIRST COMEDIAN
hurries to wrench out the plug.]

MR PARADOCK: Two in the circle two in the circle two in the circle
two in the circle [*Plug comes out.*] two in the circle [*more calmly and*
increasingly slowly] at seven and six, and six and five, and five and
four, and four and three, and three and two in the circle at six
and five, and five and four, and four and three, and three and two
in the circle at five and four, and four and three, and three and two

in the circle at four and three, and three and two in the circle at three and two, and one, and nought.

[BRO PARADOCK *unbends and mops his brow.*]

BRO PARADOCK: I thought I was never going to get back. Who unplugged me?

SECOND COMEDIAN: You were shorting.

BRO PARADOCK: You were pressing the wrong buttons. You can't do all that about pi r squared and compound interest on a compto-meter. That's not what it's for. Of course I was shorting.

FIRST COMEDIAN: You went haywire.

BRO PARADOCK: I'm not surprised.

MRS PARADOCK [*getting up*]: I expect you'd all like some coffee after that.

SECOND COMEDIAN: Thank you, Mrs Paradock. We would.

MRS PARADOCK: You and Hamster will want it black, I expect, after your drunken orgy.

FIRST COMEDIAN: Yes, please, Mrs Paradock. I think we finished up both those two bottles your husband opened for us.

SECOND COMEDIAN: I feel terrible.

MRS PARADOCK: I shan't be long. You'll feel better for a cup of coffee.

[MIDDIE PARADOCK *goes out.* BRO PARADOCK *and the two* COMEDIANS *dispose themselves about the room as the lights fade out. A spotlight reveals a technician in a white coat on right. The living room remains in darkness while the technician comes forward and addresses the audience.*]

TECHNICIAN: I don't want to hold up the action for more than a minute or two, and in fact I have no intention of holding it up for as long as that. What we are doing here on the technical side is rather new and I have been asked to come out here on the stage and as quickly as I can without holding up the action longer than absolutely necessary to give you in a few words if I can just what it is we are trying to do on the technical side. You are not going to be approached in any way. Please be quite at ease on that score. This is not audience participation in any new and more exasper-

ating form so do please relax and be quite natural. What we a
doing is by way of being an experiment and it is an experiment v
can only carry through successfully by at some stage in the produ
tion taking the audience – that is your good selves – into our co
fidence. We do this as much for our own sake as yours. We wa
you to be quite spontaneous. And that is why I am here now. T
take you into our confidence. It is as I say a new technique and w
do have of course a huge barrier to break down of prejudice if n
outright hostility from those who are not fully conversant wit
what we are trying to do. Any opportunity of making our aims an
methods more widely known is something we are always very gla
to have extended to us and I on this occasion am very grateful t
both you and those responsible for this production for bein
allowed to put you in the picture. This is a technique which ca
be used for any kind of stage production. Any production wha
ever that it is possible to mount on a stage where we have appara
tus installed comes within our scope. But it is absolutely essenti
in every case for the audience to be as it were receptive to the nee
if we are to be one hundred per cent effective, of as I say comple
spontaneity. What we want, briefly, are your reactions. As yo
know all of us react in the theatre. Laughter. Laughter is nothin
more or less than a reaction. If we instinctively feel something t
be funny, we laugh. In other words, we react. Now we have literall
thousands of feet of microfilm on which we have recorded thes
reactions as and when they have occurred. These recordings w
match up with recordings made on other reels of microfilm, record
ings of whatever on the stage has acted as the stimulus for eac
reaction recorded. Let me illustrate. At one point in the per
formance, shall we say, a witticism comes into play. This witticisr
is picked up by our very sensitive detectors which also break
down into molecules. There is a reason for this. An author wh
makes use of our records gains a complete and accurate pictur
not only of the effectiveness of a given witticism as a whole, but
enabled to see, as though under a microscope, just which *part* o
that witticism achieved maximum response. So you can see ho

essential it is that every member of the audience should react at optimum spontaneity from beginning to end of the performance. This ensures that at any given stage in the production the laughter response index which we pass on to the author and producer is as accurate and reliable as science can make it. Because that of course is what we are out to do. We hope in time with the cooperation of theatre managements and audiences all over the country to build up in microfilm a library which will embody the case histories in terms of audience reaction of a sufficiently large and representative number of productions of all kinds to do away with the need for inspired guesswork on the part of author or producer. Will this be funny? Or is one part of this likely to be more funny than some other, perhaps less funny, part? This is the kind of question the writer of comedy is always having to ask himself, and it's the kind of question we on the technical side feel we can supply a reliable answer to. And not only of course the writer of comedy. In tragedy too – where of course the response to be successful must always be a rather different response from that evoked by comedy – I hope I'm not holding up the action too much, but what we do feel we want to get established, and get more and more established, is the very real part we on the technical side can play. As I say, the writer of tragedy with his stock-in-trade of pity and terror is working just as much in the dark as his colleague of the comic muse. How much pity? Just what degree of terror? And so on. If there was audience resistance, what caused it? This is another question which, by classifying the laughter and tears we pick up, we can often answer for the bewildered author. If his audience according to our records are viscerotonic endomorphs this may explain why his play, written shall we say, for cerebrotonic ectomorphs, fails to achieve saturation impact. And now I think I have held up the production long enough. I would only like to say in conclusion that we have the technique, and are only waiting for the green light to go right ahead and take the guesswork out of the inspiration for the ultimate benefit of you, the audience. Thank you for listening to me – and before I do finally finish I would like to say how much we have been helped, very materially helped, by the way everyone responsible for this production down to the author himself has done everything possible to give us all the facilities we have asked for. And of course you, the audience, have given us what is our very life-blood – your spontaneity. Thank you very much.

[*He goes out. Lights come up in the living room.* BRO PARADOCK *and the two* COMEDIANS *are in various parts of the room, silent and blank.* MIDDIE PARADOCK *enters with a tray of coffee cups and a jug of coffee.*]

MRS PARADOCK: Did you think I was never coming?

MR PARADOCK: Ah, coffee.

MRS PARADOCK: Get the books out, Bro, will you?

FIRST COMEDIAN: Don't get them out for me, Mrs Paradock. I never read.

MRS PARADOCK: Perhaps Bug would like a book with his coffee.

SECOND COMEDIAN: I do like a short book with coffee. Thank you, Mrs Paradock.

MRS PARADOCK: Now come on. Here's a place for you, Bug. Help Hamster to a chair, Bro. He's wearing his shoes crooked this week and I know they're hurting him. There are plenty of books at your elbow, Bug, and more in the bookcase if you want them. Hamster: now what are you reading?

FIRST COMEDIAN: Nothing for me, thank you, Mrs Paradock. Just the coffee.

MRS PARADOCK: I can't get used to you not reading with your coffee.

SECOND COMEDIAN: He never has, Mrs Paradock.

MRS PARADOCK: Are we all settled? Come on, Bro. What are you going to have? Fiction, biography? I think I'll help myself to this textbook.

SECOND COMEDIAN: It looks rather nice.

MRS PARADOCK: Yes. Now we can all have a good read with our coffee.

MR PARADOCK: Shall I see what's on the wireless while we're reading?

MRS PARADOCK: That's right, Bro. See what's on. It ought to be the service.

MR PARADOCK [*looking at his watch*]: It'll be starting.

[BRO PARADOCK *tunes in the wireless and all except* FIRST COMEDIAN *continue reading throughout. The prayers heard from the wireless are intoned in a voice of cultured Anglican fatuity, and the responses said in low-toned earnestness by a small chorus of voices, which is joined by* FIRST COMEDIAN *in an undertone.*]

PRAYER: ... weep at the elastic as it stretches:

MR PARADOCK: It's started.

RESPONSE: And rejoice that it might have been otherwise.

PRAYER: Let us sing because round things roll:

RESPONSE: And rejoice that it might have been otherwise.

PRAYER: Let us praise God for woodlice, and for buildings sixty-nine feet three inches high:

RESPONSE: For Adam Smith's *Wealth of Nations* published in 1776:

PRAYER: For the fifth key from the left on the lower manual of the organ of the Church of the Ascension in the Piazza Vittorio Emmanuele II in the town of Castelfidardo in Italy:

RESPONSE: And for gnats.

PRAYER: How flat are our trays:

RESPONSE: Our sewers how underground and rat-infested altogether.

PRAYER: As the roots of a tree strike downwards:

RESPONSE: So fire burns.

PRAYER: As a river flows always towards its mouth:

RESPONSE: So is sugar sweet.

PRAYER: Let us laugh therefore and be glad for the Balearic Islands:

RESPONSE: And sing with joy in the presence of dyspepsia.

PRAYER: Let us give praise for those who compile dictionaries in large buildings, for the gallant men and women on our beaches, for all those who in the fullness of time will go out to meet whatever fate awaits them, for the tall, the ham-fisted, the pompous, and for all men everywhere and at all times.

RESPONSE: Amen.

PRAYER: Let us give thanks for air hostesses and such as sit examinations, for the Bessemer process and for canticles, that all who live in France may be called Frenchmen and that nothing may be called useful that has no purpose.

RESPONSE: Amen.

PRAYER: Let us talk and itch and swim and paint:

RESPONSE: Let us talk and itch and swim and paint.

PRAYER: Let us make music, water, love, and rabbit hutches:

RESPONSE: Let us make music, water, love, and rabbit hutches.

PRAYER: Let us be brave and punctual:

RESPONSE: And vituperative and good-looking.

PRAYER: Let us laugh with those we tickle:

RESPONSE: Let us laugh with those we tickle.

PRAYER: Let us weep with those we expose to tear-gas:

RESPONSE: Let us weep with those we expose to tear-gas.

PRAYER: Let us throw back our heads and laugh at reality:

RESPONSE: Which is an illusion caused by mescalin deficiency.

PRAYER: At sanity:

RESPONSE: Which is an illusion caused by alcohol deficiency.

PRAYER: At knowledge which is an illusion caused by certain bio-chemical changes in the human brain structure during the course of human evolution, which had it followed another course would have produced other bio-chemical changes in the human brain structure, by reason of which knowledge as we now experience it would have been beyond the reach of our wildest imaginings; and by reason of which, what is now beyond the reach of our wildest imaginings would have been familiar and commonplace. Let us laugh at these things. Let us laugh at thought:

RESPONSE: Which is a phenomenon like any other.

PRAYER: At illusion:

RESPONSE: Which is an illusion, which is a phenomenon like any other.

PRAYER: Let us love diversity:

RESPONSE: Because there is neither end nor purpose to it.

PRAYER: Let us love simplicity:

RESPONSE: Because there is neither end nor purpose to it.

PRAYER: Let us think, and think we think, because leaves are green and because stones fall and because volcanoes erupt in a world where seas are salt.

RESPONSE: Amen.

[*The introductory bars of 'Sweet Polly Oliver' in an orchestrated version are heard from the wireless.* FIRST COMEDIAN *gets to his feet.*]

FIRST COMEDIAN: I think this is where we stand, isn't it?

[*The* SECOND COMEDIAN, BRO, *and* MIDDIE PARADOCK *have become aware of the music and begin to stand. Rather self-consciously they join in the hymn-like singing of 'Sweet Polly Oliver'. There is a momentary silence when the song ends, and then to neutralize their embarrassment they all try to be excessively normal.*]

MRS PARADOCK: Now. Have we all had enough coffee?

SECOND COMEDIAN: It was splendid coffee, Mrs Paradock. You must show me how you make it.

MR PARADOCK: Middie's coffee is made by a secret process, Bug. Wild horses wouldn't drag it out of her.

FIRST COMEDIAN: In that case we'll be making up ingenious excuses for coming round here every evening for coffee, Mrs Paradock.

MRS PARADOCK: You're both very welcome. Bro and I need some good comedians in the house to prevent us quarrelling all the time.

SECOND COMEDIAN: That's a bargain then, Mrs Paradock. We supply the comedy, you supply the coffee.

FIRST COMEDIAN: And if our comedy's as good as your coffee, Mrs Paradock, we shall all be more than satisfied.

MRS PARADOCK: Well, if no one wants any more coffee I'll clear away the cups.

[MIDDIE PARADOCK *puts the cups and saucers on to the tray and takes this outside.*]

FIRST COMEDIAN: Did you know that a female cod can be the mother of eight million eggs?

MR PARADOCK: No.

FIRST COMEDIAN: Eight million!

SECOND COMEDIAN: It's the apotheosis of irresponsibility.

MR PARADOCK: There'd be no counting them – not if there were eight million of them. Except on the fingers of eight hundred thousand pairs of hands.

SECOND COMEDIAN: Eight hundred thousand people to count the eggs of a single cod! It's ludicrous.

MR PARADOCK: And yet they call a female god a goddess.

FIRST COMEDIAN: There's no accounting for it.

SECOND COMEDIAN: I'm not sure that I want to account for it. It's one of those things my imagination wilts at.

MR PARADOCK: I always thought you had a pretty strong imagination.

FIRST COMEDIAN: He hasn't. Not for that sort of thing. He picked up an imaginary chair yesterday. I thought he was handling it remarkably easily, and when he sat down on it I knew why. It just crumpled up under him.

SECOND COMEDIAN: I should think Bro has got a strong imagination. Let's see you lift an imaginary chair, Bro, by the back legs.

MR PARADOCK: How?

FIRST COMEDIAN: Get hold of it by the two back legs. Keep your arms straight out in front of you and see if you can bring it up to shoulder height. And hold it there.

MR PARADOCK: Where do I get the chair from?

SECOND COMEDIAN: Imagine it.

MR PARADOCK: Shall I?

FIRST COMEDIAN: Go on.

[BRO PARADOCK *squats on his haunches, gets up and removes his jacket, squats again, and adjusts his position before going through the motions of taking a grip on the back legs of a chair. His efforts to stand up with it are successful but strenuous.* FIRST COMEDIAN *picks up a chair which he places in* BRO PARADOCK'S *outstretched hands. He holds this chair without effort.*]

MR PARADOCK: That's extraordinary! I'd never have believed it.

SECOND COMEDIAN: You were letting your imagination run away with you.

MR PARADOCK: I'd never have believed it. The one I imagined I was lifting was twice as heavy as this one.

FIRST COMEDIAN: You've just got a strong imagination. You're like me. I use it to develop my muscles.

SECOND COMEDIAN: Why don't you two have a contest of strength? We'll ask Mrs Paradock for a pair of scales when she comes in. See which of you can hang the heaviest weight on them.

FIRST COMEDIAN: What do you say, Bro?

MR PARADOCK: I'm game if you are. [*He goes to the door, opens it, and puts his head out.*] Middie! Have we still got those scales?

[MIDDIE PARADOCK *is heard off:* 'As far as I know. What do you want them for?']

MR PARADOCK: I'll go and get them now.

[BRO PARADOCK *goes out. Several seconds later* MIDDIE PARADOCK *comes in, followed by* BRO PARADOCK *with the scales.*]

MRS PARADOCK: I hear you're going to have a trial of strength between you.

SECOND COMEDIAN: Not me, Mrs Paradock. It's these two.

MRS PARADOCK: I'm surprised Bro's got a strong imagination – I'd never have said so.

SECOND COMEDIAN: Who's going to hold the scales? Shall I hold them while you two get ready?

MR PARADOCK: Isn't it going to be a bit heavy for you when we both put weights on the end?

FIRST COMEDIAN: Don't worry about Bug. His imagination isn't as strong as yours and mine, Bro. He won't register more than a pound or two.

SECOND COMEDIAN: I shall be all right. Now then. Here it is. As soon as you're both ready.

MR PARADOCK [*looking at* FIRST COMEDIAN]: Shall we start?

FIRST COMEDIAN: Right. Here goes.

[*Both pretend to be lifting massive weights, with which they stagger towards the scales held by* SECOND COMEDIAN. *As they simultaneously hang their weights on opposite arms of the scales,* SECOND COMEDIAN'*s arm dips slightly as he takes the strain. The balance remains horizontal.*]

MRS PARADOCK: Nothing in it. Fancy that.

MR PARADOCK [*panting*]: I don't know what was in it. It weighed like cement.

MRS PARADOCK: Bug seems to be managing it without much difficulty.

FIRST COMEDIAN: Better put it down now, Bug. It's putting too much strain on the scales. You'll have the joint starting.

SECOND COMEDIAN [*lifting each load on to the floor in turn*]: I don't know about cement. It feels like something a whole lot lighter than cement to me.

MRS PARADOCK: You must be stronger in the muscles, Bug.

FIRST COMEDIAN: It's his imagination, Mrs Paradock. It isn't equal to it.

MRS PARADOCK: Is that what it is?

[*Silence.*]

MRS PARADOCK: You forgot to ring up about the elephant, Bro.

MR PARADOCK: I thought you'd seen about it.

MRS PARADOCK: I have now. They're delivering it in the morning.

SECOND COMEDIAN: As for elephants, I must say we've started a fine lot of hares this evening. Don't you think so?

MR PARADOCK: March hares.

FIRST COMEDIAN: We've started them all right. A whole lot of mad March hares streaking hell for leather across the open country.

SECOND COMEDIAN: And not one but will drop in its tracks before these worthy people pick up the scent.

[*All turn to gaze thoughtfully at the audience.*]

MRS PARADOCK: What a shame we can't give them a run for their money with tortoises.

CURTAIN

ACT TWO

Evening next day. The living room. BRO PARADOCK, *hands in pockets, is staring thoughtfully out through the window.* MIDDIE PARADOCK *turns away from the window.*

MRS PARADOCK: It'll have to stay out.

[BRO PARADOCK *turns slowly away and crosses the room.*]

MR PARADOCK: What are the measurements?

MRS PARADOCK: You don't need measurements. A thing that size in a pre-fab.

MR PARADOCK: I thought we were living in a bungalow.

MRS PARADOCK: People will think we're trying to go one better than everybody else.

MR PARADOCK: It's only once a year for goodness' sake! You should have kept the measurements.

MRS PARADOCK: I should have gone for it myself instead of ringing. [*Turns to look out of the window.*] Look at it. Look at its great ears flapping about. Surely they know by now what size we always have.

MR PARADOCK: Perhaps they've sent us the wrong one.

MRS PARADOCK: It's big enough for a hotel. If you had a hotel or a private school or something you wouldn't need a thing that size.

MR PARADOCK: I suppose not.

MRS PARADOCK: And supposing it goes berserk in the night? I'm not getting up to it.

MR PARADOCK: Why should it go berserk in the night any more than a smaller one?

MRS PARADOCK: We'll have old Mrs Stencil round again if it does – threatening us with the R.S.P.C.A.

MR PARADOCK: You should have been in when they came with it, then you could have queried the measurements.

MRS PARADOCK: I can't think what we're going to call it. We can't call it Mr Trench again.

105

MR PARADOCK: The only time we've not called it Mr Trench wa
three years ago when we had to make do with a giraffe.

MRS PARADOCK: And look at the fuss we had before they'd take i
in part exchange.

MR PARADOCK: Of course they made a fuss. There was something
wrong with it.

MRS PARADOCK [looking through the window]: Imagine calling
clumsy great thing that size Mr Trench.

MR PARADOCK: Why not?

MRS PARADOCK: We can't go on year after year calling it M
Trench.

MR PARADOCK: You talk as if it were the same animal every time

MRS PARADOCK: You can hear the neighbours, can't you? They'
think we never launch out.

MR PARADOCK: I know what you want to call it.

MRS PARADOCK: It looks all the time as if we were hard up for
name to give the animal.

MR PARADOCK: You want to call it Oedipus Rex, don't you?

MRS PARADOCK: It's better than Mr Trench year after year. A
least it sounds as if we knew what was going on in the world.

MR PARADOCK: Oedipus Rex! [Wags a finger archly through th
window.] Ah, ah! Only the edible blooms remember, Oedipus.

MRS PARADOCK: If you say it in that tone of voice of course i
sounds ridiculous.

MR PARADOCK [in same tone]: Oedipus! Oedipus! You're letting tha
glass take all your weight!

MRS PARADOCK: Anything else would sound equally as ridiculou
if you said it like that.

MR PARADOCK: It isn't Mr Trench we want a change from.

MRS PARADOCK: The only thing to do is ring up the Zoo. Tell them
to come and collect it.

MR PARADOCK: And be without an elephant at all?

MRS PARADOCK: Tell them to come and collect it and the sooner the
better. I'd rather not have one.

MR PARADOCK: I beg to differ.

MRS PARADOCK: We did without one the year we had a giraffe instead.

MR PARADOCK: I know we did without one the year we had a giraffe instead. And look at the trouble we had getting it changed. I don't want that all over again.

MRS PARADOCK: It's the R.S.P.C.A. I'm worried about.

MR PARADOCK: They haven't been round yet. In any case you wouldn't get the Zoo at this time. They'll be closed.

MRS PARADOCK: I don't know why they couldn't send us what we asked for in the first place.

MR PARADOCK: Is it any use trying to get hold of Eddie on the phone?

MRS PARADOCK: Yes. Ring Eddie up. Or Nora. Nora'd be sure to know what to do. They used to keep pigeons and things. They had a room full of nothing else but different kinds of birds when they were all living at No. 89, and white mice and things.

MR PARADOCK: It'll have to stay outside tonight.

MRS PARADOCK: I'm not having it in the kitchen if that's what you're leading up to.

MR PARADOCK: If it starts straying all over the place during the night we shall have the R.S.P.C.A. making a lot of difficulties.

MRS PARADOCK: Not if we get it changed first thing. Get on to Nora.

MR PARADOCK: If we're getting it changed first thing in the morning, where's the sense in thinking up a name like Oedipus Rex for it now?

MRS PARADOCK: Because I'm not calling it Mr Trench six years running. You can if you like. I'm not.

MR PARADOCK: I didn't want to call it Mr Trench the year it was a giraffe. That was your idea. It was your idea it would make a pleasant change to be giving the name to a giraffe instead of an elephant. Now you complain about calling it Mr Trench six years running.

MRS PARADOCK: I think we'd be better off without it.

MR PARADOCK: How would we?

MRS PARADOCK: I do really. I think we'd be better off without
We've done nothing except bicker ever since they came with it.

MR PARADOCK: We weren't in when they came with it.

MRS PARADOCK: That's the whole point.

[*Both relapse into silence.* BRO PARADOCK *takes up a paper.*]

MR PARADOCK [*looks up after an interval from his paper*]: If we'r
going to change the name at all I can't see what you've got agains
Hodge for that matter.

MRS PARADOCK: Hodge is all right for a monkey.

MR PARADOCK: We'll go through some names and see what we ca
agree on. Hodge.

MRS PARADOCK: Hodge for a monkey. Gush for an elephant.

MR PARADOCK: Admiral Benbow.

MRS PARADOCK: Hiram B. Larkspur.

MR PARADOCK: Playboy.

MRS PARADOCK: Killed-with-kindness Corcoran.

MR PARADOCK: New-wine-into-old-bottles Backhouse.

MRS PARADOCK: 'Tis-pity-she's-a-whore Hignett.

MR PARADOCK: Lucifer.

MRS PARADOCK: Stonehenge.

MR PARADOCK: Haunch.

MR PARADOCK: ⎫
MRS PARADOCK: ⎬ Splinter.

MR PARADOCK: Thank God we can agree on something. Now I ca
ring Eddie.

MRS PARADOCK: Why ring up Eddie when you've got Nora who'
had experience with animals? She could probably suggest some
thing.

MR PARADOCK: So you keep saying. [*Dialling.*]

MRS PARADOCK: Well?

MR PARADOCK: Is that Mrs Mortice? . . . Oh. . . . Will you? Thank
you.

MRS PARADOCK: You've decided to ring Nora then.

MR PARADOCK [*ignores her*]: Hallo. Nora? . . . Yes, thank you, Nora
And how are you? . . . Oh? And what's that, Nora? . . . A what?

... Hold on a moment, Nora.... Yes.... Yes.... Hold on, Nora. Wait till I fetch Middie.

MRS PARADOCK: Don't say they've got ours.

MR PARADOCK: It's a snake. She says they ordered a snake and they've got one that's too short.

MRS PARADOCK: Too short for what?

MR PARADOCK: She says they're worried about the R.S.P.C.A.

MRS PARADOCK [*takes up phone*]: Nora?... Yes, Bro was telling me. Isn't it maddening?... Yes.... Yes – they've done exactly the same with us.... No. About ten times too big. I don't know what the vanman was thinking about. A thing that size in a bunga-low.... Not indoors, no. We've got it out at the back.... Yes. I think you're quite justified.... No.... No.... Not till the morn-ing, Nora. Bro thinks they'll be closed now anyway.

MR PARADOCK: Why not ask her if she'd like to have Mr Trench and we'll take the snake off her.

MRS PARADOCK: What?... No, I was talking to Bro, Nora. I think he's got some suggestion to make. I'll get him to tell you himself. [*Puts her hand over mouthpiece.*] You talk to her. She's on about this snake of theirs.

MR PARADOCK: What about it, Nora? If yours is on the short side it might do us very nicely ... and you're welcome to Mr Trench. ... Yes. We don't need anything.... No trouble at all, Nora.... Yes? Well, that's better still.... I'll come round with it then.... No.... No, I'll remember.... Yes – in about half an hour, then. Good-bye, Nora.

MRS PARADOCK: Thank goodness we rang them up.

MR PARADOCK: Did she say how short this snake was?

MRS PARADOCK She didn't give any measurements, if that's what you mean.

MR PARADOCK: I thought perhaps you might have thought to ask her what the measurements were.

MRS PARADOCK: Why didn't you ask her for the measurements yourself as far as that goes?

MR PARADOCK: How was I to know whether you'd asked already?

MRS PARADOCK: You heard me talking to her.

MR PARADOCK: What have you done with my gumboots?

MRS PARADOCK: What do you want gumboots for to go down the road a few doors with an elephant? Where are your other shoes?

MR PARADOCK: These are my other shoes I've got on.

MRS PARADOCK: And I should come straight back with Mr Trench. We don't want Mrs Stencil asking a lot of questions.

MR PARADOCK: I notice you're all for calling it Mr Trench now you know it's a snake.

MRS PARADOCK: What are you going to bring it back in? You can't have it on a lead like a canary.

MR PARADOCK: In any case I thought we'd settled on Hodge for a name.

MRS PARADOCK: Hodge for a jackal. Gush for an anaconda.

MR PARADOCK: Admiral Benbow.

MRS PARADOCK: Hiram B. Larkspur.

MR PARADOCK: Playboy.

MRS PARADOCK: We'll see how short it is first.

MR PARADOCK: The only thing I've ever seen on a lead is a dog. I've never seen a canary on a lead.

MRS PARADOCK: A dog on a lead then.

MR PARADOCK: I hate this job.

MRS PARADOCK: You say that every year.

MR PARADOCK: I've never had to do it before.

MRS PARADOCK: You say it about other things.

MR PARADOCK: If it comes to that, how do you know it *is* an anaconda?

MRS PARADOCK: What else would it be? We shall have the R.S.P.C.A. round while you stand there.

MR PARADOCK: Good God!

[*He goes out.*]

MRS PARADOCK [*slowly moving her head from side to side*]: Admiral Benbow!

[BRO PARADOCK *comes back into the room with collar turned up. He turns it down and shakes rain from his jacket.*]

MRS PARADOCK: You're not back already?

MR PARADOCK: I'm not going in this rain.

MRS PARADOCK: It's barely started.

MR PARADOCK: I don't want to get mixed up in a lot of rain. I haven't got a hat for that sort of thing.

MRS PARADOCK: You've got an eye-shield. What's wrong with that?

MR PARADOCK: You gave it away.

MRS PARADOCK: I don't mean that one. I mean the one you wear for tennis.

MR PARADOCK: But that's to keep the sun out of my eyes.

MRS PARADOCK: Can't you wear it back to front?

[*Pause.*]

MR PARADOCK: What a coincidence! Uncle Fred! That's just what Uncle Fred used to do. When he was at sea. He used to wear an eye-shield back to front rather than be put to the expense of a sou'-wester. It deflected the rainwater from his neck and the elastic band passed conveniently across his mouth like a horse's bit.

[*A knock at the door.* MIDDIE PARADOCK *goes to open it.*]

MRS PARADOCK: That would be too ingenious for you, of course.

[NORA *is at the door.*]

MRS PARADOCK: Nora! You're drenched! Come in.

NORA: I thought I'd better come over with this as soon as I saw it was raining. [*Fumbles in her handbag.*] I'm afraid I get terribly wet in these showers. I just haven't got that kind of a hat, I suppose. [*Takes out a pencil box.*] There, I said it was short, didn't I?

MRS PARADOCK: Good gracious. Do I open it?

MR PARADOCK: That's never an anaconda.

MRS PARADOCK: Would Nora have brought it over if it had been? Perhaps I'll leave it in its loosebox. We don't want it eavesdropping. [*She puts the box, without opening it, on the mantelpiece.*]

NORA [*looks into the mirror*]: Goodness! My make-up.

MRS PARADOCK: Let me see. Oh, no. I think she's done very well, Bro, don't you? I admire you for coming out in it at all.

MR PARADOCK: It's a very good attempt, Nora. It takes a pretty good hat to manage a shower like that one. I didn't even try it. Not with my poor old hat.

NORA: I don't know about that, Bro. I wouldn't mind having a hat like yours anyway.

MRS PARADOCK: Hats aren't everything in this world. Far from it.

MR PARADOCK: I know they aren't everything.

NORA: Some people seem to get by quite nicely without them. In fact I've often noticed it's the ones who haven't any hats at all who live the most satisfying lives in the long run.

MR PARADOCK: It isn't so much having the hats as knowing how to make the best use of them.

MRS PARADOCK: We can't all be blessed with hats.

MR PARADOCK: Look at Mrs Blackboy's husband and the showers he's got through in his time with that plastic shopping bag he carries round on his head.

NORA: Or Bella for that matter. Bella's up half the night sometimes weatherproofing that old straw beehive she goes out in whenever she's got rain to cope with.

MRS PARADOCK: And a lot of those who are supposed to have such wonderful hats are going around half the time in other people's. I haven't got much time for them. They got them out of Christmas crackers more likely than not.

MR PARADOCK: I don't like to see the time Bella spends on millinery. That sort of thing's all right if you've got millinery in your make-up. Otherwise leave it alone.

MRS PARADOCK: Bro's not much of a one for millinery.

MR PARADOCK: I don't get the time. I've got other things to do. Nora and I prefer to leave the showers to the ones with the hats, unless we're compelled to tackle them. And then we don't do too badly, eh, Nora?

MRS PARADOCK: Nora's got plenty of hats, as you well know. Take no notice of him, Nora. He's only acting the fool. You shouldn't be so rude to people, Bro. It's lucky Nora knows you.

NORA: Oh, I've never made any pretensions to hats.

MRS PARADOCK: You're too modest, Nora.

MR PARADOCK: I've always known what I could do, and I've always known what I couldn't do. That's one of the reasons why I never became an air hostess.

NORA: Hasn't your Myrtle got a fine little hat on her head? I was noticing it only the other day.

MRS PARADOCK: I don't know where she gets it from then! Although I must say she didn't do too badly in her storm-test last week. I will give Myrtle her due – she doesn't seem to worry much what weather she goes out in.

MR PARADOCK: She gets it from Stan if she gets it from anybody. Or Uncle Fred.

NORA: Do you know what I think? It would never surprise me if Myrtle didn't turn out to be something of a storm-breaker before she's finished. She's got the hats for it.

MRS PARADOCK: You're joking, Nora.

MR PARADOCK: What about Uncle Fred, then? He did very nicely for himself with his eye-shield.

MRS PARADOCK: Exactly. It's Uncle Fred's eye-shield that got him where he was – you couldn't call him a natural storm-breaker. [*To* NORA] Uncle Fred was Bro's uncle in the navy, Nora.

MR PARADOCK: He used to wear his eye-shield back to front so as to protect his neck from the rainwater.

MRS PARADOCK: Anybody would think he was a positive sou'-wester man the way you talk.

MR PARADOCK: It wasn't that he didn't have a sou'-wester, so much as that he could never get round to putting it on.

MRS PARADOCK: He never had one. You know perfectly well he used to borrow quite shamelessly from the other men whenever there was an important storm at sea and he couldn't get by with just his eye-shield.

NORA [*loudly*]: Aha! Whose is the waste-paper basket! It looks rather interesting.

MRS PARADOCK: That's Mr Malden's. We lent him a couple of lampshades Myrtle has grown out of for his little boy; he said we were welcome to his waste-paper basket if we could make anything of it.

MR PARADOCK: It might be all right for Myrtle when she's older. It looks to me like one he had when he was at school.

NORA: I rather think Myrtle's father has got his eye on it, too, if I'm not too much mistaken.

MRS PARADOCK: He's tried it on for size. Didn't you, Bro? One night last week. But he won't be seen out in it.

MR PARADOCK: That sort of thing's all right for the summer.

NORA [looks through the window]: Thank goodness it seems to have stopped raining for the time being anyway.

MRS PARADOCK: Oh splendid. Now you can take Mr Trench across to Nora's, Bro.

NORA: I'll have to be going, then. I don't want to be out when you call, Bro.

MRS PARADOCK: That would never do, would it?

MR PARADOCK: It was lucky you got here when you did, Nora. I was just setting out. We might have missed each other.

NORA: We might.

MRS PARADOCK: Not if you were both going the same way.

MR PARADOCK: We could hardly be going the same way when Nora was going in one direction and I was going in the other. How could we have been going the same way?

MRS PARADOCK: If you like, Nora, I'll hold Bro back for a few minutes. That'll give you time to get in and turn round before he comes knocking on the door. [She holds him by the collar.]

NORA: If you're sure it won't throw you out?

MRS PARADOCK: Of course it won't. It's no trouble keeping Bro back for twenty minutes or so. Especially when you're helping us out by taking the elephant off our hands.

NORA: It'll be nice to get something with some size to it, believe me. I only hope you find you can make do with Bees' Wedding there. It was hopelessly short for us.

MRS PARADOCK: You've got the upstairs as well, of course, haven't you?

NORA: And the cellar. We just can't do with anything smaller. We've managed in the past with a rhinoceros – we had that one the year before last, but it was barely large enough.

MRS PARADOCK: This one's a ridiculous size for us in this bungalow. We always like to have an elephant, of course, if we can, but we can't cope with one this size.

NORA: What have you called it?

MRS PARADOCK: To tell you the truth, Nora, we haven't called it anything yet. [BRO, *still held firmly by the collar, has a barely perceptible spasm.*] We've hardly had time to get round to discussing names at all, and when we do we only seem to quarrel.

NORA: Are you like that too? We quarrel all the time over names.

MRS PARADOCK: Oh yes. We lose all control. Names and food. It's the only thing worth quarrelling about after all, isn't it?

NORA: Every animal we've ever had all the time we've been here has been called 'Retreat from Moscow', whether it's been the one we ordered or not. We just can't agree on anything else, and so every year we end up calling it 'Retreat from Moscow'.

MRS PARADOCK: Never mind, Nora. Perhaps we'll be able to do without animals altogether one of these days.

NORA: What a hope! But I mustn't keep you standing there with Bro. If you could just let him come on to us in about twenty minutes that'll give me time to open the gate at the back.

MRS PARADOCK: Good-bye, then, Nora. We'll be calling in on Sunday, remember.

NORA: Make it as early as you can. Good-bye, Middie.

MRS PARADOCK: Good-bye.

[NORA *goes out and* MRS PARADOCK *closes the door, releasing* BRO PARADOCK *who crosses the room straightening his jacket.*]

MR PARADOCK: What did you mean about that waste-paper basket? Telling her I tried it on.

MRS PARADOCK: Nora knew what I meant. It's just a private joke between us.

MR PARADOCK: I should think so.

MRS PARADOCK: I was surprised at you if it comes to that. Starting her off on all that long rigmarole about hats. You know what always happens whenever we get on to that subject.

MR PARADOCK: I thought most of what she said was very sensible.

MRS PARADOCK: Bringing Uncle Fred into it like that.

MR PARADOCK: There was no need to disparage him in front of her and make everyone feel uncomfortable.

MRS PARADOCK: There was no need to bring Uncle Fred into it in the first place and then leave it to Nora to change the subject.

MR PARADOCK: Change what subject?

MRS PARADOCK: About the waste-paper basket. That was only to get you off Uncle Fred.

MR PARADOCK: I thought you said that was a private joke between the two of you.

MRS PARADOCK: So it was.

MR PARADOCK: I can't for the life of me in that case see how it was Nora changing the subject.

MRS PARADOCK: There's no point in raking over it all again now. I just get tired that's all of hats hats hats every time anyone calls. Especially Nora.

MR PARADOCK: It happened to have been raining.

MRS PARADOCK: I know it happened to have been raining.

MR PARADOCK: Then we can let the matter drop. Where are my gumboots?

MRS PARADOCK: You don't need gumboots to go down the road a few doors with an elephant. Where are your other shoes?

MR PARADOCK: These are my other shoes I've got on.

MRS PARADOCK: And I should come straight back with Mr Trench. We don't want Mrs Stencil asking a lot of questions.

MR PARADOCK: I notice you're all for calling it Mr Trench now you know it's going to somebody else.

MRS PARADOCK: We've been through all this before. For goodness' sake pull yourself together. We shall have the R.S.P.C.A. round while you stand there.

MR PARADOCK: Perhaps we shall. Perhaps we shan't.

[*He goes out.* MIDDIE PARADOCK *sits down at the table with a glossy magazine.*

The lights fade out in the living room and a half-light reveals two cleaners who as they sweep perfunctorily, resting between bouts, are overheard in conversation.]

FIRST CLEANER: I didn't tell you about Len. He goes down the school of building twice a week now, when he's not working.

SECOND CLEANER: There's a lot of chances for them these days. More than what we had when we was their age.

FIRST CLEANER: He misses his darts now he can't go down The Grapes Tuesdays.

SECOND CLEANER: Like Charlie with his wireless.

FIRST CLEANER: He won the darts championship the other week, his team.

SECOND CLEANER: He misses his wireless. He always goes to the cupboard first thing when he gets in off leave. 'Mum,' he says, 'what you done with the soldering iron?' He come home Sunday.

FIRST CLEANER: Len'll have to go soon.

SECOND CLEANER: Goes back Sunday night. He's put in for apprentice fitter but he don't know if he'll hear anything.

FIRST CLEANER: He was talking about getting deferred but I said to him if you get deferred you'll only have it hanging over you.

SECOND CLEANER: Charlie's made one or two pals where he is. They get a bit fed up with all the routine.

FIRST CLEANER: They all do. It's only natural.

SECOND CLEANER: Everything has to be done to orders and that.

FIRST CLEANER: What Len's hoping is he'll get in the Raf. That's what he's started down at the school of building for, so he can say he's done something.

SECOND CLEANER: How's Gran?

FIRST CLEANER: Up and down. She can't get about like she used.

SECOND CLEANER: You heard about Mrs Jarvis?

FIRST CLEANER: Flo told me.

SECOND CLEANER: She'll have his pension but it's not the same.

FIRST CLEANER: Mr Braithwaite went round from the chapel. Spoke very nice. Said to keep praying and that. The Lord will provide, Mrs Jarvis, he said.

SECOND CLEANER: He can't give her what Jarvis could.

FIRST CLEANER: Sh! You'll have them dirty old men out the back listening.

SECOND CLEANER: It's true, isn't it? I reckon she'll miss him that way unless she can find somebody else.

FIRST CLEANER: I didn't tell you what old Mrs Croskett told me when she was round Mrs Jarvis's.

SECOND CLEANER: I didn't know she'd been round there.

FIRST CLEANER: She's been round there twice. So's Mrs Blench. They both said you wouldn't have thought there was nothing wrong with him to see him eat the night before, and then next day he came over funny at work.

SECOND CLEANER: Remember last winter when he was down with the gastric and nobody couldn't say what it was?

FIRST CLEANER: I'll tell you when I started putting two and two together a bit – you know he had that great thick overcoat? The one he had for when he was going anywhere? She's got that out, so Mrs Croskett was saying, and she's got all the seams unpicked and she's going to put a bit of felt lining under it after she's cut it up, and make mats out of it.

SECOND CLEANER: Isn't that Else over there coming across?

[MIDDIE PARADOCK *appears as though relaxing off the set.*]

FIRST CLEANER: I didn't know you'd decided to have another go at the stage, Else.

MRS PARADOCK: It's only while Fred's on night work. I thought I'd keep my hand in. I never expected to see you here though.

SECOND CLEANER: You used to be all for gay parts.

MRS PARADOCK: This one's not so bad. It makes a change.

SECOND CLEANER: I don't know how you can remember your lines – it sounds like a lot of rigmarole to me.

FIRST CLEANER: Everything's that trend nowadays.

MRS PARADOCK: It's all right if you don't think about it. A lot of it's supposed to be symbolic, but you get used to it.

SECOND CLEANER: I don't know, I'm sure.

FIRST CLEANER: How's Fred, Else?

MRS PARADOCK: Fred's fine, thanks, Mrs Gride. We're going down the tabernacle Sundays now. There's a new man there. Mr Brice. Took Mr Jabez' place Christmas. He gets a good crowd Sunday evenings.

SECOND CLEANER: That's nice.

MRS PARADOCK: Fred's very taken with him. We're going to go to the midweek service when he's on early turn if I can get away.

FIRST CLEANER: Wasn't Edie telling us about a Mr Brice?

MRS PARADOCK: We saw Edie there Sunday. He was ever so good on What the Church Means to Me. He's going through all different aspects: at home, you know, and at work and that. Next week it's What the Church Means to Me on Holiday. He gets a lot going up the mercy seat every Sunday. Fred was on at me to go up but I had my old coat on.

SECOND CLEANER: You feel everybody's looking at you like when Mrs Leakey stood up and give testimony that time we had the women's meeting in the Temperance Hall.

FIRST CLEANER: The Temperance Hall was when we went down Eastbourne with the outing.

SECOND CLEANER: That's right. Surely you remember Mrs Leakey? Kep' on all the way back in the coach about she's saved, she's saved all the time.

MRS PARADOCK: It's the thanksgiving Sunday week. Why don't you and Mrs Gride come over?

SECOND CLEANER: We'll see what the weather does, Else dear. It's a long way with my legs – the journey knocks me over.

FIRST CLEANER [nodding towards the set]: You look as if you're wanted, Else.

MRS PARADOCK [waves her hand]: It's only Sam but I suppose I'd better go. Must be time. I expect you'll both be gone by the time I'm finished so I'll say good-bye. Good-bye, Mrs Gride. Remember me to Len. Good-bye, Mrs Quiller.

[*She goes back to the set, which remains in darkness. The rest of the stage remains dimly lit. A spotlight is turned on to the cleaners.*]

FIRST CLEANER: Goodness! They've turned the lights on us!

SECOND CLEANER: That'll be Bert's idea of a joke.

[*They gather up buckets and mops and hustle each other out.*]

SECOND CLEANER: They've properly caught us with our trousers down.

FIRST CLEANER: Sh! You'll have us locked up!

[*Blackout. Lights in set go up.* MIDDIE PARADOCK *is sitting at the table as before reading a glossy magazine.*

She puts it away, and begins a game of patience.]

MRS PARADOCK [*without looking up*]: Come in.

[*She continues in thought, places two more cards on the table, looks towards the door, and repeats 'Come in'. When nothing happens she impatiently puts down the cards and goes to the door. As she opens it to find no one there, the two* COMEDIANS *enter by the door behind her, sit at the table and continue the game of patience. She turns away from the door, closing it, and speaks half to herself, and half to the two at the table, whose presence she takes for granted.*]

MRS PARADOCK: I made sure that was somebody at the door.

[*She stands for a moment watching the game.*]

MRS PARADOCK: Don't you two ever get tired of patience?

FIRST COMEDIAN: We've been drinking again, Mrs Paradock.

MRS PARADOCK: So you've taken my advice, have you?

SECOND COMEDIAN: We feel a whole lot tipsier for it.

MRS PARADOCK: Isn't that what I told you? You never listen to me.

SECOND COMEDIAN: It was that delicious ambrosia you gave us when we were here last week, Mrs Paradock. That was what put us on to drinking.

MRS PARADOCK: It's a very stimulating drink. Bro and I keep coming back to it and the surprising thing is we're always finding something fresh to make us drunk in it. I'm glad you both like it.

FIRST COMEDIAN: We've gone on to other things since, of course. What was it we were drinking last week-end? Bug said he couldn't remember when a drink left him so well oiled.

SECOND COMEDIAN: Raven's Blood – but I thought the name was the weakest part of it. What I enjoyed was the glass in the middle of the bottle. I spent a long time over that – just savouring it.

MRS PARADOCK: Bro's in the middle of a good bottle now. I'll get him to pour you out drops of it when he comes in.

FIRST COMEDIAN: Where is Bro, Mrs Paradock?

MRS PARADOCK: He's out with an elephant, but he should be back. We had one delivered that was too big for what we want, so we've done a sort of switch with Mrs Mortice. She's left us this snake. [*Takes down pencil box from shelf.*] And Bro's taking our elephant round to her. [*Opens box.*]

FIRST COMEDIAN: It looks hardly long enough for a snake.

MRS PARADOCK: You can have them lengthened but we shan't bother.

SECOND COMEDIAN: I think snakes are too long for what you generally want them for. People just like to go one better than everybody else.

MRS PARADOCK [*glances out through the window*]: Here's Bro now. [*She goes to open the door.*] You've been a long time.

[BRO PARADOCK *comes in, swaying a little, but otherwise normal in his manner.*]

MR PARADOCK: I've been in the pub on my way back. Hallo, Bug. Hallo, Hamster, old boy. I got stuck into a bottle in the pub and I couldn't tear myself away. I'm trying to remember what it was called. You two would enjoy it.

MRS PARADOCK: You look as if you've been having a good old drink, doesn't he, Bug? His eyes are all bloodshot. . . .

SECOND COMEDIAN: I think Mrs Paradock is the only one of us who – [*Pause.*]

MRS PARADOCK: Finish what you were going to say, Bug.

SECOND COMEDIAN: No, I'd rather leave it at that, Mrs Paradock.

MR PARADOCK: You were in the middle of a sentence, for God's sake!

FIRST COMEDIAN: He does that sometimes. He often leaves a sentence unfinished. It's more effective. It's like a sawn-off shotgun.

MRS PARADOCK [*grimacing*]: I don't like the sound of that remark

MR PARADOCK: What's wrong with it?

MRS PARADOCK: I don't like the sound of it. It sounds as if it's on the turn to me.

MR PARADOCK: It would have turned before now if it was going to turn.

SECOND COMEDIAN: It's only the sound of it, Mrs Paradock.

MRS PARADOCK: That remark will be paradoxical tomorrow morning when it comes out of the subconscious. You can't tell me anything about paradoxes.

FIRST COMEDIAN: Reminds me of an old stage designer who after a lifetime of faking stage props to look genuine had to admit defeat for the first time when he had to fake something to look bogus.

SECOND COMEDIAN: Talking about paradoxes, what about the platoon sergeant who sent his men into a wood to take cover and when they got there, said: 'You can take it easy, now, lads. We're out of the wood!'

MRS PARADOCK: You men. You're all as bad as one another, with your horrible paradoxes.

MR PARADOCK: Let's put the case of someone forgetting his lines on the stage at the exact point where he's supposed in the play to pretend to have forgotten them.

FIRST COMEDIAN: I don't think I follow. You're a bit too drunk for me.

MR PARADOCK: He has to give the illusion that he's forgotten his lines. As part of the play. All right?

FIRST COMEDIAN: Yes. I follow that.

MR PARADOCK: Now. At the precise moment when he's supposed to give the illusion of having forgotten his lines he quite forgets what it is he has to do. His mind goes blank. So what happens? There's a pause. The pause prolongs itself. But sooner or later he remembers what it is he ought to have been doing. He ought to have been giving the impression of having been at a loss for words. There's nothing he can do about it now. The audience will have to make do with the reality instead of the illusion – which would probably have been much better. They might well have had to do without both. He might well have forgotten not only that he was supposed to stumble for words, but that there was anything he was supposed to do at all. In that case he'd have gone straight on – word-perfect. Thus – the illusion of having remembered may be sustained only by forgetting, and the illusion of having forgotten only by remembering.

MRS PARADOCK: I've only one thing against these paradoxes. They're like puns – they're just plays on words when you analyse them. I don't mind good, solid, practical puns. I don't mind a pun in real life that means something. In fact I like to see somebody using his boot as a hammer, for instance. That's a practical pun.

MR PARADOCK: That can be carried too far as well.

SECOND COMEDIAN: Hamster's brother-in-law's a great practical punster. I remember the time he threw a vase at a cat. It was a beauty. It did as much damage as a genuine missile and he used it to put flowers in afterwards.

[*A knock.* MIDDIE PARADOCK *goes out.*]

MR PARADOCK: It's a pity you can't use an umbrella-stand in the breech of a fifteen-inch naval gun. If you could I should feel a whole lot happier about using a shell-case as a doorstop.

FIRST COMEDIAN: That's life, Bro. It's no use looking for an editorial in a tablecloth simply because you eat your meals off a newspaper.

[MIDDIE PARADOCK *comes in with an opened telegram which she is reading.*]

MRS PARADOCK: It's Don and that motor scooter again. I shall be glad when we see the last of that craze.

MR PARADOCK: What's he up to this time?

MRS PARADOCK: Read it. [*Hands the telegram to* BRO. *To others*] He's been parking his motor scooter on that piece of waste ground again behind Rachmaninov's Second Piano Concerto.

MR PARADOCK: Who does that belong to?

MRS PARADOCK: It doesn't belong to anybody. It's just a piece of waste ground.

MR PARADOCK: Then they can't stop him parking his motor scooter on it if it doesn't belong to anyone.

SECOND COMEDIAN: What does the telegram say, Mrs Paradock?

MR PARADOCK [*he is still holding the telegram*]: Arriving twelve-ten Euston send sandwiches. [*Hands the telegram to* SECOND COMEDIAN.]

FIRST COMEDIAN: I shouldn't let that upset you, Mrs Paradock. It doesn't mean what it says.

MR PARADOCK: The last time we had a telegram like this it was worded very differently.

FIRST COMEDIAN: I should just say nothing about the motor scooter. Say nothing to him about it. When he's gone to bed perhaps you can find a salesman to sell it to.

MRS PARADOCK: I doubt it. He bought it from a buyer.

SECOND COMEDIAN: You can set your minds at rest about the telegram. It's in code.

MRS PARADOCK: Thank heaven for that.

MR PARADOCK: How can you tell it's in code?

SECOND COMEDIAN: There's no way of telling, I'm afraid. It either is or it isn't. This one is.

FIRST COMEDIAN: I thought it was from the beginning. The moment Mrs Paradock came in with it. You can always tell with a telegram. As Bug says, it's either in code or it isn't.

[*The door opens.* DON, *a smartly dressed woman in her twenties, comes in.*]

SECOND COMEDIAN: Here's Don now.

MRS PARADOCK: Don! Why, you've changed your sex!

DON: Didn't you get my telegram?

MR PARADOCK: We got it all right, but it was in code.

DON: It shouldn't have been. I asked them to decode it before they sent it off.

MRS PARADOCK: Never mind. I always wanted a girl.

MR PARADOCK: That's the first I knew of it.

FIRST COMEDIAN: Now perhaps we can have that conversation we promised ourselves about the conversation we had at the Wordsworths'.

MRS PARADOCK: So we can. I've been waiting to hear all about it. I expect Don there's feeling like a good long conversation after travelling up to Euston since four o'clock this morning. What were the trains like this time, Don?

DON: Don't talk about them, Mother. One long compartment after another.

MR PARADOCK: Well, let's start this conversation. How was it we broke the ice at the Wordsworths'? What was it we began with? A noun clause each, wasn't it?

DON: That's right. We were all given a noun clause each – in apposition – and then we had to go round asking everyone in turn for the noun it was in apposition to, till we found the right one.

MRS PARADOCK: I suppose John was as much in demand as ever with his adverbial clauses?

DON: Oh, John! John's got a thing about his adverbial clauses.

FIRST COMEDIAN: He can be a bit childish about them too at times. Over those subordinating conjunctions, for instance, that he said were prepositions.

DON: That was Margaret. What actually happened was that he asked for subordinating conjunctions and she handed him these prepositions thinking they were adverbs or something.

SECOND COMEDIAN: And then to make matters worse she said, 'Will these do? I can never tell the difference myself'.

FIRST COMEDIAN: 'I can never tell the difference'! What a thing to say to John of all people.

DON: You know that little spot of high colour he gets on the side of his forehead whenever he's annoyed at anything. . . .

FIRST COMEDIAN: Annoyed! It was all he could do to be civil to her. [BRO PARADOCK *stands apart from the others staring tight-lipped into the distance.*]

SECOND COMEDIAN: Tell them about Joe, Hamster.

FIRST COMEDIAN: Joe?

DON: And the figures of speech.

FIRST COMEDIAN: Oh. 'Give me good plain syntax', you mean. I don't think he'd met half the figures of speech before.

SECOND COMEDIAN: I happened to look up when someone put that synecdoche in front of him. 'What's this?' he said. 'Metonymy?'

FIRST COMEDIAN: Metonymy!

DON: What about Mrs Kapellmeister then? Falling over herself almost for a transferred epithet every time one appeared. I suppose she was afraid someone else might get to them first.

MRS PARADOCK: Looking at her husband sometimes, I'm surprised to hear she didn't go for oxymoron. I've never seen anyone who looks more like the original sustained metaphor than he does.

DON: He's certainly at the opposite end of the pole from her.

MRS PARADOX: It's only zeugma that keeps them together. [*She goes across to where* BRO PARADOCK *is still morosely standing, while the others continue talking amongst themselves.*] What's the matter with you? Moping over here on your own?

MR PARADOCK: There's nothing the matter with me at all.

MRS PARADOCK: Why can't you join in the conversation then? Standing here saying nothing.

MR PARADOCK: I'm standing here saying nothing because I can't think of anything to say. I should have thought that was obvious.

MRS PARADOCK: Can't think of anything to say! Surely you could define 'consanguinity' or something.

MR PARADOCK: What chance have I had to define 'consanguinity'?

MRS PARADOCK: You've had just as much chance as anybody else. For goodness' sake come and join in the conversation even if it's only to contradict somebody.

MR PARADOCK [*reluctantly, and with the look of a martyr, he goes towards the others*]: My wife wants me to take part in the conversation.

SECOND COMEDIAN: We were just saying what a good party it was, by and large.

DON: It would have been if that girl with coordinate clause written all over her face hadn't tried to monopolize Max all evening.

FIRST COMEDIAN: At least we were spared Charles this time with his endless paronomasia.

ON: I'd rather have Charles than that one with the dreary onomatopoeia who was doing farmyard imitations with it every five minutes.

FIRST COMEDIAN: Oh no. Not farmyard imitations?

ON: He was. I thought he was never going to stop and then when Margaret asked him if he ever added to his repertoire and he did half a dozen new ones I could have killed her. It was only the thought of her adverbial clauses of concession that stopped me, I think.

SECOND COMEDIAN: I can't say they impressed me all that much. They've nothing like the sheer architectonic qualities, for instance, of successive adjectival clauses one on top of another in the hands of a master.

MR PARADOCK: Architectonic archbishops! I could give you some adjectival clauses that would scorch the seat off your pants to listen to them [*Loudly*]: This is the soldier that loved the wife that poisoned the hangman that hanged the murderer that shot the assassin that stabbed the king that won the war that killed the soldier that loved the wife that poisoned the hangman that hanged the murderer that shot the assassin that stabbed the king that won the war that killed the soldier that loved the wife that . . .

MRS PARADOCK: For goodness' sake pull yourself together! It's in bad taste. Can't you forget you're an undertaker once in a while?

SECOND COMEDIAN: I never knew Bro was an undertaker.

FIRST COMEDIAN: Neither did I. I'd noticed he was always rather partial to death. Now I see why.

MRS PARADOCK: It's his life.

MR PARADOCK: It's just that I see things from an undertaker's point of view.

MRS PARADOCK: There's no need to make everyone feel uncomfortable just because you can't arrive at a definition of 'consanguinity'. He's set his mind on defining 'consanguinity' and there's no shifting him. Everything else has to take second plac[e] when he's in this mood.

MR PARADOCK: All I want is a chance to define *something*. It doesn['t] have to be 'consanguinity'. That was your suggestion. It isn't as [?] I often get the time for defining things.

MRS PARADOCK: Or the inclination.

FIRST COMEDIAN: I think we'd better be off, Bug. Remember you'r[e] expecting a phone call at nine o'clock.

SECOND COMEDIAN: She rang this morning. [FIRST COMEDIA[N] *nudges him.*] She'll be ringing me again though at nine o'clock. [?] wasn't in this morning. No one answered the phone.

FIRST COMEDIAN: Good-bye, Mrs Paradock.

MRS PARADOCK: You're not going?

FIRST COMEDIAN: Bug's got a phone call he's expecting and I ough[t] to be getting back to my filing.

MRS PARADOCK [*out of Bro's hearing*]: He'll be all right tomorrow[.]

SECOND COMEDIAN: We'll look in, Mrs Paradock, and see how h[e] is.

DON: Don't you worry about father. We'll get him to bed with [a] hot-water bottle.

[*They go out.*]

SECOND COMEDIAN: Good-bye, Mrs Paradock. Good-bye, Bro.

FIRST COMEDIAN: Are you coming out with us, Don?

DON: I've got to go down the road a little way.

FIRST COMEDIAN: Good-bye, Bro. Good-bye, Mrs Paradock.

MRS PARADOCK: Look after yourselves.

[MIDDIE PARADOCK *closes the door and turns back to Bro.*]

MRS PARADOCK: A fine exhibition you made of yourself.

MR PARADOCK: Where's Don?

MRS PARADOCK: Gone where you can't harm her any more with your bitter words.

MR PARADOCK: I think I'll have a turn in the garden.

MRS PARADOCK: We haven't got a garden. You know that as well as I do.

MR PARADOCK: I understood we had. It's in the deeds.

MRS PARADOCK: Is it?

MR PARADOCK: I wouldn't have bought the house otherwise.

MRS PARADOCK: House? This is a bungalow.

MR PARADOCK: I wouldn't have bought it without looking pretty closely at the deeds to see if there was any mention of a garden.

MRS PARADOCK: If you can find a garden in the deeds of this place you're welcome to take a turn in it.

[*There is a pause while Bro ponders this.*]

MRS PARADOCK: I should get up to bed if I were you.

MR PARADOCK: *Up* to bed? I thought we were living in a bungalow?

MRS PARADOCK: Look, Bro. I'm trying to help you. You're being very difficult and perverse and I'm trying very hard to be reasonable with you and understand you. Don't forget I'm just as drunk as you are underneath and I'm trying to fight it for both of us. You don't make it very easy for me, Bro.

MR PARADOCK: I didn't know you were drunk too. I thought it was just me.

MRS PARADOCK: You never do think it's ever possible for me to feel a bit blotto from time to time, Bro. You think you're the only one who takes a pull at the bottle occasionally.

MR PARADOCK: I sometimes envy the man in the street who's never learned to drink for himself at all.

MRS PARADOCK: It's no good getting cynical, Bro.

MR PARADOCK: I do get cynical sometimes. The average man seems to be quite content to let the rest of us do all his drinking for him.

MRS PARADOCK: That's true, Bro, but although he's spared a lot of the hangovers, don't forget that he misses the intoxication too.

MR PARADOCK: Perhaps you're right, Middie, my dear.

MRS PARADOCK: And now we must get out of here, Bro, because the producer wants it for his critics' meeting or something in a few minutes. So up you get.

[*She helps him out. Lights fade out. Author's mouthpiece appears to right of set.*]

AUTHOR: It seemed the only way. I think we have all been trying as hard as can reasonably be expected not to show our exasperation

– I certainly have – because we do all like, naturally, to feel we've been provided with a meaning; something we can carry round with us like an umbrella for a few days. We all feel rather lost without a meaning to seize hold of; rather like a snake charmer in front of a boa constrictor and no flute. Or whatever they use. And in this search for a meaning we have some very good allies in the critics. They know a great deal about these things. They are trained to find meanings, and even if there are no meanings to be found they rarely come unprovided with spare meanings which with a little wire and string can often be fastened quite securely. So it is to the critics that for all our sakes I have decided to turn. We've got to turn somewhere. And what help I could have given you would have been worse than useless. I lay claim to no special vision and my own notions as to what it is I have in mind here may well fall pitifully short of your own far better notions. No. I am the dwarf in the circus – I give what scope I can to such deficiencies as I have. Beyond that, it is to these public servants of ours who guide us all to destinations (which even though they may not always amount to very much as destinations are nevertheless the best destinations we have), it is to the critics that we must commit ourselves. But for them we would be hard put to it to arrive anywhere at all. And it's the arriving somewhere which gives us the illusion that the journey has been worth while. No such illusion is likely to trouble any of us here, but perhaps we need not go home altogether empty-handed for all that – because here they are. Here is the first of the critics. This is, I need hardly tell you, a very welcome sight. I think we are shortly going to be led out of the wilderness. It's Mustard Short, you've probably recognized him, who has just taken his seat.

[*The critics as they arrive sit down round the table in the living room.* MUSTARD SHORT *is the first to arrive, but is closely followed by* DENZIL PEPPER *who takes a chair opposite him. When* MISS SALT *and* MRS VINEGAR *come in together they occupy the remaining seats, leaving a seat vacant at the head of the table for the* CHAIRMAN.]

It was Mustard Short as you know who last year – or was it earlier than that, in some previous incarnation perhaps? – who drew attention to some faults of structure in *Tristram Shandy*. And here is Denzil Pepper, carrying his high standards invisibly in brown paper, manoeuvring them clear of the light fittings and as ready devastatingly to unwrap them here as anywhere else. 'If this weren't in a bucket', he roars, getting a lump of soap and plunging his hands into a bucket of sulphuric acid, 'if this weren't in a bucket, I should never have guessed it was meant to be water!' He's the boy. He's the one, if anybody can, who'll unmask the shadow. In a bloody froth of fulmination, too, unless he happens to have taken a sedative. Mrs Vinegar there – she's the woman in the black suit who has just sat down on the left of Mustard Short – looks, I must say, disconcertingly the worse for tedium. Miss Salt on the other hand is clearly ready to begin digging with indefatigable trowel among whatever unfruitful clods of dramatic earth she finds at her dedicated feet, and may, for all we can tell, come upon something which will surprise us all. And now let us alert the coastguards of our minds, for the Chairman has arrived. We must try now to assume receptive postures, and be ready to give asylum to such thoughts as are shortly to come among us.

[*Lights, except in the living room, fade.*]

CHAIRMAN [*standing*]: Shall we ask a blessing? [*All stand.*] For what we are now about to bestow may we be made truly worthy.

MISS SALT: I protest!

PEPPER: I deplore!

MUSTARD: I condemn!

MRS VINEGAR: I denounce!

MISS SALT: I wish to go on record as having cringed.

PEPPER: I wish to go on record as having writhed.

MUSTARD: I wish to go on record as having squirmed.

MRS VINEGAR: I wish to go on record as having suffered agony

MISS SALT: I hail!

PEPPER: I salute!

MUSTARD: I predict!

MRS VINEGAR: I acclaim!

ALL [*loudly and in unison*]: I wish to go on record! I wish to go on record! I wish to go on record! [*Sit.*]

CHAIRMAN: We'll start at once with a discussion of the performance we have all been watching for the last hour or so, and we'll begin by deciding if we can what it is we have been present at, before going on to a consideration of its merits. Is this piece the bold experiment some people hold it to be? Is it a shameless plagiarism from the pen of a true primitive of the theatre – as someone has said – or is it neither of these things? Denzil Pepper – what do you make of this?

PEPPER: This is a hotch-potch. I think that emerges quite clearly. The thing has been thrown together – a veritable rag-bag of last year's damp fireworks, if a mixed metaphor is in order.

MISS SALT: Yes. I suppose it *is* what we must call a hotch-potch. I do think, though – accepting Denzil Pepper's definition – I do think, and this is the point I feel we ought to make, it is, surely isn't it, an *inspired* hotch-potch?

PEPPER: A hotch-potch de luxe. Only the finest ingredients. A theatrical haggis.

CHAIRMAN: Isn't this what our ancestors would have delighted in calling a gallimaufry?

[*Pause.*]

MUSTARD: 'They have made our English tongue a gallimaufry or hodgepodge of all other speeches.' Yes. The letter to Gabriel Harvey at the beginning of Spenser's Shepherd's Calendar. Yes. I'm not sure that I don't prefer the word gallimaufry to Denzil Pepper's hodgepodge.

PEPPER: Hotch-potch. No. I stick, quite unrepentantly, to my own word.

MISS SALT: I'm wondering whether what Spenser was saying there was not referring to the language itself rather than to what was said in it? Words and phrases borrowed from other languages and so on? I think perhaps – and I say this under correction: I know Mustard Short is more familiar than I am *with* the attitude to this kind of thing in James Joyce – isn't this . . . haven't we got here an actual *repudiation* on the Joycean model *of* orderliness in a way the writers Spenser was attacking had not?

PEPPER: I'm not at all happy about letting him get away with it on his own terms like that. After all, what happens when a boxer gets knocked out in the ring? He's lost the fight. It's as simple as that. He's lost the fight and it makes no difference that his manager or someone announces through the loudspeaker afterwards that lying flat on his back was a deliberate repudiation of the vertical.

MRS VINEGAR: I couldn't agree more.

CHAIRMAN: Mrs Vinegar.

MRS VINEGAR: I was bored with this play. Or whatever it is. I was bored almost from the rise of the curtain with the characters – or is characters too strong a word? – and I was even more bored by the situations they were put into.

MUSTARD: And the acting? Were you bored with the acting? I thought the cast carried it off for him exceptionally well.

PEPPER: A splendid cast.

MUSTARD: Quite exceptionally well.

MISS SALT: It was in fact an actors' play.

MUSTARD: An actors' play and of course in a way a producer's play.

CHAIRMAN: How would Mrs Vinegar feel about calling this an actors' play?

MRS VINEGAR: No. No, I thought the acting was extremely good. The production I'm less sure about, but it was quite sound. As for this being an actors' play or a producer's play, whatever that may mean, I think fifth-rate play is the only sound designation for it. No amount of talent on the stage can make a fifth-rate play into a third-rate one, although it was quite obvious that that was what they were aiming at.

CHAIRMAN: Mustard Short. Were you bored by this play?

MUSTARD: Bored, no. Exasperated at times, yes. I did, I think, suppress a mild yawn twice, but I smiled occasionally, wondered what was coming next, got annoyed and irritated fairly frequently – in fact reacted much as one does in the theatre, except for experiencing tension. There was no tension and no tears. That I think was a pity because with so much else there it would have been nice for the sake of completeness to have had those as well.

MRS VINEGAR: May I ask Mustard why, if he felt a genuine desire to yawn, he suppressed it?

MUSTARD: Politeness, I suppose – it's a vice we're all prone to in the theatre, where we could do with a lot less of it.

MISS SALT: If only to keep Aunt Edna in Surbiton.

MRS VINEGAR: The way to keep Aunt Edna or anybody else in Surbiton is to go on putting on plays like this one. And in that event I shall be in Surbiton too, I hope.

CHAIRMAN: We seem to be getting away from the play itself. Can we try to reach agreement on what kind of production this is? Is it a comedy? The play has a sub-title: The Accapictor Michmacted – A Comedy. Denzil Pepper – what do you think about this play as a comedy?

PEPPER: What do I think about it as a comedy? I believe I laughed once. So, technically, I suppose the play could be called a comedy.

MRS VINEGAR: As a matter of curiosity – what was it Denzil Pepper laughed at?

PEPPER: I really can't remember what it was.

MUSTARD: Perhaps calling it a comedy is part of the comedy?

PEPPER: Perhaps so. If someone had told me that, I would certainly have done what I could to laugh. But that's just what I'm never quite sure about – what *is* it we're being asked to do here? Are we being asked to laugh at him, laugh with him – or are we meant, God forbid, to take him seriously?

MUSTARD: It's satire, surely.

MISS SALT: What was it Swift called satire? A mirror, wasn't it, in which a man sees any face but his own. It's certainly very true here.

MUSTARD: 'Satire is a sort of glass, wherein beholders do generally discover everybody's face but their own.'

PEPPER: I would have been delighted to have caught a glimpse even of my own face!

MISS SALT: Oh, the face was there. It was impossible at times to identify it, even to distinguish it – it will take a careful reading and re-reading of the play to do that – but the face was there. Of that I'm quite certain.

CHAIRMAN: Did you, Mustard Short, discover a face you could recognize?

MUSTARD: None, I'm afraid. None whatever.

MISS SALT: A contorted face, perhaps? I thought I saw that. The human face. In the human predicament. Contorted with grief? With pain?

MRS VINEGAR: With boredom.

MUSTARD: Could he, I wonder, be satirizing satire?

CHAIRMAN: A skit on satire itself. How does that strike you, Miss Salt?

MISS SALT: Yes. Yes, I think it very likely. I'm wondering whether perhaps rather than skit the word parody would hit off better what it is he's trying for here. Could he be parodying the whole thing? The whole concept? A parody *of* a skit, if that's possible.

PEPPER: If this is a parody of a skit at all, it must be a parody of a skit *on* something.

MUSTARD: A parody of a skit on satire?

PEPPER: For a sophisticated audience. It goes without saying that it's a sophisticated audience he's got in mind here. I take it that's agreed.

MUSTARD: A sophisticated audience.

MRS VINEGAR: A sophisticated audience flagging.

MUSTARD: No. I think if I may say so Mrs Vinegar is being rather too uncompromisingly hostile to what is – let us be as fair as we possibly can about it – to what is by any standards a remarkable . . . a remarkable phenomenon.

MISS SALT: I'd rather like to take up this idea of the skit again, or the parody of it, because – and this is surely the whole point which none of us has made yet – here is a play in which the writer is imitating himself repeatedly all through the play. He is in fact actually burlesquing his own self-mimicry and in quite the most devastating way from first to last. That I think is inherent in the whole thing.

PEPPER: He's satirizing farce, of course, too. That comes across quite unmistakably. As one of the characters says somewhere in the play – this is the custard-pie farce of the intellect.

MUSTARD: Comedy. Custard-pie comedy. Of the abstract. But to get back to this point about burlesque. It is, basically, a parody of a skit on satire that he's burlesquing, and the farce is so to speak a by-product of that. I don't think he's aiming at farce at all. The farce is in a sense what we, the audience, *contribute*.

CHAIRMAN: The audience. Did anyone else, I wonder, feel – as I certainly did – that the barrier between audience and actors was being quite deliberately dismantled? Mrs Vinegar?

MRS VINEGAR: It's been done before. And done better.

MUSTARD: You mean the *Verfremdungseffekt*. The alienation effect.

MISS SALT: It's Brecht, of course – though with a very different aim from that of Brecht.

PEPPER: No. I don't see Brecht here at all.

MISS SALT: It's the Brechtian technique carried on *beyond* Brecht. Isn't that it?

MUSTARD: Beyond, and in a sense of course at a tangent to Brecht. It's as though he'd gone off on a branch line some way back which is carrying him farther than Brecht was able to go but in a quite different direction.

MISS SALT: And, of course, *facing* Brecht as he moves away from him. The farther he goes *beyond* Brecht, therefore, the farther he is retreating *from* him.

PEPPER: I can accept Brecht as starting-point. But a starting-point is something you move away from, and in my view the author of this play has been doing just that. He has been putting more and more ground between himself and his model – if that's what Brecht is, though I doubt it – and they have been getting farther and farther apart, these two, until both of them are specks on the horizon. Which is why I think we're quite wrong to be discussing this play or whatever it is as if it were The Comedy of Errors rewritten by Lewis Carroll to provide a part for Godot or somebody.

CHAIRMAN: Yes. Well, now our time is running out and I think we ought to say something about the ending – which we've none of us yet seen of course. Is it possible that some of the shortcomings of the play so far could be redeemed by the ending? Mrs Vinegar?

MRS VINEGAR: I doubt whether I could sit through any more of it. I have never begrudged danger money to steeplejacks and people of that kind, and I do think it's high time someone suggested boredom money for critics. The ending? No. I think the piece is beyond redemption. The best that can be hoped for from the ending is that sooner or later it will arrive.

CHAIRMAN: Denzil Pepper. What do you think about the ending?

PEPPER: I think it's the Russians, isn't it, who have a proverb to the effect that if you can't hold a horse by the mane, you'll never hold it by the tail?

[Pause.]

MUSTARD: You can count all the same on being dragged a reasonable distance before having to let go.

PEPPER: Possibly. I'm not sure, though, that I want to do my travelling at the tail of a runaway horse.

MRS VINEGAR: Is it travelling along the road of life we're talking about? Because as far as that journey is concerned, I broke the back of it this evening during the first act.

CHAIRMAN: And that I'm afraid will have to end the discussion if not the play, because our time is up. I'm sorry to have to apply the guillotine to a discussion which has been so lively – I think we've rarely had a livelier discussion of any play. And a play which can stimulate as much strong feeling, or even boredom! [laughter] is something we can always do with in the theatre. I'm sure we would all of us agree, whatever our individual reactions to it may have been, that we have here a play the real author of which will not be born for many years to come.

ALL: Hear, hear.

[The light in the living room fades. A half-light reveals the author's mouthpiece, who is sitting on a chair staring ahead with a quite blank expression. He starts convulsively, stands up, and looks, with no change of expression, towards the audience. As the lights come up in *the living room, revealing* BRO PARADOCK *sitting with a newspaper before him, the author's mouthpiece glances quickly in that direction, and then goes slowly out as though dazed.*

The scene is exactly the same as in Act One, Scene I. MIDDIE PARADOCK *comes into the room and begins tidying it, speaking as she does so.*]

MRS PARADOCK: There's somebody at the door wanting you to form a government.

MR PARADOCK: When?

MRS PARADOCK: He says he's working through the street directory. He's waiting outside now.

MR PARADOCK: What does he look like?

MRS PARADOCK: In an old raincoat. He's probably trying it on. I shall want this cork opened in case we have to offer him a drink.

MR PARADOCK: It's nectar if it's anything. Not ambrosia.

MRS PARADOCK: He won't be able to tell the difference.

MR PARADOCK: If he can't tell the difference between ambrosia and nectar he shouldn't be wearing an old raincoat.

MRS PARADOCK: He's only trying it on for size. I got that much out of him.

MR PARADOCK: In that case what does he want me to form a government for?

MRS PARADOCK: I should have thought that was obvious.

MR PARADOCK: Supposing it turns out to be Uncle Ted having a joke?

MRS PARADOCK: You know as well as I do Uncle Ted hasn't got a sense of humour any longer.

MR PARADOCK: He may think I look like Gladstone.

MRS PARADOCK: What if he does? You've got a good many years in front of you yet.

MR PARADOCK: Don't start on that, Middie, please.

MRS PARADOCK: You're in your prime.

MR PARADOCK: Middie!

MRS PARADOCK: A man with your constitution at your time of life is in for a good long spell of it yet.

MR PARADOCK: Can't you leave me alone, Middie. Can't you keep quiet about it?

MRS PARADOCK: You're as fit as you've ever been.

MR PARADOCK: Stop baiting me, Middie! Just shut up about being in my prime. You only keep on about it because you know it plays merry hell with my death wish!

[*Black-out. Enter, in front of living room set, a* MAN IN A BOWLER HAT *carrying a manuscript case.*]

MAN IN BOWLER HAT: Who's in charge here? Where's the producer or somebody?

[*Enter* PRODUCER *from right.*]

They've had about as much as they can take of this out there. [*To audience.*] I don't know how you feel about my breaking in on the production like this, but [*to* PRODUCER] I think we've all had about enough.

PRODUCER: You think the curtain ought to come down, sir?

MAN IN BOWLER HAT: It's unpleasant for everyone when an audience begins to get restive. [*To audience.*] I know that only too well from an experience of my own when I was foolish enough on one occasion to consent to act as chairman at a political meeting of all things. The member was speaking – or rather not the member, because as it turned out he lost his deposit – but the candidate as he was then was speaking at the time and some unruly elements . . .

[*Enter from right* AUTHOR *in high spirits.*]

AUTHOR: Well. What a waste of talent it's all been! What a waste!

MAN IN BOWLER HAT [*in sotto voce panic*]: *Pas devant les auditeurs!*

AUTHOR: *Les auditeurs.* I must say they've all for the most part taken insult after insult in a splendid spirit. Don't you think so?

PRODUCER: They've taken it very well. But I think perhaps we ought to try and get the curtain down. They'll be wanting to get away.

AUTHOR: I'll have a little chat with them. Take Henry Irving with you and get working on the curtain – it's probably jammed.

[PRODUCER *and* MAN IN BOWLER HAT *go out right.*]

AUTHOR: It's been an odd evening to say the least of it. I don't quite know whether it would be arrogant of me to take the blame on the grounds that it was I who initiated it all – or whether perhaps we ought all to share bouquets and brickbats promiscuously among us. My own contribution probably seems more important than it is because, as I say, it was my small contribution which set it all going as it were – and yet, if it comes to that, which of you with a shot or two of benzedrine couldn't have done as well or better? But there is an important point which may be overlooked unless I draw attention to it now and it's this: The retreat from reason means precious little to anyone who has never caught up with reason in the first place. It takes a trained mind to relish a *non sequitur*. So you can take comfort from that. And now one last thing. This is a delicate subject to broach but . . . we on this side of the footlights feel that some gesture from us would be more than appropriate in view of . . . of your forbearance, but on the other hand we felt that anything we might do by way of applauding the audience would seem somehow to smack if not of affectation at any rate of . . . the unconventional? We don't want to fly in the face of tradition but . . .

[*Lights come up in the living room set where the cast is assembled. Each holds a glass of a bright, purple liquid ready to respond to a toast.*]

AUTHOR: The audience!

ALL: The audience!

[*They drink.*]

CURTAIN

JOHN OSBORNE AND ANTHONY CREIGHTON

Epitaph for George Dillon

TO E.M.C.

WITH OUR LOVE

All professional inquiries in regard to this play should be addressed to the authors' agent, Margery Vosper Ltd, 32 Shaftesbury Avenue, London, w1, and all amateur inquiries should be addressed to Messrs Evans Brothers Ltd, Montague House, Russell Square, London, wc1.

EPITAPH FOR GEORGE DILLON

First professionally presented at The Royal Court Theatre, London, on 11 February 1958, with the following cast:

JOSIE ELLIOT	Wendy Craig
RUTH GRAY	Yvonne Mitchell
MRS ELLIOT	Alison Leggatt
NORAH ELLIOT	Avril Elgar
PERCY ELLIOT	Toke Townley
GEORGE DILLON	Robert Stephens
GEOFFREY COLWYN-STUART	Philip Locke
MR WEBB	Paul Bailey
BARNEY EVANS	Nigel Davenport

Directed by William Gaskill

The action of the play takes place in the home of the Elliot family just outside London.

ACT ONE

The home of the Elliot family, just outside London. Spring, late afternoon. The action takes place in the sitting room and hall. The front door being stage right. In the hall, immediately facing, are the stairs which turn off left. Flat against the staircase is a hat and coat stand, shelving hats, coats, magazines, umbrellas, etc., in the midst of which is a vase of everlasting flowers. Upstage of the hall, under the arch formed by the stairs, is the door leading into the room called the lounge. Next to this upstage is the invisible wall which divides the hall from the sitting room. The only object suggesting the wall is a door set upstage. Downstage of this, set against the 'wall' facing into sitting room is a radiogram, upon which stands a biscuit barrel and a silver-plated dish containing wax or real fruit. Nearby an arm-chair of the 'contemporary' kind faces downstage. Against the upstage wall, right, is a dining chair. Centre, an ornate cocktail cabinet and another dining chair. On the wall, flanking this, are two wall lights, in the centre of which is painted a group of wild ducks in flight.

Left centre is the door leading to the kitchen, next to which is the kitchen hatch, which, when raised, reveals the kitchen beyond. Below the hatch is a tea-trolley. Above the hatch, on the wall, is a tinted photograph of a wedding group. In the stage left wall, french windows which look out on to a small back garden. Below the french windows, a half-round occasional table; above hangs a mirror. In front of the french windows a settee, again of the utility-contemporary period. At the head a white-painted wrought-iron floor lamp. Upstage, left centre, a draw-leaf table with dining chair and arm dining chair in position. On the cocktail cabinet stands a large china model of an alsatian dog, and a photograph of a soldier in a silver frame, decorated with 'Haig' poppies.

[At rise of curtain, JOSIE is on stage alone. She is about twenty, pretty in a hard, frilly way and nobody's fool. At the moment she is not looking her best. The turban she is wearing reveals a couple of curlers above her forehead, her jumper is grubby and her slacks baggy, stained, and not very fetching. She is sprawled in the arm-chair. In

a vicious idleness she stares at a highly coloured weekly. Mozart is
on the radio, delicate, liquid. She flips through the magazine, is about
to put it down when something catches her attention.   She reads.]

JOSIE: Fancy writing up and asking *that*!

[*She laughs and goes on with her reading, fondling one of her curlers*
as she does so. Presently she throws the magazine down.]

Soppy cow!

[*She sighs and leans back, thrusts her hands into the top of her slacks,*
rubbing her stomach and frowning. She gets up and stares at her
reflection in the mirror. Pursing her lips experimentally, she watches
the effect. She leans forward and tries fluffing up her eyebrows. It
doesn't seem very successful and she sighs again.]

Oh, that damn row!

[*She goes to the radio, stabs at the knobs, then gives up and switches it*
off. Her eye catches the magazine again and she goes through it again
until she finds what she is looking for. She stares at it sullenly and
flings the paper on the floor. At the mirror again she tries several
grimaces, puts out her tongue. A little more speculation, and she goes
over to the settee, and sinks down on her knees. She stretches, and,
catching sight of the resulting white space between her jumper and
slacks, strokes herself dreamily. She slides forward on to her stomach,
her hands moving over the arm of the settee, curiosity in her fingers
and boredom in her body. She starts to sing, in a studied, offhand
way, one of those downward-inflection popular hits.]

'Why don't you Give Me . . . Give Me . . .'

[*Pause.*]

'All that you have to share.

Why don't you Give Me . . . Give Me . . .'

[*She picks her nose daintily, and turns over on her back.*]

'And tell me you really c-are . . .'

[*Her hand trails the space beside her, like a hand in rippling water,*
then stops, as she says deliberately:]

I wonder – what it *would* be like?

[*She is about to swing her legs above her head, when the front door*
bell rings.]

Good-O!

[*She rushes off to the front door, almost reaches it when she remembers something, and comes back into the dining room. Her eyes light on her handbag, and she snatches it up, taking it with her, through the hall, straight to the front door. The bell is still ringing, and she calls out:*] Oh, all right! Wait a minute! Wait a minute! [*Opens front door.*] [*We hear a voice saying:* 'Parcel for Mrs Elliot. Three pounds fifteen and ninepence to pay.'] *Miss* Elliot, if you please. I thought you were never coming. Here you are. You have been a long time. I thought you'd have been here this morning. I haven't even been able to go up the road, waiting for you to come. What? I haven't got it. Well, you'll have to change it.

[*A few minutes of change-fumbling before she slams the front door and goes into the sitting room with a square cardboard box in her arms, which she starts to open excitedly, kneeling on the floor. Off comes the string and paper, then the lid and a layer of tissue paper. She rises quickly, places the box on the settee, takes a cigarette from her handbag, which she puts in her mouth, kicks off her slippers, and goes to the radiogram, unzipping her slacks at the same time. She raises the lid, switches it on, and takes off her slacks, leaving them on the floor, one leg inside out. She selects a record from the pile beside her, and puts it on. Cigarette in mouth, she waits expectantly until the corn crake growl of a New Orleans trumpet strides off into a piece of fairly traditional jazz. She runs back to her parcel and takes out the contents, in a scurry of paper and impatience, which turn out to be a pair of black, tapering trousers. She puts them on, zipping up the sides with a little difficulty. Hands on hips, she looks down at the results anxiously then delightedly. She goes nearer to the mirror, to get a better view of herself. She bounces up and down, looking at this angle and that, patting her stomach, feeling the seat until she is finally satisfied. She lights her cigarette, then, putting her hands in her unfamiliar pockets, strikes a more or less elegant attitude and a bored expression, one black undeniably slim leg straight out in front of the other. She inclines her head back, and blows out a cloud of smoke.* JOSIE *may be funny at times, but she is never consciously so. She begins to dance, slowly at*] *first, and surprisingly well, across right, ending up by lying with her back on the floor, and her knees up. The front door opens, and* RUTH *enters hall.* JOSIE *sits up quickly.*]

That you, Mum?

[RUTH *closes the door, but makes no reply.* JOSIE *takes off her new trousers, and starts slipping them back in their box. As she is doing this,* RUTH *enters from the hall. She is about forty, slim, smartly dressed, attractive. She carries a small week-end case, which she puts down when she gets into the sitting room.*]

You're in early.

[RUTH *goes to the radiogram and switches it off.*]

RUTH: Do you mind if we do without New Orleans just for the moment?

[*She crosses and picks up Josie's old slacks from the floor.*]

Are you looking for these?

[*She throws them over, and* JOSIE *manages to catch them.*]

JOSIE: Thought you were Mum.

RUTH: I don't suppose you'd made any tea?

JOSIE [*putting on her slacks*]: I had some at dinner time.

[RUTH *goes into the kitchen, and puts the kettle on to boil.*]

You're in early.

RUTH [*off*]: Why aren't you at work today?

JOSIE: Wasn't feeling very good this morning.

RUTH [*off*]: Oh?

JOSIE: So Mum said I'd better stay indoors.

[*She is staring at the case Ruth has left on the floor.*]

Going on your holidays?

RUTH [*off*]: No – coming back. Satisfied?

JOSIE: How can you be coming back, when you haven't been away? Anyway, I haven't had a day off work for ages – it won't hurt them. [*Picking up the case to see if it is empty.*] New case?

RUTH [*off*]: I picked it up from where I left it last night – at Leicester Square Left Luggage Office. And it's full of obscene photographs.

JOSIE: Oh?

RUTH [*appearing in the doorway*]: Josie: give me a cigarette, will you?

I came all the way back in the train without one. [*Back into kitchen.*] There wasn't any post for me was there?

OSIE [*crossing to her handbag right*]: Package came for you – registered.

RUTH [*off*]: No letters?

OSIE: Just the pools. It's only a small one. Doesn't weigh anything hardly.

RUTH [*off*]: And what's inside it?

OSIE [*searching in her handbag*]: How should I know?

RUTH [*off*]: Didn't you open it?

OSIE: What do you mean? Course I didn't open it.

RUTH [*coming back in*]: If you must fry yourself food when you're feeling ill, you might have the decency to clear up afterwards. The gas stove is covered in grease and muck – it's filthy.

[*She takes off her hat, and moves to the occasional table down left, where she sees a small package.*]

Is this it? [*Examines it, and goes on, rather absently.*] You've even left the breakfast things in the sink.

[JOSIE *is holding her packet of cigarettes, watching her curiously.* RUTH *stares at the packet.*]

OSIE: Typewritten.

RUTH: You've had damn-all to do all day. It's like a slum when your mother comes in.

OSIE: Aren't you going to open it?

RUTH [*a quick glance at her*]: I said you're a slut.

OSIE: Oh, did you? I didn't hear.

[*After a momentary hesitation,* RUTH *unwraps the package.* JOSIE *slips her cigarettes back into her handbag, and moves over to the kitchen door. From a small cardboard box,* RUTH *takes out a man's wrist watch.* JOSIE *takes it in, and goes into the kitchen.*]

JOSIE: I'll get a cup of tea.

[*The watch is lying in Ruth's hand, as with the other she takes out a piece of notepaper and reads it. Then she places the box on the table. She stares at the paper, stroking her temples with her fingers, as if she felt a weight in her head. Presently, she calls out to* JOSIE *in the kitchen. The edge has gone out of her voice, and she sounds tired.*]

RUTH: Josie: be a good girl and get me that cigarette, will you?

[JOSIE *enters with a cup of tea, which she hands to her.*]

JOSIE: That man was here again this afternoon, asking for you.

RUTH: I've asked you twice to let me have one of your cigarettes. Please! I'll pay you back tonight.

JOSIE: Haven't got one. Sorry.

RUTH [*turning back to the table*]: Oh well. I suppose I'll have to go upstairs, anyway. There may be some in the bedroom somewhere.

[*She replaces the watch and note in the little box.*]

Who was here, did you say?

JOSIE: That man. I don't know who he is. The one who came on Saturday, and again the other day. That's the third time he's been.

RUTH: I thought you told him I didn't get in till 5.30?

JOSIE: I did. He said he'd come back one evening.

RUTH [*to arm-chair and sitting*]: Well, what time did he come today?

JOSIE: About four, I suppose.

RUTH: He doesn't sound very bright, whoever he is. What's he look like?

JOSIE: Not bad. Bit like Frankie Vaughan.

RUTH: Who the hell's Frankie Vaughan? [*Sipping tea.*] You make a putrid cup of tea, don't you. Doesn't he say what he wants?

JOSIE: Just that he wants to see you – that's all.

RUTH: Strange way to go about it. Calling at the time when you've specifically told him I shall be out. You didn't tell him anything, did you?

JOSIE: Tell him what? That he looked like Frankie Vaughan?

RUTH: Oh, Josie, for heaven's sake, can't you see I'm tired? All I want is a cigarette and a bath.

[*The front door opens and* MRS ELLIOT *comes in. She is a sincere, emotionally restrained little woman in her early fifties, who firmly believes that every cloud has a silver lining. She carries various carrier-bags filled with shopping. At the hall-stand she removes her coat.*]

RUTH: That's your mother. For heaven's sake make a start on that kitchen so that she can get started on the supper without having to clear up your mess first.

JOSIE [*moving to kitchen*]: O.K.

MRS ELLIOT: Are you there, Josie? [*Taking off hat.*]

JOSIE: Hullo, Mum. You're not in any trouble are you, Auntie?

RUTH: In trouble? Do you mean in the general or the popular sense?

JOSIE: What?

MRS ELLIOT [*coming into sitting room with bags*]: Hullo, dear, hullo Josie. Managed to get a seat on the train today, thank goodness. [*Into kitchen.*]

RUTH: Hullo, Kate.

JOSIE: Hullo, Mum.

MRS ELLIOT: Oh Josie, you are a naughty girl, you really are. [*Into sitting room.*] I was hoping you'd have everything nice and clean and tidy when I came in.

JOSIE: I was just going to do it.

MRS ELLIOT: Just look at it out there. It would be tonight too, when there's so much to do.

RUTH: Here, let me take that from you. [*Taking one of the bags.*]

MRS ELLIOT: Thank you, Ruth.

JOSIE: I'm sorry, Mum. Auntie Ruth was talking to me just as I was going to do it. Everyone seems a bit early tonight. [*Into kitchen.*]

MRS ELLIOT [*unpacking carrier*]: I asked Mr Beamish to let me off five minutes early. Didn't like it either. I thought I'd just miss the rush. Funny what a difference a few minutes makes. Anyway, I managed to get some shopping up the road before they closed. Oh dear, what a rush. There we are. You're back early, Ruth dear. Weren't you feeling well? Wonder if George likes parsley sauce.

RUTH: It wasn't anything. Central heating in the office, I expect.

MRS ELLIOT: Well – Josie complained she wasn't too great this morning at breakfast time, so I made her stay at home. I hope you haven't gone and caught something off of her – food poisoning or something.

RUTH: Yes.

MRS ELLIOT: You do look tired, I must say.

RUTH: Oh, I'm better now. Josie gave her *Auntie* a cup of tea.

MRS ELLIOT: You always hate her calling you Auntie don't you.

149

What can you expect dear when that's what you are? Now, I wanted you to do something for me. What was it? Josie, don't bother with those things now. Lay the table for me in here instead, there's a good girl.

RUTH: You seem a bit overloaded.

MRS ELLIOT: Well, I had to get a few extras.

JOSIE [*in from kitchen*]: Where's the fire, Mum?

MRS ELLIOT: Now try and help me a little, Josie. I'm rather cross with you over that kitchen, my girl.

JOSIE: Well, I'm doing it, aren't I?

RUTH: All right you two, I'll help, only don't go on about it, please. [*Into kitchen.*]

JOSIE: Well, she was 'going on' a bit herself just now.

MRS ELLIOT: That's enough, Josie. [*Clearing table.*] I had hoped that at least you could have had the table laid.

JOSIE: Yes, Mum, all right.

MRS ELLIOT: I'm in such a muddle, I don't know where I am. I haven't a chance to do a thing. Hope your father comes in on time.

JOSIE: What's all the panic? Don't tell me you've got somebody coming?

MRS ELLIOT: Yes, I have.

JOSIE: Who on earth is it?

[RUTH *comes in with loaded tray and puts it down, and she and* MRS ELLIOT *start laying the table.*]

MRS ELLIOT: Young George is coming, that's all.

RUTH: George?

MRS ELLIOT: George Dillon. The young fellow that works at my place. You know. I told you about him.

RUTH: Oh, did you? I don't remember.

JOSIE: Oh, him. [*She yawns loudly and flops into the arm-chair.*]

MRS ELLIOT: Of course I told you. I've often spoken about him. I've asked him down to tea lots of times. But each time some appointment seems to turn up and he can't come. Well, he's coming now, for certain. He's a very busy chap. Always on the go.

RUTH: Oh, that one. The rather superior young man who's so much younger than the rest of you. Is he still there? I thought you said the job wasn't quite good enough for him?

MRS ELLIOT: I've always felt a bit sorry for him, that's all. He seemed so much on his own all the time. And, one day, I started telling him about our Raymond, and he was most interested. He was in the services as well, you see.

RUTH: Quite a coincidence.

MRS ELLIOT: Yes. He went right through the war.

RUTH: I had the idea we all did.

[Pause.]

MRS ELLIOT: No, Ruth, some boys didn't get to see the end of it.

RUTH: I'm sorry, Kate. I've had a bit of a day, I'm afraid. I'm not in the right frame of mind to talk to young men, refined or not. If I can't do anything for you down here, I'll go and run myself a bath, if you don't mind.

MRS ELLIOT: Oh! Were you going to have a bath now?

RUTH: Yes. Why?

MRS ELLIOT: Well, I can't go into a long rigmarole now – I've too much to do before George comes. But you see – well, you've got to know sometime, I suppose – I've asked him to stay.

JOSIE: Stay? What, here?

MRS ELLIOT: It won't be for long – just till he finds somewhere else to go.

JOSIE: What's wrong with where he is?

MRS ELLIOT: He's not very happy there. I'll tell you later. Don't worry me with a lot of questions now, Josie. There's too much to do.

RUTH: Well, it's your business. It's your house – not mine. What about Percy?

MRS ELLIOT: Nothing about Percy. It's got nothing to do with him.

RUTH: You're right, of course. [Rather dryly.] It isn't his house, either.

MRS ELLIOT: There's just one thing –

JOSIE: There won't half be an atmosphere when he finds out. You know what Dad's like – he hasn't got over those budgerigars you bought yet.

MRS ELLIOT: He knows what he can do, and it won't take me long to tell him. Oh, do clear up that paper and stuff, Josie. The place looks awful. What was I saying?

RUTH: 'There's just one thing.'

MRS ELLIOT: Oh yes, Ruth. I was going to ask if you would mind very much moving out of your room for a few days, and going in with Norah.

RUTH: Why yes, I do mind. Is it really necessary? Does George Whats-his-name have to have my room?

MRS ELLIOT: No, he doesn't have to, but I thought it would be nicer – being Ray's old room, he'd like it. More like a man's room. Still –

RUTH [*quietly*]: You know, I do like to have at least some time to myself. And anyway, Norah sleeps with her mouth open.

MRS ELLIOT: Oh, very well, Ruth. Josie can go in with her. You won't mind, will you, Josie?

JOSIE [*folding up paper*]: Oh, all right. All this blessed fuss! [*Into kitchen.*]

RUTH: I'm sorry, Kate, but you do understand.

MRS ELLIOT: Never mind. I just thought it would be nicer, that's all. It doesn't matter, dear. And there's no fuss, Madame Josie, thank you. God pays debts without money, I always say.

RUTH: You haven't any aspirin, have you? I don't seem to know where any of my things are –

MRS ELLIOT: There are some in the medicine chest, I think. And if you're going up, would you mind getting some of Josie's stuff into Norah's room – as that's going to be the arrangement?

RUTH: Right.

[*She is lost in her own thoughts and does not move.* MRS ELLIOT *is too preoccupied to notice. Pause.*]

MRS ELLIOT: Only would you mind doing it now, while Josie and I get straight down here? George'll be here very soon – he's only got to pick up his bags from his digs. Is that your case?

RUTH [*picking it up, and into hall*]: I'll take it up with me. [*Taking off scarf and hanging it up.*] Is there anything else?

MRS ELLIOT: No, thank you very much, Ruth. I must get started now.

[RUTH *goes upstairs.*]

Oh, yes – [*into hall*] – Ruth, dear, would you put a clean towel in the bathroom for George? I expect he'd like a wash when he comes in.

RUTH [*halfway upstairs*]: Yes.

MRS ELLIOT: I'm sorry you're not feeling well, dear.

[RUTH *goes on upstairs.* MRS ELLIOT *returns to sitting room.*]

MRS ELLIOT: Now, where are we?

[*The table by now is almost laid, and* MRS ELLIOT *completes it.*]

JOSIE [*in from kitchen*]: Will it be the boiled pork, Mum? There isn't much left – least, not after Dad gets his hands on it.

MRS ELLIOT: He can have it all, as far as I'm concerned. Anyway, it won't worry George, he's a vegetarian. [*To cocktail cabinet.*]

JOSIE: A what?

MRS ELLIOT [*triumphantly*]: A vegetarian. Now, where's the sherry got to, I wonder? Oh, yes.

[*She finds the bottle, and puts it on the table.*]

JOSIE: Oh, one of them. He sounds a bit wishy-washy to me.

MRS ELLIOT: Well, he's not – he's a real gentleman.

JOSIE: That's what I mean. My, we are going posh, aren't we? Sherry! Anybody'd think it was Christmas.

MRS ELLIOT [*to kitchen*]: That's enough of that, young lady. Now go and get dressed and make yourself a bit more presentable, or else George will think I brought you up in the slums.

JOSIE [*idly round the room*]: George, George, George. Georgie Porgie puddeny-pie, kissed the girls and made them cry –

MRS ELLIOT [*from kitchen*]: Now do as I say, dear, please.

JOSIE: All right, Mum. [*She starts to sing.*]

'Why don't you Give Me . . .
Give Me. Give Me . . .
All that you –
All that you
Have to share . . .'

[*Her eyes light on the small package on the table down left. She moves over to it. She extracts the note from the package, and unfolds it.*]

MRS ELLIOT [*off*]: Draw the curtains before you go, will you, dear
Thank goodness the days are drawing out again, though. I'm s
sick of the winter.

JOSIE: O.K., Mum.

[*She moves to the french windows left, draws one of the curtains, an
begins reading the letter.*]

[*Reading*] 'My dear – You have just left, and I have found that yo
have *left* two pounds for me on the desk. How thoughtful of you
and, after that catechism of smug deficiencies you had just recited t
me, how very practical and how like you. I suppose you must hav
slipped it there while I was swallowed up in the damned misery c
our situation. Make no mistake – for the money, I'm grateful. Bu
your setting up as a kind of emotional soup kitchen makes me spit

[*JOSIE is seen to fold her arms to her and shiver.*]

If you had any understanding at all, you would know what a bitte
taste this kind of watery gruel must have. This is the Brow
Windsor of love all right, and the only fit place for it is the sink
If this is the kind of thing you and your pals dole out for th
proletariat and its poor, grubby artists, you had better think again
I'm just going out for some beer. PS. Was just going to post this
when I thought I would return this watch to you. It seems to be
the one thing I have left that you ever gave me. I'd like to think
that my returning it would hurt you, but I know it won't.'

[*Bell rings. The lights in the sitting room blaze on.* MRS ELLIOT ha
switched them on. The door bell goes on ringing furiously.]

MRS ELLIOT: My goodness, Josie, can't you please answer the fron
door for me? I've got milk on the stove. [*Into kitchen.*] And I aske
you to draw those curtains, didn't I?

JOSIE: O.K. [*Draws curtains.*] All right, all right, I'm coming.

[*Goes through hall to front door.*]

Oh, it's you. It's only Norah, Mum.

[NORAH *comes in, wearing outdoor clothes. She is in her middle
thirties. She has some of her mother's restraint but this is due more to
having 'been let down twice'. There is no bitterness, only a naïve
simplicity in all things and at all times.*]

MRS ELLIOT: That you, Norah?

JOSIE [*going into sitting room*]: Well, I've just said so, haven't I?

NORAH [*following her*]: Can't think where I left my key. It's probably in my other bag. I'll have a look in a minute. [*Takes off hat and coat.*] Blessed train, packed as usual. [*Fetches her slippers from under the settee and changes her shoes.*] I saw Father coming up the road, but I wasn't going to wait for *him* to let me in. Not after this morning.

[JOSIE *takes out her 'jazz' trousers and holds them against her waist dancing and humming quietly.*]

MRS ELLIOT [*in kitchen*]: Had a nice day, dear?

NORAH: Not bad, thanks, Mum. [*To Josie.*] You going to the club tonight?

JOSIE: I might. Why?

NORAH: Nothing.

JOSIE: Len's got a new motor-bike. It's a smasher.

NORAH: Fancy.

JOSIE: Mum says he can come to dinner on Sunday.

MRS ELLIOT [*in from kitchen*]: Well, Mum has changed her mind. He can't.

JOSIE: Oh, Mum! Why?

MRS ELLIOT: I'll tell you why later. For goodness' sake take that blessed box upstairs. Supper's nearly ready and there's only George and him to come.

[JOSIE *picks up box and trousers and goes upstairs, singing her favourite song.*]

NORAH: George who?

MRS ELLIOT: Young George from the office, you know the one who gave me the necklace.

NORAH: Oh, him.

MRS ELLIOT: Would you like to start your supper, dear? It's all ready, and I expect you're hungry. [*She goes into the kitchen.*]

NORAH: You know I'm never hungry, Mum.

MRS ELLIOT: Too many sweets, my girl, that's your trouble.

[NORAH *sits at her usual place at the table.*]

MRS ELLIOT: You know what a state your teeth are in already. [*In with a plate of food which she places in front of* NORAH.] I'm sure those sweets are half the trouble. There, see how you like that.

NORAH: Thanks, Mum.

[MRS ELLIOT *goes to the foot of stairs and calls.*]

MRS ELLIOT: Ruth – Ruth, dear! Don't be long will you? And don't forget that towel. [*She returns to sitting room.*] Is it all right, dear?

NORAH: Yes, thanks.

MRS ELLIOT: That's good.

[MRS ELLIOT *goes into kitchen as the front door opens.* PERCY, *her husband, comes in with a brief-case, mac, and umbrella, all of which he deposits at the hat-stand. He is a small, mean little man. Small in every sense of the word, with a small man's aggression. He goes upstairs.*]

NORAH: Mum!

MRS ELLIOT [*coming in*]: Yes, dear? Something wrong?

NORAH: He's just come in, I think.

MRS ELLIOT: Oh! [*Going to foot of stairs*]. Percy! – Was that you, Percy? [*She returns to sitting room.*] I suppose it was him, Norah?

NORAH: Of course it was. I'd know that cat-like tread anywhere. Trust him not to give a civil answer to a civil question.

MRS ELLIOT: The only time your father ever gave a civil answer to a civil question was when he said 'I will' at the wedding. Hope George isn't long, then we can all clear off into the lounge and watch the telly – leave your father to it. Anything on tonight? Not one of them morbid plays, I hope.

NORAH: There's some skating, I think.

MRS ELLIOT: That'll be nice. [*Into kitchen.*] They usually have some nice music with that.

[PERCY *comes downstairs and, after taking an evening paper from his brief-case, goes into the sitting room and sits at the table in the arm-dining-chair.*]

MRS ELLIOT [*lifting kitchen hatch*]: Will you have boiled pork or boiled eggs?

PERCY [*reading paper*]: Nothing.

MRS ELLIOT: You heard what I said – boiled pork or boiled eggs?

PERCY: And you heard what I said – nothing. Just a cup of tea.

[MRS ELLIOT *slams down hatch.* NORAH *pours out tea for her father and herself.*]

NORAH: Must put some more water in the pot.

PERCY: You'll drown it.

NORAH: And I know something else that needs drowning.

[*Into kitchen with teapot.* MRS ELLIOT *comes in with plate of food, and sets it in front of* PERCY.]

PERCY: I said I didn't want anything.

MRS ELLIOT: You'll no doubt eat it just the same. Josie! Ruth! Come along, now! And another thing: I hope you'll mind your manners, Percy, in future, particularly as I have a young gentleman from the office coming to stay here for a little while. [*To herself.*] It'll be like having Raymond in the house again.

PERCY: Accch! So you've taken to cradle-snatching, have you? Not content with taking another woman's husband, you have to pick up a 'young gentleman' as well. Where did all this happen – Dean Street?

MRS ELLIOT [*with an effort*]: Look, Percy, I'm warning you, once and for all, this is *my* house, and I have worked for every penny I bought it with, and everything in it. As far as I'm concerned, you're just the lodger here. Why you've got your knife into Jack Livings, goodness only knows. They're nice, respectable people, and well you know it. I'm sure I don't know what Mrs Livings would say if she knew about your horrible accusations. Just because Mr Livings comes in now and again to do a few useful things about the house, that's all it is – things you're too *damn* lazy to do for me.

NORAH [*mildly*]: Mum!

MRS ELLIOT: I'm sorry, Norah, but there it is. There are times when your father goes too far with his insults. And I'll have you know this too: George is a fine, clean, upright young man. And he's clever too. He's in the theatrical line, he is, and one day he's going to be as famous as that Laurence Olivier, you see, and then perhaps you'll laugh on the other side of your face.

PERCY: Accch! Theatrical line! Don't give me that nonsense. I bet you he hasn't got two ha'pennies for a penny – they never have, these people.

MRS ELLIOT: No – it's true that, at the moment, he hasn't a lot of money to throw around, but he will have, he's that type. He's used to money, you can tell that. He's very cultured.

NORAH: Not like some people we know.

PERCY: How is it he's only a tuppenny-ha'penny penpusher then?

MRS ELLIOT: He's not a clerk any longer. There was a little upset at the office today and he walked out. And a good job too, I say. Wasting his time and talent in a place like that. It's not right, and I wouldn't like to see any boy of mine going to waste like that – especially when George has so many plans and ideas to make himself famous. There isn't much he can't turn his hand to in the theatrical line, believe me. Why he doesn't only act in plays, he writes them as well. As a matter of fact, he's bang in the middle of one at the moment. I expect he'll finish it while he's here.

PERCY: That's all very interesting, I'm sure. You've got it all nicely worked out between you, haven't you? But what about me? I'm going to look a proper bloody fool, aren't I? What are the neighbours going to think, I'd like to know?

MRS ELLIOT: No more than they do now, believe me. They know very well what you're like. I haven't forgotten yesterday either – shouting and swearing at the top of your voice. At the front door too. The humiliation of it! I don't mind you swearing at the back door, but the front door – well –

PERCY: Accch! You women – nag, nag, nag.

[JOSIE *comes downstairs, and goes into the 'lounge'. She is now 'respectable'.*]

MRS ELLIOT: Is that you, Ruth? Josie? Oh, for heaven's sake don't start looking at that thing till we've had supper.

[JOSIE *comes out of lounge into sitting room.*]

JOSIE: Oh, all right. It's only the newsreel.

[*She gets a chair and sits at the table.* MRS ELLIOT *goes into the kitchen and returns immediately with two plates of food.*]

It's panel-game night, isn't it?

MRS ELLIOT: There you are. [*She places plate in front of* JOSIE.] And I may as well have mine while I'm about it. And what do you say, Miss Josie? [*Sits at table.*]

JOSIE: Sorry. Thanks, Mum.

MRS ELLIOT: That's better.

[*They are all eating now. Pause.*]

JOSIE: Silence in the pig-market, let the old sow speak first.

MRS ELLIOT: Pudding, Percy?

PERCY: No.

JOSIE: Trouble with you, Dad, is you talk too much.

PERCY: Accch!

JOSIE: Can I put a record on, liven things up a bit. Ever so sordid in here, like a mortuary.

PERCY: That blessed racket. If I had my way –

MRS ELLIOT: It's Norah's wireless.

[JOSIE *puts on a record and returns to her seat.*]

JOSIE: The girls are taking a coach up to Salisbury on Sunday. You coming, Mum?

[RUTH *comes slowly down the stairs. Halfway down, there is a knock at the door.*]

MRS ELLIOT: No, I don't think so, dear. I expect Norah will though. She's coach mad.

[RUTH *answers the front door and a man's voice is heard outside. It is* GEORGE DILLON.]

NORAH: That would be lovely.

GEORGE: I'm awfully sorry, but does Mrs Elliot live here?

RUTH: Yes, she does. Did you want to speak to her?

GEORGE: Well, as a matter of fact she asked me to –

RUTH: Oh, I am sorry. Of course, you must be George. Do come in.

[GEORGE DILLON *enters. He is a little over thirty, boyish, yet still every year his age. He is short, not good-looking, but with an anti-romantic kind of charm. He displays at different times a mercurial,*

*ironic passion, lethargy, offensiveness, blatant sincerity, and a men-
tally picaresque dishonesty – sometimes almost all of these at the
same time. A walking confliction in fact. Just at the moment he is
rather shy, feeling his way. He is carrying a suitcase and a 'carry-all'
bag.*]

GEORGE: Yes, that's right. Thank you.

RUTH: I'm Ruth Gray. Mrs Elliot's sister.

GEORGE: How do you do?

[*They shake hands.*]

I seem to think we've met somewhere before, haven't we?

RUTH: Yes, I had that feeling too.

MRS ELLIOT: There's someone in the hall. Is that you, Ruth? [*She
rises and goes into the hall.*]

RUTH: Mr Dillon has arrived, Kate.

MRS ELLIOT: Oh, good. You found your way all right, then? Glad
you remembered it was Targon Wood station you had to get out
at – most people think Pelham Junction is nearer, but it isn't really.
I didn't hear you ring the bell. I expect you're hungry, aren't you?
Would you like a wash before supper? Bring your things up.
[*Going upstairs.*] I'll show you where your room is and where you
can find the toilet.

[GEORGE *follows her up.*]

GEORGE: That's very nice of you. I couldn't find the bell, so I
knocked instead.

MRS ELLIOT: Yes, I thought I didn't hear you ring.

[*They both disappear.* RUTH *stands looking up the stairs for a
moment.*]

JOSIE: Must be nearly time for 'Classics on Ice'. I'm going to get a
good seat before that fellow pinches it. [*Rising, she puts chair under
table.*] Sounds ever so posh, doesn't he?

NORAH: I thought you were going to the club.

JOSIE: It's a woman's privilege to change her mind. [*Crosses into
hall.*] Well, what's he like, Auntie? [RUTH *does not move.*] Auntie,
what's he like?

RUTH: I don't know. Of course I don't. Why should I?

JOSIE: Oh, all right. I was only asking. Keep your hair on. [*Goes into lounge.*]

[RUTH *walks slowly into sitting room and sits in arm-chair.* NORAH *collects dirty plates.* PERCY *is still reading.* MRS ELLIOT *comes downstairs into sitting room.*]

MRS ELLIOT: Well, that's that. Have you finished, Percy?

[PERCY *folds newspaper.*]

PERCY: Where's Henry Irving?

MRS ELLIOT: Never you mind. I'd be grateful if you made yourself useful for once and made up the lounge fire.

[PERCY *rises and switches off radiogram and goes into lounge.* NORAH *takes things into the kitchen.*]

That's right, dear. Can't keep his hands off that wireless, can he? Now, Ruth, what about your supper, dear?

RUTH [*rising*]: Oh, nothing for me, thanks. [*Crosses to small table.*] I think I'll just have some hot milk and go to bed. [*She picks up the small package containing the watch. The note is missing.*] Kate.

MRS ELLIOT: Yes, dear? Why, Ruth, what is it? You look quite pale. If I were you –

RUTH: Has anyone been at this table at all? Have they, Kate?

MRS ELLIOT: My dear, I'm sure I don't know. What a funny thing to ask. Why shouldn't they if they want to?

RUTH: There was a letter of mine here. Quite personal. A private letter. Someone has moved it.

MRS ELLIOT: Now, Ruth, dear, don't go upsetting yourself over a little thing like that. I expect you'll come across it later on. You go upstairs and I'll bring you up some hot milk later on.

[MRS ELLIOT *goes into the kitchen. Then* RUTH *goes into hall, halfway upstairs she stops for a moment, then comes down again, goes to lounge door, opens it, and calls. There is the sound of the 'Skater's Waltz' from within.*]

RUTH: Josie, come here a minute, will you?

JOSIE: Oh, what do you want, can't you see I'm watching the telly?

RUTH: Come here, please, when I ask you. [*She moves to the foot of the stairs as she waits.*]

JOSIE [*at lounge door*]: What do you want?

RUTH: Shut the door and come here.

[JOSIE *goes to her.*]

JOSIE: Well?

RUTH: Where is it?

JOSIE: Where's what? I don't know what you're talking about.

RUTH: You know damn well what. Give me that letter.

JOSIE: Oh, that. Oh, yes. [*Slowly, reluctantly, she withdraws letter from her jumper.*]

RUTH: Thank you very much. Kindly learn to keep your nose clean in future, will you?

JOSIE: So that's where you've been all these week-ends, with Jock. Does he wear a kilt?

RUTH: Mind your own damned business. [*Gives her a resounding smack across the face.*]

[JOSIE *yells. Enters* MRS ELLIOT.]

MRS ELLIOT: Why, whatever's going on?

JOSIE: Going on! It's Auntie Ruth what's been going on. *Carrying* on more like – with a man – and paying him for it what's more.

RUTH: Just you dare read my letters again, and I'll do more than slap your face.

JOSIE: Don't you talk to me like that – you're not my Mum.

MRS ELLIOT: If what Ruth says is true, Josie, then I'm very ashamed. I thought I'd brought you up to behave like a lady. Never, never do that again, do you hear? Now kindly leave the room – but first say you're sorry to Auntie Ruth.

JOSIE [*after some hesitation*]: I'm sorry, Auntie Ruth. [*Goes off to lounge singing 'If Jock could love me, love me. . . .'*]

RUTH: Slut! slut! slut!

MRS ELLIOT: Ruth – that's no way to talk, and you know it. [RUTH *turns away.*]

MRS ELLIOT: So things didn't work out then?

RUTH: No – I've just walked out on him, for better or for worse.

MRS ELLIOT: But I don't understand. Josie said something about paying him –

RUTH: I don't have to buy my love – or do I? Yes, I gave him the odd pound or two, to keep him alive.

MRS ELLIOT: But surely he could do a job of work?

RUTH: Job of work? He's a writer – the original starving artist in the attic – and I believed he had promise.

MRS ELLIOT: Then why did you leave him?

RUTH: He's been a promising young man for too long. Youthful promise doesn't look too well with receding hair. I've misjudged him – he's the complete flop, and I've spent nearly six years giving all I could to him, giving my love to him – such as it is.

MRS ELLIOT: It's beyond me, dear. It's funny – you're the only one in the family who doesn't have patience or understanding. While you were enjoying yourself at college, we all had to go out to work. I can only say that college gave you a lot of funny ideas.

RUTH: That's right. Funny enough to make me do an inexcusable thing. When he told me he hadn't a penny, not even the price of a packet of cigarettes, I went to his jacket pocket, and inside I found a cheque for eight guineas for some book review or other he'd written. He hadn't even told me about it. Not only did he lie about the money, but he even kept his piffling little success from me. A brainless, cheap little lie. And that did it – the whole works collapsed, the whole flimsy works. [*She walks to the door.*] I suppose that's really why I left him. [*Exits upstairs.*]

MRS ELLIOT [*crossing to hallway*]: George! Supper's ready, dear. [*Returns to kitchen.*]

[GEORGE *comes down, looking over his shoulder. As* GEORGE *crosses hall,* NORAH *comes out of kitchen into hall. 'Skater's Waltz' comes up good and loud.*]

NORAH: Hullo.

GEORGE: Hullo.

NORAH: Your supper's in there. I'm going to watch the skating. [*She goes into lounge.*]

[GEORGE *goes into sitting room. He coughs slightly.*]

MRS ELLIOT: That's right, dear, make yourself at home. Oh, that blessed telly, it's much too loud, isn't it? [*She crosses to lounge and opens door.*] Do put that telly down a bit, there's good children. We can't hear ourselves think in here. [*She goes back into sitting room.*] There, that's better isn't it? You sit there, dear. [*He sits in* PERCY'S *place.*] They're all watching the telly, so you can have your supper in peace. And while we're alone, dear – I want you to treat this just as if it were your home, just do whatever you like, won't you?

GEORGE: That's very kind of you, Mrs Elliot. I just don't know what to say [*he puts out his hand*]. I can only say that I won't impose myself on you for one minute longer than I can help. You're so very kind.

MRS ELLIOT: I've never mentioned this before, but I'm helping you all I can because I feel that in some small way I'm helping my son, Raymond. He was killed in the war, you know. That's his picture over there.

GEORGE: Yes, I'm sorry.

MRS ELLIOT [*very simply*]: He was a lovely boy. Clever, like you, artistic, too, but somehow he didn't seem to have that drive, that sort of initiative. Well, he didn't really have much chance to get on. But *you* will, George, I'm sure. With all your talent, you just can't go wrong. You're always planning things – and all the things you've already done too. You've got your acting and your plays and I don't know what, haven't you?

GEORGE: Oh, yes, Mrs Elliot, don't you worry – the play I'm writing now is just about in the bag. I can finish it in no time here. And I've already got someone interested in it – for the West End, I mean.

MRS ELLIOT: Well, there you are – what did I say? You certainly are one for irons in the fire, aren't you? And to think we shall all come and see your piece, and sit in the posh seats. That will be nice. Well, there we are, dear. And if Ray was here now, I'd be talking to him just as I'm talking to you. What I'm trying to say is that I want you to feel that you are taking his place in the home, and if there's anything you want – anything – please don't hesitate to ask. And don't, please, ever go short of money. Ray used to send me home so much a week when he was in the army, for me to save for him when he came home. I'd like to think it's being put to good use at last by helping you.

GEORGE: Bless you, Mrs Elliot. [*He coughs slightly.*] You're so very kind and thoughtful. I just don't know how to thank you. I only hope I'll prove worthy of your kindness. I promise I won't let you down in any way. I promise you that.

MRS ELLIOT [*patting his cheek*]: Good. Now we must see about getting you something to eat. Being a vegetarian you must eat lots of strange things. You'll have to tell me about them as we go along. [*Into kitchen.*]

GEORGE: I don't want you to put yourself out.

[*He sits looking around him.*]

MRS ELLIOT [*lifting hatch*]: I've got some nice boiled cod and parsley sauce. You do eat fish, don't you? [*She sees him staring at the birds on the wall, centre.*] Yes, Ray painted those. I told you he was artistic, didn't I?

[*Hatch down.* GEORGE *rises and walks round the room restlessly, looking at the photographs on the wall, the cocktail cabinet, the general dressings. He then picks up the photograph of* RAYMOND *and looks at it steadily.*]

GEORGE: You stupid-looking bastard.

QUICK CURTAIN

ACT TWO

Summer. There is now a telephone standing on small table in hall. The french windows are open. The settee brought round to face slightly down-stage. NORAH, JOSIE, MRS ELLIOT, *and* PERCY *are sitting in their customary places at the meal table, eating. After curtain rises, a slight pause.*

MRS ELLIOT: Pudding, Percy?

PERCY: No.

[MRS ELLIOT *rises, taking plates into kitchen. As she does so, the telephone rings and she stops dead.*]

NORAH [*with awe*]: It's ringing!

JOSIE: The phone's ringing!

MRS ELLIOT: Our first call.

PERCY: What a racket – wireless, T.V., and now the blinking telephone.

MRS ELLIOT: Who's it for, I wonder?

NORAH: Answer it and see.

JOSIE: Yes, that's the best way to find out. [*Jumps up and goes into hall.*] I'll go, Mum. [*Lifts receiver.*] Yes, yes it is. Who? Yes. All right, I'll fetch her. [*Into sitting room*] It's for you, Mum. Ever such a funny man – he's got a sort of Chinese accent.

MRS ELLIOT [*giving plates to* JOSIE]: Chinese?

JOSIE: Yes.

MRS ELLIOT: But I don't know any Chinamen.

JOSIE: Well, you'd better hurry up and answer it, Mum – he's waiting.

NORAH: Perhaps he's from *Chu Chin Chow on Ice.*

[MRS ELLIOT *goes into hall, and picks up receiver.*]

MRS ELLIOT: Hullo. Yes, it is. [JOSIE *stands in doorway, listening.*] Have we what? Well, I don't know. I'll see. [*To* JOSIE] He wants to know if we've got any laundry that wants doing. [*In phone*] No, I don't think so, thank you. What are you laughing at? [*She laughs.*] Oh, you are a naughty boy, you really are – you took us all in. [*To Josie.*] It's George.

JOSIE: Oh, silly. [*She goes into kitchen.*]

MRS ELLIOT: What's that, dear? Have you? Oh, I am pleased. Yes, oh we will! All right, dear. Good-bye. [*Replaces receiver, goes into sitting room.*] Says he's got some good news – he's got a job, and something about his play. I didn't quite catch what it was. Fancy young George being the first to ring up – and I had it put in specially for him too. Isn't that nice? Oh, I must sit down a minute – the excitement's too much for me!

[NORAH *pours tea.*]

NORAH: Needs more water. [*Into kitchen.*]

PERCY: *What's* he gone and got?

MRS ELLIOT: You heard, didn't you? A job. What did you think it was?

JOSIE [*in from kitchen*]: Must be something good for him to ring up like that.

MRS ELLIOT: Yes – silly boy. He was only at the station. He'll be home in a minute. I'm so glad. That awful day he left that office, he swore he'd stick it out until he got something really worth while.

[NORAH *comes in with teapot.*]

MRS ELLIOT: And it's turned up at last. He always said he wouldn't take anything tatty.

NORAH: What's 'tatty'?

MRS ELLIOT: I don't really know, dear – George is always saying it.

JOSIE: Well, now I can really tell the whole of Targon Broadway that we've got a real actor staying with us. That's if he doesn't get too stuck up, and want to go and live in Berkeley Square or something.

MRS ELLIOT: Of course he won't. George has settled down here very well. This is his home now. There's no reason at all why he should have to go.

JOSIE: Well, he'll have to get married sometime, won't he?

MRS ELLIOT: Well, yes, there is that, of course.

NORAH: How do you know he hasn't got a girl friend already?
[*Phone rings.*]

MRS ELLIOT: Well! There it is again – twice in a couple of minutes.
[JOSIE *goes to it quickly, lifts receiver.*]

JOSIE [*on phone*]: Hullo. Who? No, I think you must have the wrong
number. You're welcome. [*Puts phone down and returns to sitting
room.*] Wrong number.

MRS ELLIOT: Oh.

JOSIE: What were we talking about?

MRS ELLIOT: George. I was just going to say that I think you're a bit
gone on him aren't you. What about poor old Len Cook now, eh!

JOSIE: Well, George will do to fill in while Len does his National
Service. I wouldn't mind going to Germany with Len though.

NORAH: You'd have to marry him first, wouldn't you? I mean it
wouldn't be very proper just to go and – well – 'live' with him –

JOSIE: Oh, I don't know. I don't mind what I do or where I go, so
long as my man's got money.

PERCY: The trouble with young girls today is that they spend too
much time thinking about love and S-E-X.

JOSIE: S-E-X? Oh, sex. Sex doesn't mean a thing to me. To my
way of thinking, love is the most important and beautiful thing
in this world and that's got nothing to do with sex.

PERCY [*producing irrelevances like a bombshell*]: Well, I may be a crank
and all that, but if I can persuade the council to close the park
gates after dark, I shall die a happy man.

NORAH: What on earth's that got to do with sex?

MRS ELLIOT: Well, I don't think we need go on with this conversation – but Josie is quite right. You keep those beautiful thoughts
dear and you can be sure you won't come to any harm. Put the
kettle on for George, there's a dear. [JOSIE *goes into kitchen.*]

[GEORGE *appears at the french window, waving a bottle of wine.*]

GEORGE: Friends, Romans, and countrymen, lend me your ears!

MRS ELLIOT: Oh, George! You did make me jump! [GEORGE *goes
up and hugs her.*] And I'm so pleased about your job dear – we're all
dying to hear about it.

JOSIE: Where is it, George, Drury Lane?

GEORGE: Could be, Josie, could be! Come on Norah, cheer up and find the corkscrew for the big Bacchanalia.

MRS ELLIOT: I'll find it. [*Goes to cocktail cabinet.*]

GEORGE: Cast of thousands, ten years in the making. Starring the one and only Mrs Elliot as Juno!

[*They all laugh with the exception of* PERCY. RUTH *comes in at the front door and stands listening at the foot of the stairs.*]

GEORGE [*assuming a thick Dublin accent*]: And you, Norah, me darlin', you shall play Ariadne.

NORAH: I'm not being a man for you or nobody.

GEORGE: And Josie, let me see, yes you'll play Semele.

JOSIE: Oh! There's a name to go to bed with!

GEORGE: And that's exactly what you do my sweet – with me, Jupiter.

[*More general laughter.* RUTH *goes upstairs.*]

PERCY: Accch!

MRS ELLIOT: There you are, Josie, what was I saying only a minute ago? [*Handing* GEORGE *corkscrew.*]

GEORGE: Now let the wine flow on this day of days. And what a day it's been. Do you know, one agent I went to see this morning looked me up and down in this duffel-coat and said: 'No, we ain't got no *Biblical* parts today.' Must have thought I looked like John the Baptist. Perhaps if I go in a kilt, he'll offer me a gangster part.

Glasses, Mrs E. Bring out the golden goblets. That's right. For in spite of George continually being told he's too young, too old, too short – in spite of his wig, glass eye, false teeth, and wooden leg, George has got himself a job. [*He hands wine to* MRS ELLIOT.] There we are.

MRS ELLIOT: I mustn't have more than one. I can't go to the meeting tiddly, can I? I don't know what Mr Colwyn-Stuart would say.

GEORGE: Josie?

JOSIE: I certainly won't say no. [*Takes glass.*]

GEORGE: And what about you, Percy. Will you have a tipple?

PERCY: Well, seeing as how you are in the money.

GEORGE: And Norah! A glass for Norah Mavourneen – me darlin' gal.

NORAH: Not for me, thank you.

GEORGE: No?

NORAH: No, thank you.

MRS ELLIOT: Oh, go on, Norah. It's no use you pretending you're teetotal. You had some on Boxing Day, I remember. Go on, be sociable.

NORAH: I really don't think I could after seeing those great fat men on the telly last night trampling on the grapes half naked. It was horrible.

GEORGE: So Norah isn't going to touch any more wine until they bath in a respectable manner? Never mind, dear, just one sip won't hurt you. [*Gives her a glass.*]

NORAH: Oh, all right then, just a sip.

MRS ELLIOT: Well, good health, George, and congratulations.

ALL: Good luck. Down the hatch, *etc.*

JOSIE: Well, now tell us what it is.

GEORGE: First of all, there's every chance of my play going on at the Trident Theatre.

MRS ELLIOT: Oh, good.

JOSIE: Where's that, George? In the West End?

GEORGE: Well, no, not exactly. Bayswater. And it means I should get plenty of managers and agents to see it.

MRS ELLIOT: Oh, good.

GEORGE: I saw Ronnie Harris this morning – you know the film man – and he said he's got a part for me coming up shortly.

NORAH: What sort of film, George?

GEORGE: Don't really know yet – to do with some Army job or something, so he says.

MRS ELLIOT: That'll be nice.

GEORGE: And finally, I've got a T.V. job coming up in three weeks' time.

JOSIE: George! You going to be on the telly?

GEORGE: Well, yes. But it's not exactly the lead, mind you, but it's something, anyway.

JOSIE: Oh, I'll say it is. Our George on the telly! What are you going to be in, George?

GEORGE: Ever heard of a play called *Hamlet*?

JOSIE: Of course I have.

NORAH: Yes, I saw that a long time ago. That's a very *old* one, isn't it. Very good though. He dies in the end, doesn't he?

GEORGE: He does indeed, Norah, he does.

NORAH: I always like a good laugh really. What I always say is –

NORAH: ⎱ There's enough misery in the world without paying to
GEORGE: ⎰ see it.

GEORGE: I don't think you really like the theatre very much, do you, Norah?

NORAH: Oh, yes I do.

GEORGE: Not really.

NORAH: Yes, but I don't ever go.

GEORGE: Oh, but you should. The theatre is like a shrine, Norah. A cathedral. Do you ever go to church, Norah?

MRS ELLIOT: The only time she goes to church is when she's got a blessed banner stuck in her hand.

NORAH: Oh, Mum. [*Rises and goes into lounge.*]

MRS ELLIOT: And talking of church – I must pop your Saviar in the oven. You'll be able to look after it, won't you? I'm off to the meeting as soon as Mr Colwyn-Stuart gets here. [*Exit kitchen.*]

GEORGE: Lord, is he coming? I'm in no mood for Mr Colwyn-pussy-Stuart. Josie, how long will you be?

JOSIE: How long will I be? Oooooh! It's jazz night! I must get changed. [*She runs upstairs.*]

GEORGE [*sinking exhausted in arm-chair*]: Tired as I am, anything would be better than having to put up with that moron.

PERCY: For once, young man, I agree with you. Thanks for the drink.

GEORGE [*absently*]: Not at all. A pleasure.

PERCY: Now that you're a celebrity, I'm surprised that you want to go jazzing at the Jubilee Hall with Josie.

GEORGE [*singing*]: 'Jazzing at the Jubilee with Josie!'

PERCY: And I certainly hope that now you are earning money, you will be able to pay for yourself instead of sponging off other people.

GEORGE [*looks at him sharply*]: What do you mean?

[*The front doorbell rings.*]

MRS ELLIOT [*in from kitchen*]: That's him now. Right on the dot as usual. Do I look all right?

[RUTH *comes downstairs.*]

GEORGE: Ravishing.

PERCY: Accch!

MRS ELLIOT [*into hall*]: Answer that, Ruth dear, will you? [*Into sitting room.*] And if you can't make an effort to make yourself a little more pleasant, you'd better go and watch the telly.

PERCY [*sitting down*]: I'm busy.

[RUTH *opens front door.*]

MRS ELLIOT: All right then. But I don't want any upsets tonight.

[GEOFFREY COLWYN-STUART *comes in and follows* RUTH *into sitting room. He wears an elegant suit, with a beautifully laundered shirt, a carefully chosen green spotted tie, and breast pocket handkerchief to match. He is a pale, balding man in his late thirties, all sweetness and light.*]

MRS ELLIOT: Oh, come in Mr Stuart, I'm nearly ready. You know everyone don't you?

GEOFFREY: Yes. Good evening everyone. Why, Mrs Elliot, you look blooming tonight.

MRS ELLIOT: Oh, not really. I haven't had a minute since I came in.

GEOFFREY: But that's the secret, isn't it? Good evening Mr Elliot. How are you?

PERCY [*half rises, turning to greet* GEOFFREY *but finally doesn't*]: How are you?

MRS ELLIOT: You've met George, haven't you?

GEOFFREY: Oh, yes, we've met several times, haven't we?

MRS ELLIOT: Yes. He's been here a long time now.

GEOFFREY: Like one of the family, in fact.

MRS ELLIOT: Well, I won't keep you long. I'll just pop upstairs and put on a spot of powder, then I'm ready. George'll keep you entertained. He keeps *us* entertained, doesn't he?

[PERCY *makes a noise like an aborted whistle, which he keeps up for the next few minutes.* RUTH *sits at the table, drinking tea.*]

MRS ELLIOT: Didn't you want to watch the television, Percy? George has had some good news today, haven't you, George? We've been ever so excited. He's going to be on the telly himself soon. You'll have to come round and see him when he is. I expect he'll tell you all about it. Make Mr Colwyn-Stuart comfortable. Don't go without me, now! [*Into hall and upstairs.*]

GEOFFREY: It's all right, you needn't hurry. We're early yet. [*Crossing left.*] What a dear she is.

GEORGE: Rather.

GEOFFREY: Mind if I sit here? [*At table.*]

RUTH: Do. There's some tea left, if you'd care for some.

GEOFFREY: No, thank you so much. I've just had dinner.

RUTH: Have you? We've just had supper. [*Removes wine to cocktail cabinet.*]

[PERCY *taps the sides of his armchair pensively.*]

GEOFFREY: And how's the world treating yóu, Mr Elliot? I suppose I should say 'how are *you* treating the world?' After all, that's what really counts, isn't it?

PERCY: Not too badly, thank you.

GEOFFREY: Your wife's been telling me that you've not been sleeping very well lately. I'm sorry to hear that.

PERCY [*rubbing his nose*]: Oh? She told you that, did she?

GEOFFREY: She mentioned it at our last meeting actually.

PERCY: The last meeting, was it? Actually?

GEOFFREY: How are you feeling now? Any better?

PERCY: Nothing the matter with me. Don't sleep so good sometimes, that's all.

GEOFFREY: Mrs Elliot says she can't persuade you to go to a doctor about it.

PERCY: Don't believe in them.

GEOFFREY: Well, I think you'll find plenty of people to support you there – including you, eh, George?

GEORGE: Right.

PERCY: I don't believe in a lot of vegetarian rot either. I'm not making *my*self ill. Meatless steaks! [*Grins.*]

RUTH: Yes, I must say, that was rather too much for me. Nut cutlet I can take, but meatless steak's a bit too much of a paradox. Do you think Oscar Wilde could possibly have been a vegetarian?

PERCY: It's just that I have a lot of things on my mind.

GEOFFREY: In your own words, Mr Elliot. Exactly. The old ravelled sleave of care, am I right, George?

GEORGE [*absently*]: Eh?

RUTH: Shakespeare, George. Aren't you supposed to stand to attention, or something?

GEOFFREY: The number of people one sees every day, with tired, haggard eyes, dark circles of care underneath them.

GEORGE: I always thought that had another significance.

GEOFFREY [*smiling*]: You're a pretty free sort of chap, aren't you? I hope you don't shock everyone in this respectable household with your Bohemian ways.

GEORGE: By 'Bohemian' I suppose you mean crummy. It's rather like calling bad breath 'halitosis', don't you think?

RUTH: He's straight out of *Trilby* – didn't you know?

GEORGE: Frankly, I always touch mine up with a brown liner.

GEOFFREY: What?

GEORGE: The rings under my eyes – helps me when I play clergymen's parts. I'm rather good at them.

GEOFFREY [*refusing to be stung*]: You know, you surprise me a little, George. You seem such an intelligent, vital young man, so much in the swim. After all, it's not even considered fashionable to be sceptical nowadays. The really *smart* thing is the spiritual thing.

RUTH: That's true enough.

GEOFFREY: And you too, Ruth. Of course, your interests are political, I know. But shall I tell you something? If I were to invite the Foreign Secretary, say, down here to speak, he wouldn't be able to half fill the Jubilee Hall.

RUTH: Are we supposed to be surprised?

GEOFFREY: On the other hand, if I were to invite someone like Billy Graham – well, take my word for it, you wouldn't be able to get within a mile of the place.

RUTH: With his message of love and all that? Love isn't everything, you know, Mr Stuart.

GEOFFREY: That's where we disagree, Ruth. I believe that it is.

RUTH: Take justice away from love, and it doesn't mean a thing.

GEOFFREY: Love can change the face of the world.

RUTH: Tell that to the poor black devils in South Africa. Why don't you do something for them?

GEOFFREY: Dear, oh dear – we're going to get involved already if we're not careful. I can see that. Oh, there's nothing I enjoy more than a good old intellectual rough and tumble, and I only wish I could stay and slog it out with the two of you, but there isn't time, unfortunately. The fact is, we've probably got a great deal in common. You know: I have discovered a new way of judging people.

RUTH: You have?

GEOFFREY: I simply ask myself whether their lights are shining.

GEORGE: What about their livers?

GEOFFREY [*laughing*]: Yes. I did phrase it badly didn't I? Perhaps I should have said 'lamps'. I ask myself whether their lamps are shining. You see, my theory is that inside every one of us is a lamp. When it's alight, the loves and hates, the ambitions, desires, and ideas inside it are burning, and that person is really alive. But there are people who go around every day, at work, at home with their families – they seem normal, but their lamps have gone out. They've simply given up. They've given up being alive.

RUTH: And are our lamps alight, do you think, Mr Stuart?

GEOFFREY: Oh, very definitely. It struck me the moment I came into the room.

GEORGE: Tell me. [*Nodding at* PERCY.] What about Mr Elliot's lamp?

GEOFFREY: Oh, yes, I think so. I think so. It's burning all right.

GEORGE: You *think* so! You hear that, Percy? You need a new wick.

GEOFFREY: Oh, I hope I didn't sound rude. I think Mr Elliot is on edge about things a little perhaps, principally because he's tired and can't sleep.

PERCY: All I said was –

GEOFFREY: People are wearing themselves out, worrying about a whole lot of things, unimportant things that don't matter one jot. You, Ruth, you worry about who's going to win the next election.

RUTH: Believe me – I no longer give a *damn*.

GEOFFREY: It's not important. And you, George, you worry about whether you're going to rise to the top of your profession. That's not important.

GEORGE: Thank you. We'll let you know.

GEOFFREY: One day – a few years ago this was – I happened to speak to a very famous clergyman – oh, he's dead now –

PERCY: He's all right then.

GEOFFREY: For years that man was in the habit of addressing as many as six different meetings in one day, often in the same number of towns. So I asked him how it was that he never seemed to get even a little bit tired. And he explained it to me. He said: 'Because I believe in every single word that I utter.'

GEORGE: Lucky him.

GEOFFREY: You could see his lamp burning at the very back of the hall. He was on fire for what he believed in. And that's the secret. It's no use sitting around moaning.

[*Enter* MRS ELLIOT *from hall.*]

MRS ELLIOT: Who's been moaning? I'm all ready. The television's started, Percy. Have you been having a little chat with George?

GEOFFREY: Well, not exactly. I'm afraid I've been rather bad mannered.

MRS ELLIOT: I'm quite sure you haven't. *You're* never bad mannered with anyone.

GEOFFREY: I have been rather monopolizing the conversation. In fact, I've a teeny-weeny feeling that George and Ruth think I'm rather an old bore.

MRS ELLIOT: Of course he doesn't. He's a very deep one, George –
I know that.

GEOFFREY: What really started us off was – we were talking about
tiredness. It's a long time since I heard *you* complaining of tiredness,
Mrs Elliot. Not since those very early days just after – just after
the end of the war. I think she's a good advertisement for the
system, don't you? No doubt, it sounds a little odd to you, but
it's all a question of what *we* call synchronizing yourself with
Providence. Of getting into step with the almighty.

MRS ELLIOT: Yes. Well, I think we ought to be getting in step
ourselves, Mr Stuart, don't you?

GEOFFREY: Yes, I suppose we had.

[*She turns to go, and* GEOFFREY *rises.* GEORGE *has hardly been
listening, but suddenly he responds, almost as an afterthought to himself.*]

GEORGE: Yes. If only it were as simple as that, Mr Stuart. But life
isn't simple, and, if you've any brains in your head at all, it's
frankly a pain in the arse.

MRS ELLIOT: George! Really!

GEORGE: I'm sorry. I apologize. But I've said it now. You see, to
me there is something contemptible about a man who can't face
it all without drugging himself up to the rings round his eyes with
a lot of comforting myths – like all these bird-brains who batten
off the National Health. I don't care who it is – you or anyone –
you must have a secret doubt somewhere. You know that the only
reason you do believe in these things is because they *are* comforting.

GEOFFREY: So you think that religion is just a series of useful untruths?

GEORGE: Yes, I do.

PERCY: Hear! Hear!

MRS ELLIOT: You be quiet!

GEOFFREY: It's all right, Mrs Elliot. George is like so many young
men – he believes that the great thing about the truth is that it
must always be unpleasant.

GEORGE: It's just that I believe it's easy to answer the ultimate
questions – it saves you bothering with the immediate ones.

MRS ELLIOT: There's such a thing as faith, George.

GEORGE: I believe in evidence. And faith is believing in something for which there *is* no evidence. You don't say: I have faith that two and two are four, do you? Or that the earth is round? And why? Because they're both easily verified.

GEOFFREY: So it all has to be verified for you, does it, George? I think I understand you better than you know.

GEORGE: Oh?

GEOFFREY: You see, I come into contact with a great many artistic people. What *do* you believe in? Yourself?

GEORGE: Right. [*Adding in vocal parenthesis*] He said, striking attitude of genius.

GEOFFREY: You have faith. You have faith in yourself – in your talent. Am I right?

GEORGE: Well?

GEOFFREY: Your talent, George. You believe in that with all your heart. And your evidence? Where is that, George? Can you show it to me?

[*Pause. They all look at him.*]

RUTH: Touché.

[GEORGE *is still for a moment. Then he laughs.*]

GEORGE: What a performance! All this Jesuit subtlety! You're too much for me. Just say that I'm like Christopher Columbus – I haven't discovered America yet. But it's there all right, waiting to be, yes, verified.

GEOFFREY: Yes, I'm quite sure it is. You see, I have faith too. I can see the lamp burning. Well, we really must be off. Come along, Mrs Elliot. Good night, everybody.

MRS ELLIOT: Yes. Well, I shan't be back late.

[*They both go into hall, and out through the front door.*]

PERCY [*rising and crossing to doorway*]: Lamps! [*Chuckling, turns.*] 'E ought to be on the bleeding stage – not you! [*Exit to lounge.*]

RUTH: Are you all right. You look a bit shaken.

GEORGE: I'm all right. I rather stupidly let the conducting of divine lip-service irritate me.

RUTH: So I noticed.

GEORGE: It's just been a pretty awful day, that's all.

RUTH: You surprise me.

GEORGE: Do I?

RUTH: Not really. You aren't very impressed with Geoffrey, I take it?

GEORGE: Right. What the Americans call 'strictly for the birds'. If there should be any heavenly purpose at all behind Mr Colwyn-phoney-Stuart, it's that he's God's own gift to the birds. Hope I didn't upset Mrs Elliot though. She's obviously pretty taken up with the whole racket.

RUTH: It might help if you weren't quite so vicious about it. You sound like a man with a secret doubt yourself.

GEORGE: Why is it you distrust me so much? I had a feeling we were the same kind.

RUTH: Did you? I suppose it's given poor Kate something to think about since Raymond was killed.

GEORGE: Tell me –

RUTH: Yes?

GEORGE: What was he really like?

RUTH: Raymond? Nice enough boy. Hard working, conscientious. Like most decent, ordinary lads of his age. [*Their eyes meet.*] You aren't remotely alike.

GEORGE: I thought you were in the habit of pitching into her yourself, hammer and sickle, over the Colwyn-Stuart.

RUTH: I should have thought that was different.

GEORGE: You mean that you're one of the family, and I'm not?

RUTH: If you like.

GEORGE: Suppose I'd better apologize.

RUTH: I shouldn't worry. I can't imagine what you could do wrong in her eyes. Well – I can imagine it all right, but I can't see you being stupid enough to lose the only good friend you've got.

GEORGE: What makes you think I haven't any good friends?

RUTH: Have you?

GEORGE: I thought you steel-hardened cadres of the far-away left had a better defence against the little jokies of right wing deviation-

ists like me. Or is it Wall Street jackal? No – I don't really look
much like a jackal. Villiers Street wolf perhaps.

RUTH: Very droll – but not very well timed for someone who i
supposed to be an actor.

GEORGE: Join my fan club, won't you?

RUTH: I'm not in the right frame of mind for shoddy little gags
[*Pause.*] I looked up the Party secretary tonight.

GEORGE: So you've packed it in at last.

RUTH: No doubt you think it's pretty funny.

GEORGE: No. I don't think it's funny.

RUTH: Seventeen years. It's rather like walking out on a lover. Al
over, finished, kaput. He hardly listened to my explanation – jus
sat there with a sneer all over his face. He didn't even have the
manners to get up and show me out. I think that's what I've hated
most of all, all these years – the sheer, damned bad manners of the
lot of them.

GEORGE: Farther left you go, the worse the manners seem to get.

RUTH: Well! The house is still fairly ringing with the bloody shovel
of *your* opinions.

GEORGE: *I* have a sense of humour. 'Bloody shovel of your opinions!'
Is that a quotation?

RUTH: Just someone I used to know. Someone rather like you, in
fact.

GEORGE: I thought you'd tied me up with someone the moment I
met you.

RUTH: Where are you going tonight?

GEORGE: Dancing, I believe. Somewhere Josie knows.

RUTH: Don't sound so apologetic about it. It doesn't suit you. Pass
my handbag, will you?
[*He does so.*]

RUTH: Looks as though you've a long wait ahead of you, my lad.
[*She offers him a cigarette.*]

GEORGE: Have one of mine. [*Fumbles in his pockets.*]

RUTH: You needn't go through the pantomime for me, George.
Take one.

GEORGE: No, thank you.

RUTH: Oh, don't look like that, for God's sake! You make me feel as though I'm – setting up as a soup kitchen or something. Please. [*She throws a cigarette. He catches it, fumbles for a light. She snaps a lighter at him, and he goes over to her. He bends over her for a light.*]

GEORGE: How young you look sometimes.

RUTH: So do you when you're silent, and no longer trying to justify yourself.

GEORGE: What's the time?

RUTH: Seven-fifteen. Where's your watch?

GEORGE: Being repaired.

RUTH: Pawned, I suppose.

GEORGE: Just as you like. I think I'll give Josie a yell.

RUTH: It won't do any good – not for ages yet. I didn't mean to hurt you just now.

GEORGE: Didn't you?

RUTH: Yes. You're quite right. I did mean to hurt you. I wish I hadn't.

GEORGE: What are you doing tonight?

RUTH: I don't know yet. I'm getting rather used to being at home every night. I *did* apologize.

GEORGE: We're neither of us as steel-hardened as we should be, are we? I used to smoke my mother's cigarettes too. Right up until the time she died.

RUTH: When was that?

GEORGE: Couple of years ago. We often used to go out together – she enjoyed that more than anything. She'd pay for the lot: drinks, meals, cinemas – even the bus fares. When the conductor came up the stairs, I would always grope in my pockets. And my mother would bring out her purse, and push my empty, fumbling hands away. 'It's all right, dear, I've got change.' I used to wonder whether perhaps there might come just *one* day when it might not have to happen. When I might actually have that two shillings or half-crown in my pocket. But it always did. It had become a liturgy. We went through it the last time we went out together – on my thirtieth birthday. During the war it was different. I was well paid then.

RUTH: What did he give you for it?

GEORGE: What?

RUTH: The pawnbroker – for the watch?

GEORGE: Fifteen shillings. I was lucky to get that – it wasn't a very good one.

RUTH: Here. [*Takes out Jock's watch from handbag, and holds it out to him.*] Well, take it.

GEORGE: What's this?

RUTH: What does it look like? Try it on.

GEORGE [*taking it*]: Are you giving me this?

RUTH: Yes, but you don't have to make a meal out of it.

GEORGE: It must have cost a fortune.

RUTH: It did. Try not to pawn it. Or, if you do, tell me, and I can renew the ticket or something.

GEORGE: I shan't pawn it, I promise you. I think it must be the nicest present I've had. How do you fix it?

RUTH: Here – [*She adjusts it for him, he watches her.*]

GEORGE: Your – friend?

RUTH: Oh, he doesn't want it any more. He told me.

GEORGE: Can you get the Third Programme on it?

RUTH: There!

GEORGE: Perhaps it'll change my luck.

RUTH: Superstitious too?

GEORGE: Thank you. Very much.

[*She still has his hand in hers.*]

RUTH: How beautiful your hands are – they're like marble, so white and clear.

GEORGE: Nonsense.

RUTH: But they are. I've never seen such beautiful hands.

GEORGE: You make it sound as if I were half dead already.

[*She looks up quickly, disturbed. Quite suddenly, he kisses her. Almost as quickly, he releases her. She soon recovers and moves away.*]

RUTH: Did you notice what I did with my lighter? My cigarette's gone out.

GEORGE: Didn't you put it back in your bag?

[*She opens it.*]

RUTH: So I did. What sort of parts do you play? On the stage, I mean.

GEORGE: Good ones.

RUTH: Stupid question deserves a stupid answer. I mean: any particular type.

GEORGE: I suppose so. Reminds me of the actor who was asked at an audition what sort of parts he played, and he replied, 'Scornful parts'. I think I play 'scornful' parts – anyone a bit loud-mouthed, around my height, preferably rough and dirty, with a furnace roaring in his belly. The rougher and dirtier the better.

RUTH: A character actor in fact.

GEORGE: I'm sorry I kissed you. So you needn't try to pay me back for it.

RUTH: Don't apologize. I was flattered for a moment. I'm sure there's an explanation somewhere, but I'd rather you didn't try to tell me what it is.

GEORGE: Just as you like.

RUTH: First time I've tasted Brown Windsor.

GEORGE: Tasted what?

RUTH [*laughing*]: The Brown Windsor of love, George. Haven't you come across it.

GEORGE: That – friend of yours sounds rather pretentious to me.

RUTH: It's funny how rhetorical gentle spirits can become.

GEORGE: He's a poet or something?

RUTH: I used to hope so.

[GEORGE *stretches himself.*]

GEORGE: God, I feel tired!

[*He looks all round the room. His eyes rest on Raymond's painted birds on the back wall, centre.*]

Blimey! Those birds! [*Goes upstage and walks around and is finally stopped by the sight of the cocktail cabinet.*] I've sat here for weeks now and looked at that. Oh, I've often marvelled at them from afar in a shop window. But I never thought I'd ever see one in someone's house. I thought they just stood there, in a pool of neon, like some sort of monstrous symbol, surrounded by bilious dining room suites and mattresses and things. It never occurred to me that anyone bought them!

RUTH: Norah's cocktail cabinet? Well, she didn't actually buy it – she won it.

GEORGE: What was her reaction?

RUTH: I think we were all a little over-awed by it.

[GEORGE *goes nearer to it.*]

GEORGE: It looks as though it has come out of a jelly-mould like an American car. What do you suppose you *do* with it? You don't keep drinks in it – that's just a front, concealing its true mystery. What do you keep in it – old razor blades? I know, I've got it!

[*He sits down and 'plays' it vigorously, like a cinema organ, humming a 'lullaby-lane' style signature tune. He turns a beaming face to* RUTH.]

And now I'm going to finish up with a short selection of popular symphonies, entitled 'Evergreens from the Greats', ending up with Beethoven's Ninth! And don't forget – if you're enjoying yourself, then all join in. If you can't remember the words, let alone understand 'em, well, just whistle the tune. Here we go then!

[*Encouraged by* RUTH'*s laughter, he turns back and crashes away on the cocktail cabinet, pulling out the stops and singing:*

'I fell in love with ye-ieuw!
While we were dancing
The Beethoven Waltz!...'

A final flourish on the invisible keyboard; he turns and bows obsequiously. RUTH'*s response has exhilarated him, and he stands in front of her, rather flushed.*]

It ought to disappear somehow, but I couldn't find the combination. [*He watches her with pleasure.*] That's the first time you've ever laughed.

RUTH: Oh, yes, you can be funny, George. These flashes of frenzy, the torrents of ideas, they can be quite funny, even exciting at times. If I don't laugh, it's because I know I shall see fatigue and fear in your eyes sooner or later.

GEORGE: Oh?

RUTH: You're burning yourself out. And for what?

GEORGE: Go on – but don't think you can kill my confidence. I've had experts doing it for years.

RUTH: I just can't make up my mind about you.

GEORGE: Meaning?

RUTH: Do you really have any integrity?

GEORGE: What's *your* verdict?

RUTH: I'm still not sure. It just seems to me that for someone who makes a religion out of being brilliant, you must be very unlucky.

GEORGE: You don't even begin to understand – you're no different from the rest. Burning myself out! You bet I'm burning myself out! I've been doing it for so many years now – and who in hell cares? At this moment I feel about as empty and as threadbare as my pockets. You wonder that I should be tired. I feel played out.

[*She applauds.*]

RUTH: Bravo! Not bad at all, George. Bit ragged maybe, but it'll do. Perhaps you may not be so bad after all. Tell me about this television job.

GEORGE: That? It's a walk-on – one line which will be drowned by the rest anyway. And if I know Lime Grove, it'll be so dark, I shan't be seen at all. All for twelve guineas. It's a fortune. But what am I going to do? How can I let them all sit in there – and probably half the street as well – staring stupidly at the telly for two and a half hours to watch me make one thirty-second appearance at the very end? What a triumph for dear old Percy! And Mr Colwyn-Stuart and his Hallelujah Chorus!

RUTH: Quite a problem.

GEORGE: As it is, I owe Mrs Elliot God-knows how much. But I suppose you knew that.

RUTH: It's not exactly a surprise.

GEORGE: She was buying me cigarettes every day up until last week.

I did manage to put a stop to that. I told her I was giving it up for my health. To my surprise, she actually believed me.

RUTH: *Are* you any good, George?

GEORGE [*almost like a child*]: That's a moron's question.

RUTH: As you like.

GEORGE: Well, ask yourself. Isn't it? Listen: all I ever got – inside and outside the theatre – is the raves of a microscopic minority and the open hostility of the rest. I attract hostility. I seem to be on heat for it. Whenever I step out on to those boards – immediately, from the very first moment I show my face – I know I've got to fight almost every one of those people in the auditorium. Right from the stalls to the gallery, to the Vestal Virgins in the boxes! My God, it's a gladiatorial combat! Me against Them! Me and mighty Them! Oh, I may win some of them over. Sometimes it's a half maybe, sometimes a third, sometimes it's not even a quarter. But I *do* beat them down. I beat them down! And even in the hatred of the majority, there's a kind of triumph because I know that, although they'd never admit it, they secretly respect me.

RUTH: What about this film you're going to be in?

GEORGE: It doesn't mean a thing. The old line. You know? Keep in touch – we'll let you know. You *don't* understand, do you?

RUTH: I just don't see much virtue in trying to ignore failure.

GEORGE: There's no such thing as failure – just waiting for success.

RUTH: George – really!

GEORGE: All right, forget it.

RUTH: I know what it is to go on waiting.

GEORGE: And do you think I don't! I spend my life next to a telephone. Every time it rings is like death to me.

RUTH [*relentless*]: What about these plays you write? You do do that as well, don't you?

GEORGE: Oh yes – you think I'm a dabbler. A dilettante who can't afford it.

RUTH: This Trident Theatre – the 'three uplifted fingers of Drama, Ballet, and Poetry –'

GEORGE: A so-called club theatre, meaning a preciously over-decorated flea-pit, principally famous for its rather tarty bar, and frequented almost exclusively by intense students, incompetent longhairs, and rather flashy deadbeats generally.

RUTH: I see. I'd like to read some of your work.

GEORGE: Thank you, I'll think about it.

RUTH: Do you charge a fee?

GEORGE: You're not being very funny yourself now.

RUTH: Perhaps your sense of humour has deserted you after all. My politics and your art – they seem to be like Kate's religion, better not discussed. Rationally, at any rate.

GEORGE: I knew you were suspicious of me, that you distrusted me. I didn't realize you detested me this much.

RUTH: George: why don't you go?

GEORGE: Go?

RUTH: Leave this house. Get out of here. If you're what you believe yourself to be, you've no place in a house like this. It's unfair to you. It's stifling. You should be with your own kind. And if you're not what you say you are, you've no right to be here anyway, and you're being unfair to everyone.

GEORGE: Are you serious? I haven't got a penny in the world.

RUTH: You'll manage. You've got to. It's your only chance of survival. Am I being harsh, George? Perhaps, as you say, we're the same kind.

GEORGE [savagely]: That's good! Oh yes! And what about you?

RUTH [off her balance]: What about me?

GEORGE: What are you doing here? All right, you've had your go at me. But what about yourself?

RUTH: Well?

GEORGE: Oh, don't be so innocent, Ruth. This house! This room! This hideous, God-awful room!

RUTH: Aren't you being just a little insulting?

GEORGE: I'm simply telling you what you very well know. They may be your relations, but have you honestly got one tiny thing in common with any of them? These people –

RUTH: Oh, no! Not 'these people'! Please – not that! After all, the
don't still keep coals in the bath.

GEORGE: I didn't notice. Have you looked at them? Have yo
listened to them? They don't merely act and talk like caricatures
they *are* caricatures! That's what's so terrifying. Put any one o
them on a stage, and no one would take them seriously for on
minute! They think in clichés, they talk in them, they even feel i
them – and, brother, that's an achievement! Their existence is on
great cliché that they carry about with them like a snail in hi
little house – and they live in it and die in it!

RUTH: Even if it's true – and I don't say it is – you still sound prett
cheap saying it.

GEORGE: Look at that wedding group. [*Points to it.*] Look at it! It'
like a million other grisly groups – all tinted in unbelievabl
pastels; round-shouldered girls with crinkled-up hair, open mouths
and bad teeth. The bridegroom looks as gormless as he's feeling
lecherous, and the bride – the bride's looking as though she's jus
been thrown out of an orgy at a Druids' reunion! Mr and Mr
Elliot at their wedding. It stands there like a comic monument to
the macabre farce that has gone on between them in this hous
ever since that greatest day in a girl's life thirty-five years ago.

RUTH: Oh, a good delivery, George. You're being brilliant, after all
They're very easy people to score off, but, never mind, go on!

GEORGE: There's Josie – at this moment putting all she's got int
misapplying half Woolworths on to her empty, characterless littl
face. Oh, sneer at me for my snobbery, for my bad taste, but, say
what you like: I have a mind and feelings that are all fingertips.
Josie's mind. She can hardly spell it. And her feelings – what abou
them? All thumbs, thumbs that are fat and squashy – like bananas,
in fact, and rather sickly.

RUTH: You should look an intriguing couple on the dance floo
tonight. I'm tempted to come myself.

GEORGE: Why don't you?

RUTH: I should hate to break up this marriage of true minds.

GEORGE: You know damned well why I'm going. People like me

depend upon the Josies of this world. The great, gaping mass that you're so fond of. You know? And for tonight, Josie is that mass, all rolled into one. And do you know what? Behind that brooding cloud of mascara, she's got her eye on George, Josie has. Because not only does she suffer from constipation, but night starvation as well. And then, there's Norah. Now what can you say about her? Norah doesn't even exist – she's just a hole in the air!

RUTH: You've a lot to learn yet, George. If there weren't people like the Elliots, people like you couldn't exist. Don't forget that. Don't think it's the other way around, because it's not. They can do without you, take my word for it. But without them, you're lost – nothing.

GEORGE: Don't give me that, Ruth. They drive you mad, and you know it. It's like living in one of those really bad suitable-for-all-the-family comedies they do all the year round in weekly rep. in Wigan. How have you stuck it here? What's the secret? Tell me. Since that mysterious divorce of yours that they all heavy-handedly avoid mentioning – and the week-end trips you don't make any more. How long is it you've been here? How long? Nine years is it? Ten years? Twelve? Oh no, Ruth – *you* can't afford to sneer at me!

RUTH: You've made your point. Don't get carried away with it. Why do I stay? Because I don't earn enough to get me out of it, and somewhere else. I spend too much on clothes, cigarettes –

GEORGE: And – 'incidentals'? [*Holding up wrist-watch.*]

RUTH: The job I do is so hysterically dull that every time I go into that office, and see myself surrounded by those imitation human beings, I feel so trapped and helpless that I could yell my lungs out with the loneliness and the boredom of it.

GEORGE: So you do!

RUTH: But, at my age, and with my lack of the right kind of qualifications, there's not much else I can do. Perhaps I haven't the courage to try. At least, I'm safe. And so I go on, from spring, through the summer, to the autumn and another winter, meaningless; just another caricature.

GEORGE: I knew it! I knew it!

RUTH: Thank you for reminding me of it.

GEORGE: The truth is a caricature.

RUTH: Is that meant to be profound?

GEORGE: You hate them, don't you? Shall I tell you why they horrify me?

RUTH: I suppose I give you what is known as the 'feed' line now. No – tell me, why do they horrify you?

GEORGE: They've no curiosity. There are no questions for them, and, consequently, no answers. They've no apprehension, no humility –

RUTH: Humility! [*Laughing.*] Good old George!

GEORGE: And, above all, no real laughter. Tell me, have you ever heard any of them, even once, laugh? I mean really laugh – not make that choked, edgy sound that people make all the time. Or, to put it more unintelligibly: I don't mean that breaking wind people make somewhere between their eyebrows and their navels, when they hear about the old lady's most embarrassing moment. I mean the real thing – the sound of the very wit of being alive. Laughter's the nearest we ever get, or should get, to sainthood. It's the state of grace that saves most of us from contempt.

RUTH: Hooray!

GEORGE: No, it wasn't really spontaneous. Singing and dancing 'Jazzing at the Jubilee with Josie'.

RUTH: Why haven't we talked like this before? A few moments ago you made me feel old. Now, I suddenly feel younger.

GEORGE: 'If you can't give a dollar, give me a lousy dime...'

RUTH: Can't say I've exactly heard *you* falling about with mirth since you came here.

GEORGE: No, you haven't. I suppose it does sound as though I'm complaining because everyone doesn't go round as if they were on parole from *Crime and Punishment*, muttering about God, and laughing their blooming heads off.

RUTH: Oh yes, you are a character! I think your little performance has done me good.

GEORGE: You're a good audience. Even if I do have to beat you down. That's all I need – an audience.

RUTH: And do you – think you'll find it?

GEORGE: I don't know.

[*He takes a deep breath, and sits down quickly, suddenly drained. She watches him, fascinated.*]

RUTH: How quickly you change! That's what's so frightening about you. These agonizing bubbles of personality, then phut! Nothing. Simply tiredness and pain.

GEORGE: I've been trailing around all day. I've had a few drinks, and nothing to eat. It suddenly hit me, that's all.

RUTH: Perhaps you have got talent, George. I don't know. Who can tell? Even the experts can't always recognize it when they see it. You may even be great. But don't make a disease out of it. You're sick with it.

GEORGE: It's a disease some of us long to have.

RUTH: I know that. I met it once before.

GEORGE: Then you must know it's incurable.

RUTH: Galloping – like a consumption.

GEORGE [*sharply*]: What did that mean?

RUTH: Nothing.

GEORGE: But do you know what is worse? Far, far worse?

RUTH: No, Brother Bones, tell me what is worse.

GEORGE: What is worse is having the same symptoms as talent, the pain, the ugly swellings, the lot – but never knowing whether or not the diagnosis is correct. Do you think there may be some kind of euthanasia for that? Could you kill it by burying yourself here – for good?

RUTH: Why do you ask me?

GEORGE: Would the warm, generous, honest-to-goodness animal lying at your side every night, with its honest-to-goodness love – would it make you forget?

RUTH: All you're saying is that it's a hard world to live in if you're a poet – particularly if it should happen that you're not a very good poet.

GEORGE: Unquote.

RUTH: Unquote. Life is hard, George. Anyone who thinks it isn't

is either very young or a fool. And you're not either. Perhaps eve
bad artists have their place in the scheme of things.

GEORGE: Scheme of flaming things! Get us with our intellectual se
on! And we're not even tight. I wish we were spending the even
ing together, all the same.

RUTH: Why are you so morbidly self-conscious? I thought all acto
revelled in exhibitionism.

GEORGE: Don't you believe it. Only insincere old bastards wh
carried spears with Martin Harvey, and have been choking them
selves silly with emotion ever since. 'Emotion, laddie – that's th
secret!' Shall I tell you a story? Yes, do tell me a story. Well,
happened to me when I was in the R.A.F. during the war.

RUTH: I didn't know you were. You've never mentioned it.

GEORGE: The one thing I never shoot lines about is the R.A.F. Just
gap in my life. That's all. Well, it happened like this: It was on
night in particular, when it wasn't my turn to go on ops. Instead
we got a basinful of what we gave the Jerries, smack bang in th
middle of the camp. I remember flinging myself down, not s
much on to the earth as into it. A wing commander type pitche
himself next to me, and, together, we shared his tin-helmet. Fea
ran through the whole of my body, the strange fear that my righ
leg would be blown off, and how terrible it would be. Suddenl
the winco shouted at me above the din: 'What's your profession?
'Actor', I said. The moment I uttered that word, machine-gur
fire and bombs all around us, the name of my calling, my whol
reason for existence – it sounded so hideously trivial and unimpor
tant, so divorced from living, and the real world, that my fea
vanished. All I could feel was shame.

[*He is lost for a moment or two. Then he looks at her quickly, an
adds brightly.*]

Gifted people are always dramatizing themselves. It provides it
own experience, I suppose.

RUTH: How pompous can you get? You had me under your spell
for a moment. Now you've broken it. I'm beginning not to know
when you're being real, and when you're not.

GEORGE: Always put the gun in the other man's hand. It's my rule of life.

RUTH: Yes. You're play acting all right. You've done it all your life, and you'll go on doing it. You can't tell what's real and what isn't any more, can you, George? I can't sit here drivelling all night. [*She turns to go.*]

GEORGE [*taking her by the arm*]: And what if I do? What does it matter? My motives aren't as simple as you like to think –

RUTH: – You're being phoney, George, aren't you? We're a pair of –

GEORGE: – What if I am? Or you, for that matter? It's just as –

RUTH [*sings*]: 'It's a Barnum and Bailey world,
Just as phoney as it can be!'
You've got us both acting it now –

GEORGE: – just as serious and as complex as any other attitude. Ruth! Believe me, it isn't any less –

RUTH: – haven't you, George? Cutting in on each other's lives –

GEORGE: – real or sincere. You just never stop standing outside –

RUTH: – fluffing your emotions –

GEORGE: – it's a penance –

RUTH: – that's the word, isn't it? You're fluffing it –

GEORGE: – the actor's second sense –

RUTH: – all studied, premeditated –

GEORGE: – watching, observing, watching me now, commenting, analysing, giggling –

RUTH: – timed for effect, deliberate, suspect –

GEORGE: – just at this moment, don't you want me more than anything else –

RUTH: ⎤ I've had my lot, George.
GEORGE: ⎮ More than anything?
RUTH: ⎮ We've both had our lots!
GEORGE: ⎬ You're as arrogant as I am!
RUTH: ⎮ You know what, George?
GEORGE: ⎮ That's one of the reasons you're drawn to me! If only
⎦ you knew – how much – at this moment –

RUTH: No, not me. Somebody else – not me!

GEORGE: I mean it, damn you!

RUTH: Strictly for the birds, George! Strictly for the birds!

GEORGE: Ruth!

RUTH: Let me go!

[*He does so.*]

GEORGE [*simply*]: I've botched it. [*Pause.*] Haven't I?

[*The descent has been so sudden, and they are both dazed.*]

RUTH: I'm not sure what has happened. Nothing I suppose. We're just two rather lost people – nothing extraordinary. Anyway, I'm past the stage for casual affairs. [*Turns away.*] You can't go on being Bohemian at forty.

[JOSIE *comes running down the stairs into the sitting room. She is wearing her 'jazz trousers'.*]

JOSIE: Ready?

GEORGE: Yes. Yes, I suppose so.

[RUTH *goes quickly out through the french windows.*]

JOSIE: Well, come on then. Had your supper?

GEORGE: No. I don't want anything. Let's have a drink, shall we, before we go?

JOSIE: Oh yes, lovely!

[GEORGE *does not move.*]

Well, what are you standing there for? What are you thinking about?

GEORGE: What am I thinking about? [*To cocktail cabinet for the wine.*] What am I thinking about? [*Pouring drinks*] Do you realize, Josie, that that is a lover's question? 'What are you thinking about?' [*Hands her a drink.*]

JOSIE: Oh, you are daft. You make me laugh when you talk in riddles. Oh, well, cheers!

GEORGE: Cheers. It'll be tonight, Josephine. [*Drinks.*]

JOSIE: Whatever are you talking about? You are in a funny mood, I must say. Let's have some music while we finish our drinks. [*She goes to radiogram.*] We don't want to get there too early, do we?

GEORGE: All the best people arrive late.

JOSIE [*looking through records*]: What shall we have? There's 'Mambo Man', 'Jambo Mambo', or 'Marmalade Mambo'.

GEORGE: Oh, let's have something to soothe my rather shabby soul,
Josie.

JOSIE: Go on, you haven't got one. What about this then?
[*She puts on Mantovani.*]

GEORGE [*screwing up his face*]: Heaven. [*They begin dancing.*] Sheer
heaven.
[*After a moment.*]

JOSIE: Bit boring isn't it – the music I mean.

GEORGE: The preliminaries always are, Josie, my girl. But they
make anticipation all the more exciting. Are you ever excited by
anticipation?

JOSIE: No, not really. Only when I see fellows like Len Cook, he's
lovely.

GEORGE: That's not anticipation, Josie, that's lust, plain lust. Although
it never is really plain. Do you know what lust is, Josie?

JOSIE: Of course I do, silly.

GEORGE: Lust, the harshest detergent of them all, the expense of
spirit in a waste of shame. Or as Jean Paul Sartre put it – sex.

JOSIE: We were only talking about sex a little while ago. Boring, I
think.

GEORGE: Do you? Shall we go?

JOSIE: All right.
[*They move into the hall. At the foot of the stairs, GEORGE stops her.*]

GEORGE: Have you ever been kissed, Josie?

JOSIE: Hundreds of times.

GEORGE: Like this?
[*He kisses her fiercely. The lounge door opens and they do not see
PERCY standing there. RUTH comes in through french windows,
switches out main lights, leaving just a glow in the sitting room.
PERCY remains silhouetted against the light from the lounge as RUTH
sits in arm-chair.*]

JOSIE: George – don't George, there's somebody coming!

GEORGE: I've never tried the etchings line – [*leading her up the stairs*]
– let's see if it really works.

JOSIE: But George –

GEORGE: Come and see my etchings. [*They are by now halfway upstairs.*]

JOSIE: What are you –

[GEORGE *smothers her with another kiss.*]

GEORGE: Silly girl.

JOSIE: But, George, what will Mum say?

[*They are swallowed up in darkness.* PERCY *moves towards the foot of the stairs and looks up. Then he moves into the sitting room and looks down at* RUTH *for a moment. She is suddenly aware of him.*]

RUTH: Why, Percy, how long have you been there?

PERCY: Long enough, I think. Quite long enough.

QUICK CURTAIN

ACT THREE

SCENE I

Autumn. One french window is open. GEORGE *is lying on the settee in his shirt sleeves. His jacket is hung on the back of one of the chairs. There are some loose leaves of manuscript scattered by the side of the settee. After a moment,* GEORGE *shivers, gets up, and puts on his jacket.* MRS ELLIOT *comes downstairs into the sitting room with a breakfast tray.*

MRS ELLIOT: Are you feeling any better, dear. You need not have got up at all, you know. [*She puts tray on table.*] Silly boy – the window open too. [*Crossing to window.*] You'll catch your death. The chrysanths have gone off. Chrysanths always remind me of Father. [*Stands at the window. Shuts it.*] Oh, dear, the clocks go back tonight. Awful, isn't it? [*Picks up tray.*] You didn't eat much breakfast, dear. [*Into kitchen*] Your bed's made and your room is done if you want to go up any time. Nearly twelve – [*in from the kitchen*] the others will be back soon. Sure you're all right, dear? Everyone's a bit down in the dumps these days. It must be the winter coming on. Not that I mind it really. It's the awful in-between that gets me down. How's the writing going? All right?

GEORGE: Oh, not too bad, Mrs Elliot, thanks. Feeling a bit whacked at the moment though.

MRS ELLIOT: Well, you mustn't overdo it, you know. I'll get in some nice cakes for your tea.

GEORGE: Please don't do that, Mrs Elliot dear, you know I don't eat them.

MRS ELLIOT: All right, dear, just as you like. [*Going to him*] I'm ever so sorry about the money, dear. Something will turn up soon I expect – don't worry, dear. Raymond's money didn't go as far as we thought it might, did it? Still, never mind. As long as I've got a shilling or two, I'll see that you're all right. Now I really must go and get some shopping done. I hate Saturdays – the crowds are awful. [*Crosses into hall, and puts on coat.*]

[*The doorbell rings.*]

Oh, that'll be the milkman. Now where's my bag? [*She picks it up from the hallstand, and goes to the front door.*] Oh yes, yes, he does. Won't you come in?

[MRS ELLIOT *stands back to admit a tall, official-looking man. He carries a brief-case.*]

MAN: Thank you.

[*They go through the hall towards the sitting room.*]

MRS ELLIOT: I'd better show you the way. He's not feeling so good today. Still, it'll be a nice break for him, having someone to chat to. [*In sitting room.*] George, dear, someone to see you. Well, I'll leave you to it, if you don't mind. [*Exit through front door.*]

MAN: You are Mr George Dillon?

GEORGE: That's right.

MAN: I'm from the National Assistance Board.

GEORGE: Oh yes, I wondered when you were coming. Please sit down.

MAN: Thank you.

[*He does so. Then opens brief-case, and extracts papers, file, etc., and fountain-pen from jacket. He studies papers for a moment.*]

Hmm. Now, with regard to your claim for assistance – you are Mr George Dillon?

GEORGE: I thought we'd cleared that up just now.

MAN [*making notes*]: And you are residing at this address, paying rent of thirty shillings a week?

GEORGE: Right.

MAN: What does that entail the use of? A bedroom, and general run of the house, I take it?

GEORGE: Yes.

MAN: May I trouble you for your rent book?

GEORGE: Well, as a matter of fact, I haven't got one. Not right now, that is. I could get you one, if it's really necessary.

MAN: You understand we have to examine your rent book, Mr

Dillon, in order to ascertain the correctness of your statement regarding the thirty shillings which you claim is being paid out by you in the way of rent each week.

GEORGE: Yes, of course.

MAN: So would you please make sure you are in possession of one, the next time I call.

GEORGE: Does that mean that I'll have to wait until then before I get any money?

[PERCY *comes in at the front door.*]

MAN: I'm afraid I can't answer that at the moment, Mr Dillon. Now, let me see. You are, by profession, an actor?

GEORGE: Yes, I am – by profession.

MAN: Have you any idea when you are likely to be working again?

GEORGE: It's rather difficult to say.

MAN: In the near future, would it be?

GEORGE: That phone might ring at this moment with something for me. Or it may not ring for months. It might not even ring at all.

MAN: You seem to have chosen a very precarious profession, Mr Dillon.

GEORGE: This money means rather a lot at the moment. I need – something – to show, you see –

MAN: Isn't there something else you could do, in the meantime perhaps?

GEORGE: Do you think I haven't tried? Incidentally, I am rather anxious that no one in the house should know about this –

MAN: Yes, of course.

[PERCY *enters sitting room, and sits down.*]

MAN: Yes. I see. Well, Mr Dillon, I can only hand in my report as I see things, and see what happens. The board is very hesitant about – paying out money to strong, healthy men.

GEORGE: Of course. Is there anything else? [*Looking at* PERCY. *The* ASSISTANCE MAN *is not quite sure what to do.*]

MAN: There's just the little matter of your last job. When was that?

GEORGE: Oh, about three months ago – television.

PERCY: Accch! You don't call that a job, do you? You could hardly
see it was him. *We* knew it was him all right – but you had to be
sharp to catch him.

MAN: Well, that'll be all I think, Mr Dillon. [*Rising.*] You won't
forget your rent book, will you?

PERCY: Rent book. Rent book! He hasn't got one! Shouldn't think
he's ever paid any!

GEORGE: He knows that, you idiot. Well, I'll show you to the door,
shall I?

[GEORGE *shows him into the hall. They get to the foot of the stairs,
and the* MAN *turns.*]

MAN [*officialdom relaxing*]: You know, you people are a funny lot. I
don't understand you. Look what you do to yourselves. And all
for what? What do you get out of it? It beats me. Now take me
and my wife. We don't have any worries. I've got my job during
the day – secure, pension at the end of it. Mrs Webb is at home,
looking after the kiddies – she knows there'll be a pay-packet
every Friday. And in the evenings, we sit at home together, or
sometimes we'll go out. But we're happy. There's quite a lot to
it, you know. [*Quite kindly.*] What could be better? I ask you? No,
you think it over, son. You think it over.

[*He goes out of the front door.* JOSIE *comes downstairs in her dressing-
gown.*]

JOSIE [*quietly*]: Ruth home yet?

GEORGE: No. Not yet.

JOSIE: Know where she is?

GEORGE: She's at the doctor's.

JOSIE: Doctor's? What for?

GEORGE: For me. [*Crossing to sitting room.*]

JOSIE: For you? Thought you didn't believe in doctors.

GEORGE [*turns*]: I don't. She's picking something up for me.

JOSIE [*going to him:*] I should have thought you could have done that
rather well yourself. What's she picking up for you?

GEORGE: What's called a report. You know? Making no progress,
but he mustn't try so hard. Unpromising.

JOSIE: Oh, I see. [*Crossing through into kitchen.*] Think I'll have some hot milk.

[GEORGE *goes into the sitting room after her, and picks up the scattered leaves of his manuscript.*]

PERCY: Well, young man – you're at it again I see.

GEORGE: Yes, I'm afraid I'm not getting very far with it though.

PERCY: I don't mean that. I mean you're busy fleecing money from someone else again.

GEORGE: What the hell are you talking about?

PERCY: Not content with taking the money we bring home, you're even trying to get hold of the money we pay in income tax. You're getting it all ways, aren't you, George?

GEORGE: I certainly am! Look here, Percy, you'd better be careful what you say –

PERCY: And I think you'd better be careful what *you* say. Telling a government official barefaced lies like that! That's a case – [*leaning forward with infinite relish*] – for the assizes, that is!

GEORGE: All right, I admit it. But Mrs Elliot knows that she'll get back every penny, and more, for looking after me as she has.

PERCY: Accch! I don't believe it. Anyway, you don't think she'll be very pleased when she finds out where it comes from, do you? Assistance Board! To think of us having someone like that at the door. What'll people think of that? I know all about you my lad. I've checked up on you at my firm – you owe bills all over the place. Don't be surprised if you don't have the police after you soon – for debt. *Debt!* [*Thrilling with horror*] Imagine that! Police coming to my house – to me that's never owed a farthing to anybody in all his life.

[*Doorbell rings, followed by violent knocking.*]

PERCY: And it wouldn't surprise me if that was them already. I know a copper's knock when I hear it.

[*Exit quickly into kitchen.* GEORGE *sinks into arm-chair, exhausted. Doorbell and knocking again. Pause.* BARNEY EVANS *comes in through the front door. He is wearing a rather old Crombie overcoat, an expensive but crumpled suit, thick horn-rimmed glasses, and a rakish brown Homburg hat. He is nearly fifty, and has never had a doubt about anything in all that time.*]

BARNEY: Anyone there? Anyone at home? I say?

GEORGE: In here. Come in here.

BARNEY: Where? [*To sitting room.*] In here? Oh yes. Good. Sorry to butt in on you like this. The fact is – [GEORGE *rises.*] Oh yes, you must be who I am looking for.

GEORGE: Oh? Sit down, will you?

BARNEY: No, no, no – I can't stop a minute. I found I was passing your door, so I thought I'd just pop in for a few words. I haven't a London office any longer – just for a moment, you see. I'm just on my way to Brighton, as a matter of fact.

GEORGE: For the week-end?

BARNEY: Business and pleasure. [*Thoughtfully.*] Business – mostly. Look, I'll come straight to the point, Mr –

GEORGE: Dillon. George Dillon.

BARNEY [*producing a script from his pocket*]: Oh yes. It's on here. George Dillon. Been in the business long?

GEORGE: Well – a few –

BARNEY: Thought so. Didn't ever play the Palace, Westport, did you?

GEORGE: No, I didn't.

BARNEY: Face seemed familiar. Well, now – to get down to it –

GEORGE: Is that my script you've got there?

BARNEY: That's right.

GEORGE: How on earth did you get hold of it?

BARNEY: Andy gave it to me.

GEORGE: Andy?

BARNEY: André Tetlock. You know him, don't you?

GEORGE: Oh – the Trident. Is he a friend of yours then?

BARNEY: Andy? I knew him when he was a chorus boy at the old Tivoli. You wouldn't remember that. Why, it was me put him back on his feet after that bit of trouble. You know that don't you?

GEORGE: Yes?

BARNEY: He hadn't even got a set of underwear – I had to get that for him. Silly fellow! [*Sucks in his breath deprecatingly*.] Still, he's all right now. That was my idea – that bar, you know. Oh, he did it up himself, mind you – Andy's very clever with his hands. But it was my idea. And now that bar's packed every night. Can't get within a mile of the place. He doesn't have to worry whether he puts on a show or not. Get some odd types there, of course, but you know Andy – so everybody's happy. And as long as he can find enough authors willing to back their own plays with hard cash, *he* won't go without his bottle of gin, believe me. [*Produces a packet of cheroots.*] Got a match? I take it you *don't* have any capital of your own?

GEORGE: Right.

BARNEY: Yes, he said you'd told him you hadn't any money to put up yourself.

GEORGE [*lighting his cheroot for him*]: I rang him about it weeks ago. I remember he said he'd liked the play, but he'd passed it on to someone else.

BARNEY: Liked it! That's a good one. Andy doesn't *read* plays – he just puts 'em on. Provided of course he can make something out of it! Now, I've read this play of yours, and I'm interested. Are you willing to listen to a proposition?

GEORGE: Of course.

BARNEY: By the way, I'm Barney Evans. You've heard of me, of course?

[GEORGE *hesitates, but* BARNEY *doesn't wait.*]

Now, Andy's a friend of mine. I've done a lot for him – but he's only in the business in a very small way. Oh, he does himself all right. But it's small stuff. You wouldn't get anywhere much with him – You know that, of course?

GEORGE: Yes.

BARNEY: I'm only interested in the big money. Small stuff's not worth my while. I take it you *are* interested in money?

GEORGE: Is that a rhetorical question?

BARNEY: Eh?

GEORGE: Yes, I am.

BARNEY: That's all right then. I don't want to waste my time. This the first play you've written?

GEORGE: My seventh –

BARNEY: Dialogue's not bad, but these great long speeches – that's a mistake. People want action, excitement. I know – *you* think you're Bernard Shaw. But where's he today? Eh? People won't listen to him. Anyway, politics are out – you ought to know that. Now, take *My Skin is my Enemy!* I've got that on the road at the moment. That and *Slasher Girl!*

GEORGE: *My Skin is my* – Oh yes, it's about the colour bar problem, isn't it?

BARNEY: Well, yes – but you see it's first class entertainment! Played to £600 at Llandrindod Wells last week. Got the returns in my pocket now. It's controversial, I grant you, but it's the kind of thing people pay money to see. That's the kind of thing you want to write.

GEORGE: Still, I imagine you've got to be just a bit liberal-minded to back a play like that.

BARNEY: Eh?

GEORGE: I mean – putting on a play about coloured people.

BARNEY: Coloured people? I hate the bastards! You should talk to the author about them. He can't even be civil to them. No – I know young fellows like you. You're interested in ideals still. Idealists. Don't think I don't know. I was an idealist myself once. I could tell you a lot, only I haven't got time now. But, make no mistake – ideals didn't get me where I am.

GEORGE: No?

BARNEY: You spend your time dabbling in politics, and vote in some ragged-arsed bunch of nobodies, who can't hardly pronounce the Queen's English properly, and where are you? Where are you? Nowhere. Crushed down in the mob, indistinguishable from the masses. What's the good of that to a young man with talent?

GEORGE: I should have thought you had a vested interest in the masses.

BARNEY: Most certainly. I admit it. And that's why I believe in education. Education – it always shows, and it always counts. That's why I say let them who've got it run the whole show. We're not going to get anywhere with these foreigners once they see they're no longer dealing with gentlemen. They're always impressed by an English gentleman. Just because they've got no breeding themselves, they know how to recognize it in others when they see it. Oh, yes. I could tell you a lot you don't know. However, I am diverting from what I came about.

[*He sprays his ash over the floor thoughtfully.*]

To get back to this play of yours. I think it's got possibilities, but it needs rewriting. Acts One and Two won't be so bad, provided you cut out all the highbrow stuff, give it pace – you know: dirty it up a bit, you see.

GEORGE: I see.

BARNEY: Third Act's construction is weak. I could help you there – and I'd do it for quite a small consideration because I think you've got something. You know that's a very good idea – getting the girl in the family way.

GEORGE: You think so?

BARNEY: Never fails. Get someone in the family way in the Third Act – you're halfway there. I suppose you saw *I Was a Drug Fiend*?

GEORGE: No.

BARNEY: Didn't you really? No wonder you write like you do! I thought everyone had seen that! That was my show too. Why, we were playing to three and four thousand a week on the twice-nightly circuit with that. That's the sort of money you want to play to. Same thing in that: Third Act – girl's in the family way. Course, in that play, her elder sister goes out as a missionary and ends up dying upside down on an ant hill in her birthday suit. I spent six months in the South of France on what I made out of that show. [*Motor-horn toots outside.*] Here, I'll have to be going. As I say, you rewrite it as I tell you, maybe we can do business together and make some money for both of us. I'll read it through again, and drop you a line. In the meantime, I should redraft the whole thing, bearing in mind what I said. Right.

GEORGE: I'll have to think about it. The fact is – I'm not feeling up to much at the moment. I'm completely broke for one thing.

BARNEY: O.K. then. You'll be hearing from me. You take my advice – string along with me. I know this business inside and out. You forget about starving for Art's sake. That won't keep you alive five minutes. You've got to be ruthless. [*Moves into hall.*] Yes, there's no other word for it – absolutely ruthless. [GEORGE *follows him.*]

[BARNEY *picks up his hat from stand and knocks over the vase. He looks down at the pieces absent-mindedly.*]

BARNEY: Oh, sorry. Now you take Hitler – the greatest man that ever lived! Don't care what anyone says – you can't get away from it. He had the right idea, you've got to be ruthless, and it's the same in this business. Course he may have gone a bit too far sometimes.

GEORGE: Think so?

BARNEY: I do. I do think so, most definitely. Yes, he over-reached himself, no getting away from it. That's where all great men make their mistake – they over-reach themselves.

[*The car horn toots more insistently.*]

Hullo, blimey, she'll start smashing the windows in a minute. [GEORGE *follows him as he hurries to door.*] Well, you just remember what I said. Tell you what – I'll give you a ring on Monday. I'll be busy all the week-end. [*Opens door.*] By the way, that girl?

GEORGE: What girl?

BARNEY: The girl in your play – what do you call her?

GEORGE: Oh, you mean –

BARNEY: Build her up. Build her right up. She's – she's a prostitute *really* isn't she?

GEORGE: Well –

BARNEY: Of course she is! I've just had an idea – a new slant. Your title, what is it? [*He doesn't wait for a reply.*] Anyway, it won't bring anybody in. I've just thought of a smashing title. You know what we'll call it? *Telephone Tart*, that's it! *Telephone Tart*. You string along with me, George, I'll see you're all right. [*Exit.*]

[JOSIE *looks in from kitchen.*]

JOSIE [coming in with a glass of milk]: It's all right, he's gone. [Sits in arm-chair.] Don't know what all the fuss was about.

PERCY: Well, I hadn't shaved, you see. I should hate to let George down in front of his friends – what few he has got.

JOSIE: Oh, you are daft, Dad. You don't know what you're talking about half the time.

[GEORGE comes slowly into sitting room.]

JOSIE: Who was it, George? Teddy-bear coat and all!

GEORGE [smiling wryly]: I suppose he's what you might call the poor man's Binkie.

JOSIE: What? Whatever's that? What's that, George?

[RUTH comes in front door into sitting room.]

GEORGE: Oh, never mind. It doesn't really matter. Hello, Ruth.

RUTH [after a slight pause]: Hullo.

GEORGE: Well, did you go to the doctor's?

RUTH: Yes.

GEORGE: Well – [laughing] – don't stand there with the angel of death on your shoulder – what did he say?

RUTH: George – just come in here, will you, for a minute.

[GEORGE follows her into lounge.]

JOSIE: Well, of all the – I like that, I must say! We're not good enough to know what's going on! [Rising and going up to radiogram.] I'm sure I don't want to hear what she got to say to George. Them and their secrets. [She puts on Mambo record very loud.]

[JOSIE then picks up a magazine and glances at it viciously, her foot wagging furiously. After a moment she gets up and goes over to the window and looks out in the same manner. PERCY watches her all the time. She catches him doing it.]

JOSIE: Well, had your eyeful?

[She walks over-casually towards the lounge door.]

Real heart-to-heart they're having, aren't they?

[Over to mirror as RUTH comes out of the lounge and goes into the sitting room and says something to PERCY. MRS ELLIOT comes in at the front door, laden as usual. She goes into sitting room and switches off the radiogram.]

MRS ELLIOT: Whatever do you want that thing on like that for, Josie? I could hear it halfway down the street. I thought you weren't well?

[*Pause.*]

Why, what is it? What's the matter with you all? What is it, Ruth?

PERCY: George has got T.B. [*In a voice like sandpaper.*]

MRS ELLIOT: T.B., George. I don't believe it. It isn't true. There must be some mistake –

RUTH: There's no mistake. It's quite true, Kate. The doctor will be coming up soon to let us know what the arrangements are.

MRS ELLIOT: Does this mean that he'll have to go away?

[RUTH *nods her head.*]

George – poor old George. [*She moves into hall and up the stairs.*] George dear, where are you? He won't like this at all, will he? George –

[PERCY *comes out of room to foot of stairs as* MRS ELLIOT *is half-way up.*]

PERCY [*calling up loudly*]: You'll have to burn everything, you know! All his sheets, blankets. Everything will have to be burnt, you know!

JOSIE: Oh, my God. Auntie Ruth! What's going to happen. What about me?

RUTH: You?

JOSIE: Yes, that's what I want to know – what's going to happen to me?

QUICK CURTAIN

SCENE 2

Winter. MRS ELLIOT *is on stage alone. She is looking up the stairs.* GEORGE'S *hat, coat, and suitcase are standing in the hall. She is looking very anxious. She picks up the hat and coat, and hangs them up carefully on the hallstand. Then she goes back to the sitting room. She goes over to*

208

the wedding group picture, and stares up at it. As she is doing this PERCY
*comes in at the front door. He takes off his hat and coat, hangs them up
beside* GEORGE'S, *and comes into the sitting room.*

PERCY: So he's back then?

MRS ELLIOT: Yes.

PERCY: Where is he?

MRS ELLIOT: Upstairs – talking to Josie.

PERCY: Upstairs?

MRS ELLIOT: Yes. She wasn't feeling too good this morning, so I
told her to stay in bed. I didn't want to take any chances. I think
she was over-excited at the thought of George coming back.

PERCY: Excited, was she?

MRS ELLIOT: Of course she was. She's thought about nothing else
for weeks.

PERCY: Well, well! She's in for a bit of a shock, isn't she?

MRS ELLIOT: Listen to me, Percy. I've told you – you're to keep
out of this. It's nothing to do with you. The only two people it
need concern at the moment are George and myself. Above all,
I don't want one word of this to get to Josie's ears. We've no idea
what might happen if she was to get a shock like that. And in her
present condition. If you so much as open your mouth about it to
her – you can pack your bags and go. You understand? Besides,
we don't know yet that it's true – not for certain. We've only got
your word for it, and we all know what a nasty mind you've got.
It would please you to think something rotten of George. You've
always been against him. You're jealous of him – that's why.

PERCY: Me? Jealous of him! That wreck!

MRS ELLIOT: He's a gentleman – which is something you'll never be.

PERCY: Oh, he is, is he? Perhaps that's why he can't even earn the
price of a cup of tea!

MRS ELLIOT: That's all *you* know.

PERCY: And what does that mean, exactly?

MRS ELLIOT: Never you mind. But there's a lot you don't know
about George. George will come out tops in the end – you wait.

PERCY: Seems more like there was a lot *all* of us didn't know about him.

MRS ELLIOT: You don't understand, Percy. And what's more, you never will. You think everyone's like yourself. George is an artist –

PERCY: And what's *that* supposed to mean?

MRS ELLIOT: He's sensitive, proud – he suffers deeply. Raymond was like that – you never liked him, and he was your own son. That boy's gone through a lot – he doesn't have to tell me that. I could tell the first time I ever spoke to him. I knew he was a good fellow, that all he wanted was a chance to bring a little pleasure to other people. I don't think that's so much of a crime, anyway. Oh, he's never said anything to me, but I've known what he's been going through all these months. When he's come back here in the evenings, when he couldn't get a job or any kind of encouragement at all, when people like you were sneering at him, and nobody wanted him. He didn't think I knew when he was feeling sick with disappointment. He didn't think I knew he was trying to pass it off by making us laugh, and pretending that everything was going to be all right. And I've never been able to tell him because I can't express myself properly – not like he can. He's got a gift for it – that's why he's an artist. That's why he's different from us. But he'll have his own way in the end, you mark my words. He'll show them all – and you. God always pays debts without money. I've got down on my knees at night, and prayed for that boy. I've prayed that he'll be well, and get on, and be happy – here – with us.

PERCY: With us?

MRS ELLIOT: If that's what he wants. And I believe it is. I know we're not the kind of people George is used to, and probably likes being with – he must have felt it sometimes. Not that he's ever said anything – he's too well brought up for that. He just accepts us for what we are. He's settled in here. And while he's been in that hospital all these weeks, he's known he's got somewhere to come back to. He's known that somebody wants him, anyway, and that's a great deal when you're laying there in bed, and you don't know

properly whether you're going to live or die. To know that someone is counting the days until you come home.

PERCY: What's he look like?

MRS ELLIOT: A bit thin. But who wouldn't look thin on that
hospital food? I'll soon feed him up.

PERCY: Did you manage to have a word with the doctor?

MRS ELLIOT: No, I didn't.

PERCY: Well, why not?

MRS ELLIOT: Because I wasn't going to ask the doctor a lot of
questions behind George's back, that's why. He's back – that's all
I care about, that's all I want to know at the moment. Things will
work themselves out somehow. George won't let us down.

PERCY: Well, we shall soon see, shan't we? He's a long time up
there, don't you think? And what's he going to do about his wife?

MRS ELLIOT: How do I know what he's going to do? Why can't
you shut up about it! You've talked about nothing else for days
now.

PERCY: You mean to say you didn't tackle him about it?

MRS ELLIOT: I didn't have an opportunity. I couldn't bring it up on
the bus, could I? Besides, I couldn't start on him straight away.
And as soon as we got back, he wanted to go up and see Josie,
naturally.

PERCY: Well, you wait till he comes down. If you're afraid to tackle
him about it, I'm not.

MRS ELLIOT: I meant what I said, you know. If you try and cause
trouble in this house, you can go.

PERCY: I think it's disgusting. Carrying on in someone else's house –
a married man at that! Do you know what? It's my belief that
there was something between him and your sister Ruth – and that's
why she decided to pack her bags, and go, all of a sudden.

MRS ELLIOT: Oh, don't be so childish, for heaven's sake, Percy.
You've got sex on the brain. I must admit you could have knocked
me down when Ruth told me she was going to find herself a room
somewhere. I mean – it seemed a bit suspicious. She didn't even
give a proper explanation. Just said that she felt she had to 'get out

of it'. It seemed a funny thing to say, and especially after all these years. Of course, she always was a dark horse. But, as for her and George – it's ridiculous. Why, she's old enough to be his mother.

PERCY [*as he goes to lounge*]: Oh, you women – you go on and on.

    [RUTH *appears at front door – unlocking it, enters, leaving door open.* RUTH *enters sitting room.*]

RUTH [*quietly*]: Kate. Kate.

    [GEORGE *comes downstairs – shuts front door. Then goes towards sitting room – meets* RUTH *face to face in the doorway.*]

RUTH: Hello, George. Are you better?

GEORGE: You're not really going, are you?

RUTH: I was coming to collect my things this morning – but I couldn't.

GEORGE: In fact it's quite a coincidence meeting you.

RUTH: No. Not really. I suppose it was silly of me to come when I knew you'd be back. I always seem to let myself in for farewells.

GEORGE: We both ought to be pretty good at them by now. [*Pause.*] Are you really leaving then?

RUTH: Not again, please. There's only a few minutes.

GEORGE [*very quietly*]: What's going to happen to me?

RUTH: George – don't! Try and help a little.

    [*Pause.*]

GEORGE: Isn't it hell – loving people?

RUTH: Yes – hell.

GEORGE: Still sounds rather feeble when you say it though. Rather like 'shift me – I'm burning'. What are you going to do?

RUTH: I don't know. Maybe find some scruffy wretch with a thumbnail sketch of a talent, and spend my time emptying bits of brown cigarette stubs from his saucer – generally cleaning up.

GEORGE: Did you ever look up your – friend?

    [*He lifts up the wrist-watch.*]

RUTH: Yes. I did. Soon after you came in here. But he wasn't at the same place any more. His landlord gave me his new address. Number something Eaton Square.

GEORGE: But of course, my dear – everyone lives in Eaton Square.

RUTH: Apparently, she's in publishing. She's just published his book last week. But I mustn't be unfair – she didn't write the reviews as well. They fairly raved. He's on top of the world.

GEORGE: You know I've been waiting for you to tell me that you're old enough to be my mother. Still, mothers don't walk out on their sons – or do they?

RUTH: How's Josie – have you seen her yet?

GEORGE: God! What a farce! What pure, screaming farce!

[*He starts to laugh.*]

RUTH: For heaven's sake!

GEORGE: Sorry. I just thought of something. How to make sure of your Third Act. Never fails! [*Roars with laughter.*] Never fails! [*Subsides almost immediately.*] Don't panic. I'll not get maudlin. I probably would start howling any minute, only I'm afraid of getting the bird from my best audience.

[*He looks away from her, and adds in a strangled voice, barely audible.*] Don't leave me on my own!

[*But he turns back quickly.*]

You haven't mentioned my – success – once.

RUTH: I didn't know whether you expected me to congratulate you or not.

GEORGE: Second week of tour – I've got the returns here. Look: Empire Theatre, Llandrindod Wells – week's gross takings £647 18s. 4d. Long-hair drama gets a haircut from Mr Barney Evans!

RUTH: I simply can't bear to go on watching you any longer.

GEORGE: But don't you think it's all very comic? I seem to remember some famous comedian saying once that he'd never seen anything funny that wasn't terrible. So don't think I'll mind if you laugh. I expect it. We should be both good for a titter, anyway. That's why religion is so damned deadly – it's not even good for a giggle. And what's life without a good giggle, eh? That's what I always say! Isn't that what you always say, Ruth?

RUTH: Let go of my hand. You're hurting me.

GEORGE: Well – isn't it? No. Perhaps it isn't. We never really had the same sense of humour, after all.

RUTH: Please don't try to hurt yourself any more by trying to hit back at me. I know how you feel. You're overcome with failure. Eternal bloody failure.

GEORGE: But I'm not a failure, I'm a – success.

RUTH: Are you, George? [*She turns away.*]

GEORGE: Listen! I'll make you laugh yet, before you go. Just a trip on the stage-cloth, and Lear teeters on, his crown round his ears, his grubby tights full of moth-holes. How they all long for those tights to fall down. What a relief it would be! Oh, we should all use stronger elastic. And the less sure we are of our pathetic little divine rights, the stronger the elastic we should use. You've seen the whole, shabby, solemn pretence now. This is where you came in. For God's sake go.

[*She turns to go.*]

GEORGE: No, wait. Shall I recite my epitaph to you? Yes, do recite your epitaph to me. 'Here lies the body of George Dillon, aged thirty-four – or thereabouts – who thought, who hoped, he was that mysterious, ridiculous being called an artist. He never allowed himself one day of peace. He worshipped the physical things of this world, and was betrayed by his own body. He loved also the things of the mind, but his own brain was a cripple from the waist down. He achieved nothing he set out to do. He made no one happy, no one looked up with excitement when he entered the room. He was always troubled with wind round his heart, but he loved no one successfully. He was a bit of a bore, and, frankly, rather useless. But the germs loved him. [*He doesn't see* RUTH *as she goes out and up the stairs.*] Even his sentimental epitaph is probably a pastiche of someone or other, but he doesn't quite know who. And, in the end, it doesn't really matter.' [*He turns, but* RUTH *has gone.*]

[*Bell rings,* PERCY *opens door.*]

NORAH [*coming in*]: Only me. Forgot my key again. Is George back yet? [*Into room.*] George! You are back!

GEORGE: Yes, Norah, I'm back again, with a face like the death of kings.

NORAH [*rushes to him*]: Oh, George, you look fine! Doesn't he, Dad? I thought you'd look awful – but you look fine. [*Kisses him as* MRS ELLIOT *comes in from kitchen.*]

GEORGE: Here – mind my ribs!

NORAH: Oh, we'll soon feed you up, won't we, Mum?

[*She takes him into sitting room,* PERCY *follows.*]

MRS ELLIOT: We certainly will. We're going to look after him from now on. He can sit in here all day and rest, and – keep himself happy. Can't you, George?

GEORGE: Rather.

MRS ELLIOT: He can lie down on the settee in the afternoons with his books and things, and – oh, I forgot! We got you a little home-coming present, didn't we, Norah?

NORAH: Shall I go up and get it?

MRS ELLIOT: If you like, dear, I don't know whether George feels up to opening presents. He must feel all in after that journey. I expect he'd like a bit of a rest.

GEORGE: I'm all right. I'd like a cup of tea though.

MRS ELLIOT: It's all ready. And I'll get you something to eat in no time.

NORAH: All right, then. I'll go and get it. I'll just pop in and have a look at Josie. Have you seen her, George?

MRS ELLIOT: He's been in there ever since he came in, haven't you, George?

NORAH [*crossing to and up stairs*]: She's been so excited at the thought of you coming back. She's talked about nothing else for days. [*She laughs.*] Isn't love grand!

[*Exit.*]

MRS ELLIOT: It's true, George. She's been quite a changed girl since you went away. I'm afraid she did used to be a bit on the lazy side sometimes, but not now – you wouldn't know her. Why, Sunday we spent practically all evening getting your room ready and look-ing nice. And Norah's been the same. Why, she's even booked seats for a coach ride for all of us down to the seaside.

PERCY: Well? How are you feeling, George?

GEORGE: Sorry, Percy. I haven't had a chance to say hullo yet, have I? [*Offers his hand.*]

PERCY [*shakes perfunctorily*]: How have they been treating you?

GEORGE: Oh, not too bad, thanks. But it's certainly good to be back. You've all given me such a welcome.

PERCY: It's quite a nice place down there, I believe.

GEORGE: It's all right.

PERCY: Nice country.

GEORGE: Oh, lovely.

PERCY: Isn't that near Tunbridge Wells?

GEORGE: Not far.

MRS ELLIOT: I don't suppose he wants to talk much now, Percy. Let him have a rest first. He's tired.

PERCY: They say that's a nice town.

GEORGE: It's pleasant enough.

PERCY: Ever been there, George?

GEORGE: What are you getting at?

PERCY: I think you *know* what I'm getting at.

GEORGE [*to* MRS ELLIOT]: What is it? You're upset about something, aren't you. I could tell something was wrong when you met me at the hospital. And all the way home on the bus.

PERCY: I suppose you didn't happen to be in Tunbridge Wells on June 22nd, 1943, did you?

[*Pause.*]

GEORGE: I see.

MRS ELLIOT: George – it's not true, is it? I was sure he'd made a mistake.

GEORGE: No, he hasn't made a mistake. I *was* married in Tunbridge Wells, and it was in 1943. The middle of June. It poured with rain. How did you find out?

PERCY: Through my firm, as a matter of fact. As you know, it's our job to check on people's credentials, etc., for hire purchase firms and the like. Well, last week, I found myself checking on a certain Ann Scott, on behalf of a building society. She's contemplating buying some big property in Chelsea. Good report – excellent banker's references and all that. Living in large house in upper-class district. And it seems her married name is Mrs George Dillon. Well? What have you got to say?

GEORGE: Well?

MRS ELLIOT: Oh, dear.

GEORGE: What do you want me to say?

MRS ELLIOT: I don't know, George. I'm so upset, I don't know where I am. I suppose it's not your fault, but –

GEORGE: But, my dear, I don't see what there is to be so upset about. This doesn't change anything.

MRS ELLIOT: But – but what about Josie?

GEORGE: Nothing is changed, I tell you. It's simply that neither my wife nor I have ever bothered about a divorce. She's had other things to think about, and I've never had the money. But it's all easily settled. There's nothing to worry about. I promise you.

MRS ELLIOT: You're not just saying this, George? I'd rather –

GEORGE: Of course not. I've come home, haven't I?

MRS ELLIOT: Yes, you have. You've come home, thank heaven.

GEORGE: You see, my wife never was anything. With Josie, it's different. I know exactly where I am.

MRS ELLIOT: She loves you, George. She really does.

GEORGE: Yes. I know.

PERCY: It said on my report that she's an actress, this wife of yours. [PERCY *feels cheated, and is desperately looking round for something else.*]

GEORGE: Right.

PERCY: She must do pretty well at it then.

GEORGE: She does.

PERCY: Can't say I've ever heard the name.

GEORGE: On the contrary, you know her very well.

PERCY: What do you mean?

GEORGE: I mean that somebody must have slipped up rather badly in your report. They seem to have left out her stage name.

PERCY: Stage name?

GEORGE: We both thought 'Ann Scott' a bit commonplace.

PERCY: Who is she then?

GEORGE: Well, you've always told me that she's the only one in your favourite television parlour game who's really any good at all. In fact, you've said so many times.

PERCY: You don't mean – What? Not *her*!

GEORGE: Her.

PERCY: Well, I'll be . . .

GEORGE: Yes. It's always puzzled me why you should admire her so much. Or anyone else for that matter.

MRS ELLIOT: But George – honestly, I don't know where I am. Now that – well – now that you're a success, how do you know that your wife won't want you back?

GEORGE: Somehow, I don't think that will influence her!

PERCY: What are you talking about? Now that he's a success?

MRS ELLIOT [*recovered and triumphant*]: Well, I don't see why he shouldn't know now, do you, George?

GEORGE: No, I don't see why not.

MRS ELLIOT: George has had his play put on. It's on tour at the moment, and last week it made – tell him how much it made, George.

GEORGE: £647 18s. 4d. [*Flourishing returns.*]

MRS ELLIOT: And he gets five per cent of that every week, so perhaps that will shut you up a bit.

PERCY [*staring at returns*]: Well! Fancy that! Why didn't somebody tell me?

MRS ELLIOT: Why should they? Well, I mustn't stand here wasting time. You must be hungry, George.

[*Phone rings.*]

MRS ELLIOT: Do answer that, Percy, will you? Wish Norah would hurry up.

[PERCY *goes to phone.* NORAH *comes down stairs carrying parcel into sitting room.*]

NORAH: Josie says she won't be long, she's going to get up.

PERCY: What's that? Oh, yes, hang on a minute while I find my pencil. All right – go ahead.

NORAH: Well, George, here we are – I can't wait to see his face when he opens it, Mum.

GEORGE: Well –

MRS ELLIOT: No, wait till Josie comes down. She'll want to be with him when he opens it.

NORAH: Oh, blow that. She's got all the time in the world with him now. If he won't open it, I will.

PERCY: Yes. Yes. I've got that. Who? What? What name? Right. Good-bye.

MRS ELLIOT: All right then. I don't suppose she'll mind. Go on, George, open it.

[GEORGE *starts opening the parcel.*]

PERCY [*coming in*]: That was for you, George. A telegram.

GEORGE: Oh, who from?

PERCY: Somebody called Barney. I've got it written down here.

GEORGE: Read it out, will you? I'm busy at the moment.

PERCY: It says 'Playing capacity business. May this be the first of many smash hits together. Welcome home – Barney'.

MRS ELLIOT: Well, wasn't that nice of him?

GEORGE: Yes, good old Barney. Now, what have we here?

[*Stands back to reveal a portable typewriter.*]

Well! Look at that!

MRS ELLIOT: I hope you like it, George.

GEORGE: Like it! I should think I do! I think it must be the nicest present I've had. What can I say? [*He kisses them both.*] Thank you both. Thank you for everything.

MRS ELLIOT: That's all right, George. Believe me, all my prayers have been answered. Mr Colwyn-Stuart prayed for you too, every week you were away. All I want is for us all to be happy. Come along now, sit down, while I get the supper. Give him a chair, Percy, you look all in, dear.

PERCY: Oh, sorry. Here you are.

NORAH: It'll be nice, having George for a brother-in-law.

GEORGE: Yes, of course it will, Norah. It's about time you got married yourself, isn't it?

MRS ELLIOT: She almost has been -

NORAH: - Twice.

GEORGE: I'm sorry.

MRS ELLIOT: The last one was an American.

NORAH: Yes. The last time I saw him, we were going to get a bus t
Richmond. He just simply said suddenly: 'Well, so long, honey
it's been nice knowing you' and got on a bus going in the opposit
direction. It's swimming on the telly tonight. I think I'll go an
watch it, if you'll excuse me.

[*She goes into lounge. Slight pause.*]

MRS ELLIOT: Well, I don't know. What with one thing and another
That's right, George dear. Just you relax from now on. And yo
let him alone, Percy. I've always believed in you, George. Always
I knew he'd come out tops.

[MRS ELLIOT *goes into kitchen.* GEORGE *leans back, tired.* PERC
*turns on radio. Jazz - 'If you can't give me a dollar, give me a lous
dime.'*]

PERCY: Not too loud for you, George?

GEORGE: No - fine. [*Pause.*]

PERCY: I can't get over it you know.

GEORGE: What?

PERCY: Your wife, I mean. Big star like that. Surprised she couldn'
have helped you on a bit all this time. Still, you're doing all righ
yourself now, by the look of it. Turned out to be Bernard Shaw
after all, eh? I suppose you'll be writing some more plays when you
start feeling better again?

GEORGE: I dare say.

PERCY: I see. Same sort of thing?

[RUTH *comes down slowly with suitcase.*]

GEORGE: Yes. Same sort of thing.

PERCY: Well, that's good, isn't it? What was the name of that
theatre again?

GEORGE: The Empire Theatre, Llandrindod Wells.

[*The sound of* JOSIE'S *voice singing comes from upstairs. From the
lounge, the telly is playing music.*]

PERCY: Well, I don't think it would do any harm if we all have a little drink on this. [*To cocktail cabinet.*] If we're going to start living in style, we may as well get into the way of using this, eh? [*He opens the cocktail cabinet, revealing all its hidden glory.* RUTH *exits through front door.*]

PERCY: Now, where are we. [*Staring into cabinet.*]

MRS ELLIOT: That's right. Let's have a little drink.

GEORGE [*in a flat, empty voice*]: Yes, let's have a little drink – to celebrate.

PERCY: Music too, would not be inappropriate. [*Putting on record.*]

GEORGE: Music too, would not be inappropriate.

[JOSIE *sings, off.*]

PERCY: Well, we can't leave the blushing bride upstairs all on her own, can we? I'll give her a yell, shall I, George? [*He goes out, calling upstairs.* GEORGE *goes to the door. He looks trapped and looks around the room and the objects in it; he notices the birds on the wall.*]

GEORGE: Those bloody birds!

[*Enter* MRS ELLIOT. *He stares at her as if for the first time, then his face breaks into a mechanical smile.*]

Come on, Mum, let's dance!

[*They dance together for a few moments.*]

SLOW CURTAIN

THE PENGUIN SHAW

All the plays are complete with Shaw's original prefaces.

FOUR MODERN VERSE PLAYS

PL 37

T. S. Eliot
THE FAMILY REUNION

Christopher Fry
A PHOENIX TOO FREQUENT

Charles Williams
THOMAS CRANMER OF CANTERBURY

Donagh MacDonagh
HAPPY AS LARRY

NOT FOR SALE IN THE U.S.A. OR CANADA

—

FOUR ENGLISH COMEDIES

Edited by J. M. Morrell

PL 33

Jonson · VOLPONE
Congreve · THE WAY OF THE WORLD
Goldsmith · SHE STOOPS TO CONQUER
Sheridan · THE SCHOOL FOR SCANDAL